To: Hiromi

Xmas '05

Tomoko

THE CINNAMON CLUB
COOKBOOK

THE CINNAMON CLUB
COOKBOOK
IQBAL WAHHAB & VIVEK SINGH

A.

Publisher and Project Editor Jon Croft Commissioning Editor Meg Avent Editor Jane Middleton
Design Matthew Le Maistre Smith and Ian Middleton at Design United Photographer Jean Cazals Stylist Sue Rowlands
ISBN 1 904573 01 0
First published in Great Britain in 2003 by Absolute Press, Scarborough House, 29 James Street West, Bath BA1 2BT
T: 44 (0) 1225 316013 F: 44 (0) 1225 445836 email: info@absolutepress.co.uk Website: www.absolutepress.co.uk
Reprinted 2004
A CIP catalogue record of this book is available from the British Library
Printed and bound by Lego, Italy

The Cinnamon Club Cookbook

ACKNOWLEDGMENTS

There are many people without whom there would never have been a Cinnamon Club or a Cinnamon Club Cookbook, so if we do not mention you here, please forgive us.

Percy Marchant, who introduced us in the first place, David Cabriel for designing the restaurant so tastefully, John Turner for running the company and keeping us in check, Jori White for placing us on the map so well, our friends and family for supporting us when the going got tough in the early days.

The Cinnamon Club is a team effort but some have been particularly helpful in producing this book – Laurent Chaniac for recommending a wine with each dish and writing what we consider a seminal essay on matching wines with spice, Jes Soor for the cocktail recipes, our opening pastry chef Candido Santos for devising some stunning desserts and Hari Hara Kumar for assisting with recipe co-ordination.

Much of the culinary style we developed was with the help of Eric Chavot, whose endless enthusiasm, creativity and support will not be forgotten.

When Jon Croft, our publisher, first suggested we write a book we didn't hesitate to accept his offer. The commitment and enthusiasm that he has shown from the outset has made this book what it is. It has been a great pleasure to work with each member of the team that helped produce this book – Meg Avent for seeing the commission through, Jane Middleton for her meticulous editing of the recipes, Matthew le Maistre Smith and Ian Middleton for the stunning design and Jean Cazals for his breathtaking photography.

A lot of work has gone into this book – Vivek having to take catering volumes and applying them to domestic situations and Iqbal for having tried and tested each and every recipe in his home. We hope you enjoy reading it and cooking from it as much as we enjoyed producing it.

Iqbal Wahhab, and Vivek Singh 2003

SOME NOTES FOR AMERICAN READERS

Below are the American terms for some of the ingredients used in the book:

Aubergine = Eggplant	Digestive biscuits =	ground beef/lamb/veal
Beetroot = Beets	whole wheat biscuits/graham crackers	Plain flour = all-purpose flour
Caster sugar = superfine sugar	Double cream = heavy cream	Prawns = shrimp
Coriander = cilantro (when referring	Fresh yeast = compressed yeast	Red or green pepper =
to the green, leafy herb rather than	Greek yoghurt = thick, strained yoghurt	red or green bell pepper
the seeds)	Icing sugar = confectioner's sugar	Shrimps = very small shrimp
Cornflower = cornstarch	Marrow = vegetable marrow/	Single cream = light cream
Courgette = zucchini	marrow squash	Sweetcorn = corn
Dark Chocolate = bittersweet chocolate	Minced beef/lamb/veal =	Tomato purée = tomato paste

INTRODUCTION

My mother tells the story of how from the age of four, I would tug at her sari while she was standing at the stove cooking and demand to see the curries she was preparing whereupon she would have to lower the pot to mini Iqbal eye level. So not only have I always been keen on how food *tastes*, but also on how it *looks*.

I would say that alongside the French, the Indian sub Continent has the world's greatest cuisine. What I admire so much about French cuisine is the delicate manner in which often rich ingredients can be combined with a saucing process that uplifts the palate through a layer of refined flavours. Indian cuisine of course varies (as does French) through its various regions but what brings this term to life is the common factor of spice. No cuisine in the world can produce so many styles of flavours from its sauces and marinades.

The studied balance between the beauties of these two cuisines has shadowed much of my professional life. From varied previous media careers and enterprises

I had both promoted and written about French and Indian cuisines and restaurants, predominantly the latter, and it has been a charmed existence to have been able to make a living by spending much of each day of the last ten years in a different restaurant in the company of chefs, restaurateurs and food writers.

The French domestic dining experience is very similar to the Indian one and very different to the British one in that it is a communal family affair – the time when everyone is together and they talk, they laugh and they enjoy their food. In British homes food is often more of a chore, something to be done and got out of the way – which is probably why you don't see many British restaurants.

Food is not timeless; it lives in a social, national and international context and continuum. It has its own values and as an essential part of the kit of culture, it draws from its environment. In its raw, unmodified form, Indian cuisine as rendered by classically trained chefs and promoted by spirited restaurateurs has been able to show its stature on the world stage. But does it stop there? Where further could it go? It was with these thoughts – a grown up version of my childhood demands – with which The Cinnamon Club started.

For many years I had run a public relations consultancy specialising in Indian food. I represented some of London's best Indian restaurants. One day Jori White, an American woman from another restaurant PR company came to see me offering a clutch of highly reputed European restaurant clients in return for a partnership in the firm. Watching Michelin starred operations from the inside, with the attention to detail that went into service, wine pairings, the creation and presentation of dishes, left me wondering why that same 'wow' factor was not present with my Indian clients' establishments.

One reason was that chefs at Michelin operations were in their kitchens at 7am checking what was available in the markets that day and setting up their stocks and sauces. Chefs at Indian restaurants were barely in before 11 – a menu comprising lamb and chicken dishes that rarely changes doesn't encourage excess application. The opportunities to develop, experiment and innovate were thereby severely diminished. More importantly, most of their owners (only a handful of the 8000 Indian restaurants in the country are chef-owned) were averse to change. The curry house explosion had served them well; they had grown up through the ranks and had much more experience than did I on what made their businesses work. So whenever I would go and visit them and propose change on more modern and perhaps European lines, they would dismiss my suggestions as romantic and fanciful.

With busy restaurants to back their claim, they maintained that their business wasn't broken and therefore didn't need fixing. there was also a consensus of opinion to the effect that the British dining public only had a certain level of expectations from Indian restaurants and that innovation was therefore perilous.

Where did this thought process come from? One explanation was that first generation settlers had not become part of the British social fabric and thus through lack of opportunities to integrate more fully, remained unable to understand the psyche of their customers and therefore invariably double-guessed their expectations of Indian dining. This explains why Indian restaurants twenty and thirty years ago looked like a mixture of a mosque and a pub – minarettes to portray the east and velour seats to emulate the much loved drinking dens.

Seen from a different perspective, the reason why Indian cuisine hadn't grown was because it had not been encouraged to – a curry was a curry. In the early 1990s restaurant critics who knew their achar from their elachi were few and far between. The critics and the guides continued to judge restaurants on more rarefied French dining criteria. Indian, and indeed Chinese, dining in their traditional incarnations were based on a variety of dishes shared from bowls passed around a table. Restaurant and food critics judged dishes by presentation - the way a dish was constructed on a plate. Restaurants were also often judged by the quality of their wines. Again, traditionally Indian and Chinese cuisines were better served with other drinks – tea for the Chinese, water or beer with Indian food. So automatically it meant that these cuisines would be left behind when it came to the top echelons of critical acclaim. I detected and wrote about this bias.

One day a friend of mine told me she shared a flat with a Michelin Guide inspector and that if I could convince her of the validity of my widely reported attacks in the national press she would take up the case with her friend. I took her to lunch at one of the restaurants I

considered to be a worthy contender for a Michelin award. My friend soon showed me how I was expecting too much. There was a mango chutney splat on the menu, one of the plates was chipped and my wine glass was being refilled before hers. I realised then that I had to tackle the problems of the Indian restaurant scene from within. This experience helped me realise that food was often considered to be but a small part of a restaurant's dining experience. Service, location and atmosphere are consistently ranked higher than food in consumer surveys about what motivates people to choose one restaurant over another. Sadly, these were elements invariably missing from the existing Indian restaurant scene. That is not to say that food should not be the main concern – it should – just that the dining experience in the round was being ignored by so many in the Indian restaurant world.

The successful formula popularised in the 1980s – north Indian menus, Raj-inspired decor and the poppadom/lager combo – was by the mid 1990s beginning to look jaded. Having won Britain's hearts, the curry house experience was beginning to lose its charm through over-familiarity. Restaurants would operate the principle of cloning – choosing a location in close proximity to another, taking their rival's menu to the local printer and asking them to typeset it with their name on, changing the price of the odd dish in the spirit of originality.

It is no surprise, then, that restaurant owners would observe that over time their customers invariably didn't look at the menu – they knew what they wanted and invariably it was onion bhaji followed by chicken tikka masala and a pint of Carlsberg. This was deemed a good thing. The mid 1990s however, saw a new spirit of adventure in the British public when it came to food. A huge new dining out culture had emerged from increased travel abroad and television programmes exploring numerous national cuisines. The Italians saw the writing on the wall and moved on from the traditional trattorias with their caricatured moustachioed waiters wielding enormous pepper grinders.

They also, crucially, moved their culinary product along. People were making Spaghetti Bolognese and Lasagne at home – they wanted something more from their local Italian restaurant.

With some notable exceptions, Indian food as served in restaurants stayed put. The customers they had weaned on curry were repaying the favour by cooking those same dishes at home from jars of sauces and buying increasingly acceptable ready-made meals from the supermarkets. Some younger restaurateurs embraced change and are today enjoying the rewards from having done so. The older generation – the settlers – will sadly see their restaurants wither and die with them.

How do you go about opening a restaurant like The Cinnamon Club? The project needed a spectacular venue. Against the odds the owner of a Grade II listed building in the heart of Westminster – for 100 years previously it had been the Westminster public library – selected us from a list of the 300 biggest restaurant operators in the country (in other words there were 300 of them and me) to become the occupiers of a 12,000 square feet of prime London space, thus enabling me to begin to realise a fantastic dream.

But what exactly was the dream? It was certainly to do more than just create another posh Indian restaurant. It was a mission to see how far a cuisine could go if taken in a new direction. My view was this: Indian cuisine as served either here or in India had become stuck in a rut. Only marginal degrees of innovation were occurring, with restaurateurs and chefs feeling the pressure to remain true to ancient recipes and traditions. Whilst the prevalent view in culinary circles

was that the quest for authenticity was the most important motivating factor for a chef, my feeling was that authenticity is a strait-jacket which stifles inventiveness – as if every dish has to be made a certain way just because some old sage with a long beard sitting at the top of a mountain in Lucknow decreed it. Ironically it needed someone with no previous experience to defy this resistance to change. In those early days, and indeed even now, it was sacrilege to defy tradition. And yet the principles of dining in the sub continent are these: we don't eat starters, we share food from dishes placed in the middle of a table, we don't drink wine with our meals and on the whole we don't use knives and forks. Very few Indian restaurants would survive if they followed tradition fully rather than in the manner that suits them. Food travels and Indian food has travelled very well to Britain and is very well served by those serving 'traditional' dishes in five star environments. But Indian food has more than travelled – it has arrived and has a permanence in British culture from which has developed a strength to allow it to unravel itself in whatever terms it sees fit. To break with tradition would mean setting up a new template.

To take that childhood-long obsession of food looking beautiful as well as tasting great, to recognise that we eat with our eyes and with our imagination, meant cracking the issue of presentation. This meant more than taking curry out of a bowl and making it look pretty on a plate – it meant redefining the all-important process of saucing. Indian dishes typically have their sauces cooked 'up' with all their ingredients simmered together slowly to give one big spice 'hit'; so to serve them in bowls for people to share makes sense – that is, when you know how to eat it. Rather than take this as the opportunity to savour items with varying flavours and ingredients, the British have instead taken this as license to compile a plate invariably containing vegetables, seafood, chicken and possibly also lamb, each with their own sauce, which then gets mushed together to form the gloop that to date has been the mainstream curry house experience. Would you eat from a plate that contained fish and chips, mushy peas, roast chicken and steak and kidney pudding? What would the British do if they went to a British restaurant in Delhi and saw that this was how Indians were eating British food?

So instead of trying to get the public to break with the habit of a lifetime, I saw that what was needed to make the Indian dining experience more sophisticated was to produce dishes individually rather than in batches. This is where the French part of the hybrid comes in; to make these kinds of individually plated dishes would involve 'reducing' sauces rather than cooking them up. For us this would have to involve a fine understanding of spicing – the sequence in which they are added needed to be much more accurately judged in this process so as to allow each spice's individual oils and aromas to be released and its impact maximised upon the others. This is what makes French cooking stand out – the ability to layer flavours through a sauce.

Directly associated with this from the outset was the vow that The Cinnamon Club would be a poppadom free zone. It would be no more than a half-measure to devise this style of cooking and yet allow the old curry-house rituals to remain. Beer – which has a respectable place on the Indian dining table - would only be served from bottles and in small, elegant glasses. The layering of flavours from the sauces to be served would lend themselves more successfully to wines as the qualities of acidity, tannin, oak and fruit allow for a greater enhancement of flavour than a one-hit beer or lassi (over 2000 wines were tasted and paired in the process of selecting our first list). But was any of this possible? Were there chefs capable of sharing this vision, let alone performing it?

Transport yourself now to the tranquil and palatial surroundings of the Rajvilas in Jaipur, once voted by Tatler as the most luxurious hotel resort in the world. A maximum of 70 guests are crammed into 35 acres of sculptured gardens, tents and villas, each with their own private garden. In 1999 a close friend hired it out for his wedding party. We are gathered having poolside drinks on the first evening of the party and he asks me if I have found a chef yet for the Cinnamon Club. I tell him I haven't and he points out the chef running the party's barbecue and says: "You should talk to him." I did straight away. At the age of 26, Vivek Singh had become head chef of India's most prestigious hotel. Unlike most ambitious chefs, at catering college he had chosen Indian cuisine as his speciality – hotel bosses always encouraged potential recruits to concentrate on continental food– and he had travelled around India with the Oberoi group, who had groomed him for fast track growth.

After graduating through catering college, abandoning parental hopes that he would follow his father's footsteps as an engineer, he first went to Bombay and worked in their flight services kitchens and then spent two years at The Oberoi Grand in Calcutta, their largest and oldest hotel, as a senior chef before his big posting to Rajvilas. It transpired that Vivek had been reading Escoffier from the age of 20 and had devoured books by the US chef Charlie Trotter and the British genius Marco Pierre White, always thinking of how their skills and applications could be honed to Indian flavours.

So it came as a mutual shock to find that someone on the other side of the world had been thinking in exactly the same way as them. Most of the top Indian restaurant owners in London had at various stages made approaches to Vivek, but he hadn't seen the point of uprooting himself thousands of miles away to do the same thing but in a different country.

For the next two days, the wedding party went travelling and sight seeing, whilst Vivek and I talked food. On the final day I re-joined them; a coach had been arranged for one of their expeditions and I was the last to get on board, holding everyone up. "Hey Iqbal," someone shouted from inside. "What were you doing – poaching the chef?" "Yes, actually," I replied. Cheers all round. A lawyer friend who was sat behind me tapped me on the shoulder and said: "Do you know that makes your trip tax deductible?"

Part of the appeal that Vivek held for me was the pro-active way he allowed his mind to work. In essence he went from asking 'Why do we do things this way?' to 'Why not do things a different way?' So for example, he would not just ask why spinach is cooked to a pulp but more importantly why can't spinach be cooked in a manner that retains its texture and colour. The notion of doing things a different way would result in him one day serving a vindaloo of pig's cheeks at The Cinnamon Club – precisely born out of this logic.

He had started early with these thoughts. Working at the Oberoi flight services kitchens, which produced over 2000 meals a day for international airline passengers, Vivek began his career with the ultimate in batch cooking where mass production went by strict rules of preparation. Taking a linear approach to this, Vivek dissected the cooking process by analysing core values of ingredients, spices, colours, flavours, oils and textures. To make a chicken tikka, for example, meant applying a certain spice mix to chicken to give it a certain colour, texture and flavour. But what if we used different spices, another marinade or an alternative cooking process? What would the end result be? From the charts he created for this exercise, Vivek found that the permutations and combinations open to him from the ten kebabs the factory made could in fact be turned into 80 more dishes. This cross-fertilising was the technical solution to my more amateur view that we are held back by the rules.

In unearthing this thought, Vivek's eyes were opened to the virtually endless possibilities of where Indian cuisine could go. Developing this thought over time, Vivek also mixed and matched the powers of our five senses opening up the possibilities of both balancing and challenging flavours and tastes.

It is easy to drift into a "change for change's sake" mentality and avoiding that is successfully achieved by fully understanding the ingredients we work with – not just the values of each spice, herb and oil but also how they interact with each other. The best way to do this is by a process of deconstruction. Once everything is broken down to their core components we are much more likely to understand how best they can be re-assembled to create something new, and desirable. Vivek's view was that, as in other creative realms, everything is subject to evolution and that this exercise was one that was required to be done, whose time had come.

I returned to India a few months later with the dual purpose of sourcing materials with our interior designer David Gabriel and also to recruit further chefs. Upmarket British Indian restaurants invariably had head chefs from Indian five star hotels, but then set them up to work with a British Asian kitchen team. My worry was that a local staff's skill sets would be so different from those who have been formally trained in India as to create more problems than they solved. So I decided to bring the whole kitchen team from India. No restaurant has ever started with 18 chefs on work permits, simply because nobody before had asked for so many – a classic case of the perceived glass ceiling. Vivek had arranged for chefs from all over India to come for a day of interviews and trials in Jaipur. By the end of what was a very long day, the last person we saw was mumbling and his eyes were half shut. I asked Vivek to ask him what his problem was. Vivek spoke with him in his native Telugu and then turned to me and said that he had travelled for 18 hours from Bangalore to be there and had now been up for 30 hours awaiting an interview. If you've ever eaten a biryani at The Cinnamon Club, it will have been made by that man.

The chefs we recruited came from all parts of India had all held senior positions at an early age within a five star hotel. Most are graduates and all have been acclaimed in their particular fields: for instance Bhagwan Singh, who came to us from the Rambagh Palace, has represented India to display Rajasthani cuisine in six international food festivals. We explained to them all that we were seeking from them was their ability to render the specialities of their particular region in its traditional form but that they needed to be open-minded about how we would then 'twist' the dishes. None of the chefs, Vivek included, had ever ventured west of India and so it was important that having harnessed this huge wealth of culinary expertise spanning all the main regions that we set a framework for placing those skills within a European formula. An early e-mail to Vivek read: "Think in terms of both sensory and visual impact – dishes will have to not only taste stunning but look stunning too. This may involve adopting more European styles of cooking and sauce reductions."

I had met Eric Chavot, the hugely talented two Michelin starred chef of Knightsbridge's Capital Hotel, in a parallel universe in which I occasionally wrote for the food pages of The Financial Times, with whom I had a fantastic brief – go anywhere, write on anything, the smarter and more luxurious the better. I took him to Cannes for a weekend where my arduous mission was to review a French restaurant run by an English chef and took the opportunity to discuss my project with him. Eric had no great understanding of Indian food outside of his local take-away but over the course of the weekend soon grasped what I wanted to achieve and immediately began fine-tuning my thoughts.

I gave him an example of a Cinnamon Club dish as I saw it – tandoori calf's liver with masala mashed potato. Whilst I had understood flavours and ingredients, Eric taught me the importance of textures; that dish, he said, would need something crisp on top, like a refined bhaji. We exchanged many crazy ideas – one of his was a tower of mini naans with different toppings on each, one of mine was a chicken and foie gras kebab. Luckily we got these out of our system before we met Vivek – otherwise he might have run a mile from us. Eric said he would happily get involved in helping Vivek create this new style of cooking – with the one condition that I took him to India.

The flight to India with Eric also involves a journalist friend called George Dorgan who has been commissioned to write a magazine feature on the story of The Cinnamon Club. Dayanita Singh, India's leading social photographer, has been brought in to follow us on our travels around the country and the BBC have a TV crew filming me for a documentary on The Cinnamon Club for their Trouble at The Top series. George and I spend part of the flight telling Eric about sangri beans. Vivek had made a dish with local Rajasthani beans called sangri, which are dried, thin and black with a grass like quality and are a revelation of flavours and textures. We don't know them in this country unless you have either been to Rajasthan or The Cinnamon Club – along with all of our spices, we decided we would bring these beans to Britain for the first time.

Like everyone when they first visit Rajvilas, Eric is stunned. The hotel, incidentally, by this stage knows their main man is going to be leaving to join me and instead of banning me or putting snakes in my bed, are perfectly charming and accommodating. Eric meets Vivek and the first photo shoot is arranged – an outdoor display of Vivek cooking the famous sangri beans. Eric looks at them and shrieks in best primadonna French chef voice: "Flippin' eck – all ze way over you talk about these flippin' things and what is it? It's hay! You have flippin brought me to India to eat flippin' hay!"

Bemused by the hammed up performance, Vivek begins cooking the beans. At the end, Eric tries them and he grabs me aside from the others and says: "That man can make hay taste like this? For a French chef our life is easy – we have fantastic ingredients like foie gras to start with. But look what he can do with hay!" From that day to this, Vivek and Eric have been the best of friends and have established a uniquely successful collaboration to empower Vivek to become, like Eric, a world-class chef.

I want to just briefly interrupt my story by going back in time to the beginnings of Indian food in the British Isles and start, appropriately, with Queen Victoria who would have chicken curry, rice and dhal served to her twice a week at Osborn House in the Isle of White, where she stayed. Although she never went to India, Benjamin Disraeli made Victoria Empress of India and in 1887 in her Golden Jubilee year she was presented with two Indian servants, who started as waiters and then quickly moved to the kitchen. They were not impressed with the curry powder mixes available and instead shipped in their own selections. Indian cuisine in Britain thus started with grandeur and now has it back.

Another story drawn from the vaults of curry legend is the fact that the man who first sold Indian food in Britain is also the same fellow who brought us aromatherapy. The fascinating life of Dean Mohamet is largely ignored. The son of a Bengali senior army official who died when he was ten years old in 1769, Dean was semi adopted by an ambitious and well connected officer called Godfrey Evan Baker, from Cork. Fifteen years later Baker returned to Ireland and took Dean with him. Dean wrote and published 'The Travels of Dean Mohamet' in 1794, the first book ever to have been written and published by an Indian in English.

Dean married Jane Daly, settled down and at the turn of the century he and his family moved to London and went to work for the Honourable Basil Cochrane in central London's Portman Square for whom he developed the notion of 'shampooing' – a therapeutic massage later to become known as aromatherapy. In 1809 he went on to open The Hindostanee Coffee House at 34 George Street, just by Portman Square. Coffee houses in those days did not actually sell coffee and this one was no different in that respect but they were the height of fashion. An advertisement for the restaurant ran as follows:-

Hindostanee Coffee-House, No. 34 George-Street, Portman square—Mahomed (he changed the spelling of his surname around this time), East-Indian, informs the Nobility and Gentry, he has fitted up the above house, neatly and elegantly, for the entertainment of Indian gentlemen, where they may enjoy the Hoakha, with real Chilm tobacco, and Indian dishes, in the highest perfection, and allowed by the greatest epicures to be unequalled to any curries ever made in England with choice wines, and every accommodation, and now looks up to them for their future patronage and support, and gratefully acknowledges himself indebted for their former favours, and trusts it will merit the highest satisfaction when made known to the public

The restaurant did not do well. Indian families had their own staff that cooked for them and Portman Square was some way apart from the hub of coffee house life in the City. In 1812 Mohamet filed for bankruptcy. He moved to Brighton and set up Mahomed's Bath House where he returned to the art of shampooing, this time bringing in traditional Indian herbal mixtures and remedies and received a royal warrant in the process. The father of British curry died at the age of 92.

Many have subsequently also laid parental claim over British curry. Edward Palmer, a returning army officer married to a daughter of the Nizam of Hyderabad, launched The Veeraswamy in 1926 just off Regent Street. At around the same time Shafi's opened in Gerrard Street, now home to Chinatown.

The mass popularisation of the curry, though, is due to the efforts of the Bangladeshi community. The north-eastern region of Sylhet is celebrated throughout the sub-Continent for the quality of its cooks. Sylheti cooks were originally engaged as galley chefs by the East India Company on the ships headed back to London and were often so badly treated (beatings and tortures were commonly recorded) that once they came close to the docks, they would jump ship to avoid more of the same on a return journey. With the skills that they had, they would often become cooks. If a large enough Indian settlement was in the same area, Indian cafes were formed. Thus the birth of the Bangladeshi owned restaurant (after Independence in 1947 this country was called East Pakistan and then after a liberation war in 1971 became Bangladesh). Equipped in the early days with little in the way of formal education, mainstream labour market opportunities were not open to them – they had to fend for themselves and curry was their lifeline. These cooks lived in cramped and squalid conditions – often as many as ten men sharing the same room, using it in shifts.

Once they began to own their own businesses or gained employment through other restaurants, they started bringing their families over, thus becoming the facilitators of the curry boom, moving across the country throughout the 1960s and 70s and opening Kohi Noors, Taj Mahals and Light of Indias wherever they could.

The 1980s saw the growth of posh curry – upmarket Indian restaurants in expensive parts of London, often owned by Indian hotel groups or wealthy Indian businessmen and hardly ever by Bangladeshis. But we should all be thankful to the endeavours of this community, who suffered the constant verbal abuse from drunken customers that came to be the caricature of the curry house experience, and who rose above it to make their dishes the country's most sought after. Without

the groundwork the Bangladeshi community put in to popularising this cuisine, restaurants like The Cinnamon Club would probably not exist.

So now back to the story and the beginnings of The Cinnamon Club. With the largest middle class in the world at 100 million, India (and in this respect Pakistan and Bangladesh too) is unlike most other countries in having domestic help available to more than an elite few. This has many implications; in terms of dining out, it means that Indians don't tend to eat out in Indian restaurants – they have servants and cooks who can produce food for them at home. Going out tends to mean Chinese or Thai and, more recently, pasta. The Indian roadside cafes, dhabas, serve rustic spicy food typically targeted at the country's maniac truck drivers, and there are also the very cheap thali houses where for a few rupees you can have a compartmentalised aluminium tray with various vegetarian goodies assembled on it. The five star hotels have their perfunctory Indian restaurants, but tend to promote Oriental and even French cuisine. No wonder there is a curry drain to Europe – their loss, our gain! One of the implications of all this is that little innovation is taking place within the domestic cuisine.

Naturally, given such a wide depth and breadth to all the regions' culinary styles, there may be an argument for saying there is little need to innovate until we first fully explore. Certainly, when Eric, Vivek and I went on our travels across India, there were many revelations for us. The purpose of the culinary voyage was to identify the essential and special elements of the Indian culinary repertoire that I wanted Vivek to bring to The Cinnamon Club table and with Eric's help to interpret into the western five star environment that was being planned. It was not a trip for the faint hearted. On occasion Eric would sit out some adventures and wait with the press team following us as Vivek and I delved further, such as the three hours we spent at Bombay's Crawford Market – their Billingsgate Fish Market but lacking some of the hygiene standards.

In Bombay we visited numerous street vendors of savoury snacks. The challenge I gave Vivek and Eric was to take street snacks and make them into amuse bouches; from the first day at The Cinnamon Club, we have as a result been able to do without poppadoms.

Visits to the spice markets of old Delhi were a revelation. Vivek didn't know what was available in Britain and I didn't know what was available in India. The huge array of spices put to shame what is available in here, where importers focus on mass-market quality. The varieties of chillies available alone made it clear to us that we had to create our own supply route.

Every fortnight at the restaurant, we receive a consignment of all our spices as well as our Rajasthani sangri beans, specially pressed Bengali mustard oil and whatever else we require for the dishes of the moment. For example, if Vivek wishes to offer a lamb shank cooked in rogan josh style, we go to the root, or in this case, the bark of the matter. For most westerners, this dish is shorthand for medium hot lamb curry in a tomato sauce. The real derivation of this dish, however, requires the redness of the sauce ('rogan josh' means red juice) to come from the bark of a Kashmiri tree called rattan jyot, so Vivek and his team are empowered to use the right ingredients for their dishes as opposed to what local markets here can offer.

The flying over of our spices gives us great pride – it may not be the most commercially expedient decision ever made and not all diners may notice the difference but for us it stands as a pillar to our vow not to compromise on quality.

Vivek spent much of his first three months in London with Eric in his kitchens at The Capital. When not with Eric at the Capital, Vivek was to be found with me visiting markets, meeting our future suppliers and seeing what top end European restaurants were offering. The culinary language we spoke became increasingly developed and fine-tuned.

We tested out adaptations of familiar dishes. Chicken korma was turned into a roulade of breast stuffed with spinach and apricot with an aromatic sauce. More invented dishes included char-grilled sea bream with pomegranate extract, a loin of rabbit with dried fruits in a mustard marinade or zucchini flower stuffed with spiced corn and mushroom.

After more than our fair share of the usual building and money traumas, The Cinnamon Club opened in April 2001. For all the talk and all the hype (and we had a lot of it), there was no way to know whether the British public would actually take to this new style of cooking in sufficient numbers to justify the multi million pound investment in it. We had some trials and from the first day the food critics were in. One, from The Daily Telegraph, said to me: "You know Iqbal, we English don't expect so much fuss from a curry." I could have hit him. Luckily, he was in a minority. The opening reviews were fair to good – I, of course, had been expecting wild and ecstatic endorsement.

What though would the discerning Asian customers think of The Cinnamon Club? Would we be chastised for having bastardised a great cuisine? Many in the early days would bound up to me and remonstrate at not being able to share dishes. I asked them to at least try it out once The Cinnamon Club way and if after that they were not pleased, then all they had to do was not come back. Most of them have in fact become regulars

– our most scrutinising community has in the main given us their support, providing an ironically neat twist to the tale of authenticity.

The commitment of the 65-strong team at The Cinnamon Club is probably unparalleled. They have joined us from some of the best hotels and restaurants in Britain and India and they come in on their days off to help out or to learn new skills. They, along with our professional team, are deeply committed to the Cinnamon Club vision and we constitute our own family.

Our efforts have paid off – nearly two thirds of our opening team are still with us, a minor miracle for a restaurant. We were also given the prestigious 'Investor in People' award at a very early stage. People have taken significant salary cuts to come and work for us, such is the attraction that The Cinnamon Club has created for itself. It was an early lesson for me that you can tell the world that you are building what you hope will be the most fabulous Indian restaurant ever, but unless you fully involve all your team in that process, you will never reach anywhere near that goal. As part of their induction process, each new recruit is taken to lunch in the restaurant by a senior member of the team. I regularly host lunches for a cross section of bar, floor and kitchen members and after a hard night's service, I encourage everyone to get together and have a drink and a joke so as to revive their spirit before venturing home.

Luckily we have taken an ever-growing dining clientele with us on our voyage and a science has emerged which underpins our passion. Sales of drinks and dishes are analysed on a daily basis, our food and wine suppliers are spoken to on a daily basis and we both create and anticipate future demand by engaging with our customers and acting upon staff feedback. The thrill in the kitchen is for Vivek and his team to see what they can do with what a particular fish or meat supplier brings in for them. Our evening menu changes daily, keeping both us and our diners constantly engaged in the dynamic nature of the Cinnamon Club vision.

THE TERM "INDIAN" AS USED IN THE CINNAMON CLUB COOKBOOK

"Indian" is used throughout this book to denote food from the Indian subcontinent. Pre-partition India, previously enclosing what are now called Pakistan and Bangladesh, saw a communality of culinary traditions that were especially pronounced through the influences of the Mughal emperors. Royal dishes such as Biryani and Korma remain common from Pakistan, through much of India and into Bangladesh.

THE DIFFERENCE BETWEEN FUSION COOKING AND CINNAMON CLUB COOKING

As you will find when you go through the recipes, we have taken core essential Indian styles of cooking with all their flavours and adapted or 'extended' their logic. So we might, for example, use a typical saucing style from Kerala and rather than cook a fish in it, sear a piece of say sea bream and place it on top of the sauce. That mysterious but distinct place where extensions stop and fusions start was brought home clearly to me when visiting Tabla, New York's smartest Indian restaurant. A highly impressive place with an equally impressive chef, their menu contained dishes such as 'Loin of beef with hand-cut pommes frites, haricots verts and horseradish raita'.

Iqbal Wahhab, 2003

THE CHEFS

Above left to right: Himmat. S. Nathawat Curry Chef; Rakesh Ravindran Nair Grill chef; Mor Singh Pastry Chef; Rajeev Kumar Tandoor Chef; Narayan Prasad Adhikari Asst.Pastry Chef; Shambhu Chimire Tandoor Assistant Manoj Kumar Mehta Curry assistant; Bhagwan Singh Speciality Rajasthani Chef

Below left to right: Hari Hara Kumar Sous Chef and Hyderabadi speciality Chef; Suman Kharel Pastry assistant; Abdul Yaseen Tandoor Chef; Vivek Singh Executive Chef Thangavel Murugavel South Indian Chef; Sanjeev Chimire Grill assistant; Kishore Das Breads and Bengali speciality chef

TECHNIQUES

For the purposes of this book, if I were to mention cooking techniques that are specific to India or just used in Indian cooking, you would not be able to cook half the recipes here. Quite rightly as a sign of the times, you will notice that the cooking techniques used for various recipes in the book are not just Indian but some quite Western or European as well. As we have done with the rest of the concept, even in cooking we have tried to use the best of both the worlds and hence you will commonly see techniques such as searing, oven roasting, grilling etc used in many of our recipes.

We are also aware of the limitations that many recipe books present in terms of availability of equipment and also techniques and therefore each and every recipe has been tried in a Western domestic kitchen to ensure that techniques are easy to follow and most of them are easy to reproduce with the equipment commonly available in our kitchens.

I must mention Iqbal who very painstakingly cooked every single recipe in his kitchen and literally transformed his kitchen into a laboratory for well over 6 months. Without him, we wouldn't have had the confidence in our recipes as we have now. Another person without whose help we would never have been able to try everything is Hari Hara Kumar who very diligently packed ingredient by ingredient for the trials that carried well over 6 months. In his own words at the end of the whole process, his ability to weigh, measure and pack ingredients is far better than any skilled grocer back in India!!

All of us at the Cinnamon Club feel that food is not timeless and does not exist in a vacuum. Like everything else in this world, food, cooking and eating habits are constantly in a state of flux. As with any successful cuisine, it's important to constantly assess and analyse methods, procedures, quality, timing and seasons so as to be able to respond to a constantly changing environment. I believe that it is essential to have both the flexibility and the ability to first de-construct a cuisine, assess what is not necessary or can be done away with, analyse what new influences can be brought in and then re-construct the elements back in to create something that is truly evolving and in step with the times.

Vivek Singh, 2003

TANDOOR COOKING WITHOUT A TANDOOR

In India, particularly in the north, meat, fish and some vegetables are marinated and then cooked on skewers in clay ovens called tandoors, which are traditionally coal fired. The skewers rest on the sides of the oven, exposing the food to intense heat from the flames. The juices dripping on to the burning coals create a smoke that imparts a characteristic flavour to food cooked in tandoor ovens.

Tandoor cooking is almost impossible to recreate at home, although a barbecue can be used in some recipes to good effect. However, if you do not have access to a tandoor oven, or even a barbecue, there is no need to despair. For the recipes in this book, I have broken down the cooking process that takes place in a tandoor and devised a method that works equally well in a domestic kitchen. All you need to do is alter the marinating sequence and the end result is just as good. Traditionally most foods are marinated for a few hours before they are skewered and cooked in a tandoor. I have divided the marinade into two separate components, the first and second marinade. The first marinade is applied to the food and left for 15–30 minutes. Then, instead of applying the second marinade immediately, the meat or fish is seared quickly in a hot pan. After the second marinade has been applied, the cooking is finished in the oven. The first marinade draws out a little moisture from the meat or fish but it also helps the seasoning and spices permeate better. Searing the meat or fish before applying the second marinade ensures that the juices are sealed inside rather than flowing out and rinsing away the marinade.

MARINATING

One of the things we did before opening The Cinnamon Club was to look long and hard at traditional cooking methods and question whether they were still relevant. In India it is usual for meat to be marinated for long periods, sometimes up to 12 hours, particularly before being cooked in the fierce heat of the tandoor. However,

meat and poultry have changed considerably over the last few decades. Most of the meat available now is farmed, and far less game is eaten. We realised that long marinating periods really aren't necessary, as the meat is already quite tender and better-quality cuts are more readily available. Marinades were also used to preserve meat and extend its life but modern refrigeration has made this unnecessary.

However, marinades still have two useful functions to perform. They are an unbeatable way of flavouring food with spices and aromatics, and they also protect it from intense heat, thereby keeping it moist. This makes marinating a particularly good technique to apply to fish, whose delicate flesh benefits not only from the flavours of the marinade but also from its protective role in the oven.

Some people simply combine all the spices and then mix in the meat or fish, but I prefer to use the two-marinade method described above. Initially just salt, ginger and garlic pastes, and sometimes lemon juice, are applied and left until the meat or fish has absorbed their flavours. The second marinade contains a more complex mix of spices, plus yoghurt and sometimes cheese. Because a little moisture has been drawn out during the first marinating period, the meat or fish takes to the second marinade much better. This double marinade also contributes to the subtle layering of flavours in the final dish.

TEMPERING

Tempering refers to the process of adding whole or broken spices to hot oil or ghee to release their flavours into it. In many northern Indian dishes, whole spices are added to the oil or ghee at the beginning of cooking, then followed up with onions, tomatoes, garlic, ginger and other ground or pasted spices to make the final dish.

However, some dishes, such as lentils or beans, are finished by adding hot ghee or oil that has been tempered with spices such as chillies, cumin, garlic etc. This is often referred to as baghar.

For certain southern Indian dishes, such as Sambhar (see page 32) and Lemon Rice (see page 135), the oil is heated and then mustard seeds, curry leaves, white and yellow lentils, whole chillies etc are added and the mixture is used to finish the dish. This is usually a very fast process and it is vital to follow the correct sequence and timing when adding the various ingredients, otherwise some might burn while others stay undercooked. It is also important to maintain the oil or ghee at a fairly high temperature to extract the full flavour from the spices, thus adding both flavour and texture to the finished dish.

SMOKING

This technique is used in Muslim cooking to impart a smoky flavour. After the meat or fish has been marinated, it is transferred to a large container with a small bowl in the centre. A piece of burning charcoal is placed in the bowl and sprinkled with spices, such as cloves or cardamom. Then some ghee or oil is poured over the charcoal to generate plenty of smoke, the container is covered with a lid or aluminium foil and left for about 20 minutes in order for the smoke to permeate the food. The meat or fish is then fried, grilled or cooked in a tandoor.

As it may be impractical to handle burning charcoal in a domestic kitchen, I have devised an alternative method of smoking food for recipes such as Home-smoked Lamb Kebabs (see page 65) and Clove-smoked Tender Beef Kebabs (see page 66). Simply heat ghee or oil to smoking point in a small pan, add twice the usual quantity of spice, then discard the spices and add the oil or ghee to the dish. It's not quite the same as the real thing but it gives the dish plenty of flavour.

SEARING

The process of sealing in the juices of meat or fish by placing it on a hot pan until it forms a crust is called searing. Some foods, such as scallops, are cooked completely in this way, while others, like venison and lamb, may require further cooking in the oven. This European technique is not commonly used in Indian kitchens but at The Cinnamon Club, in our endeavour to combine the best of both worlds, we rely on searing quite a lot. Whereas in traditional Indian cooking, meat is generally cut into small pieces and cooked in batches in a sauce, at The Cinnamon Club we use larger cuts of meat, such as a whole steak or chicken breast, and sear them in a hot pan, then serve them with a separate sauce. We also use this technique very effectively to recreate the tandoor cooking effect at home (see Tandoor Cooking on page 26). When searing, use a heavy-based pan and make sure it is moderately hot before you add the meat or fish. Resist the temptation to move the food about the pan – leave it well alone for a few minutes, then lift one edge to check that it has formed a good crust before turning it over.

DUM COOKING

Dum is a method of braising ingredients in a very little liquid in a sealed container so the steam does not escape. The pot may be sealed by placing a heavy, tight-fitting lid over it and then either putting a heavy weight on top or sealing the join with strips of dough, which solidify when they become hot. In this way, all the flavours mingle together in the dish, the nutrients are preserved, and none of the cooking juices are lost.

STORING SPICES

Most basic spices, such as cumin, coriander, chilli and turmeric, can be bought ready-ground. More aromatic spices, however, such as cardamom, cinnamon, cloves, mace and star anise, should be bought whole and then ground just before use. Both ground and whole spices should be stored in airtight containers in a cool, dark place. Use ground spices within two weeks and whole spices within six months.

EQUIPMENT

Most of the recipes in this book do not require any special utensils. Traditionally in India a lot of heavy copper pots and pans are used but they can be quite difficult to maintain. Stainless steel pans with alloy bottoms are easily available nowadays and work well on different heat sources. A good set of pots and pans is always a worthwhile investment for any enthusiast.

CAST IRON FRYING PAN

When you are searing meat and fish, a large, cast iron frying pan is invaluable, as it can be transferred directly to the oven to complete the cooking.

MORTAR AND PESTLE

A brass or stone mortar and pestle is a useful item to have, as it enables you to grind spices to exactly the required texture.

FOOD PROCESSOR

A food processor is the most effortless way of making spice pastes. Choose a heavy-duty model with a powerful motor.

SPICE MILL

In Indian homes, spice mixes are made into a paste by grinding them on a stone slab with a little water, using another piece of stone. For larger quantities, people use wet stone grinders, which are motorised versions of the same concept. Grinding the spices with water means that the spices contribute to the body of the sauce and the water prevents them burning.

With changing times, more and more households have done away with stone grinders and use electric spice mills instead. They save a lot of time and mess.

BASICS

GINGER PASTE
Makes about 6 tablespoons
175g/6oz fresh ginger, peeled
5 tablespoons water

Chop up the ginger and process it to a paste with the water in a food processor or blender. The paste will keep for 1 week in the fridge.

GARLIC PASTE
Makes about 6 tablespoons
175g/6oz garlic, peeled
5 tablespoons water

Chop up the garlic and process it to a paste with the water in a food processor or blender. The paste will keep for 1 week in the fridge, but if you substitute oil for water it should keep for 2 weeks.

GINGER AND GARLIC PASTE
Makes about 8 tablespoons
100g ginger peeled
75g/3oz garlic peeled
175 ml/6 fl oz water

Chop up the ginger and garlic and blend it to a fine thick paste using water.

Almost all recipes require ginger paste and garlic paste, there are certain preparations where more of garlic paste is required in that case the pastes could be made separately.

FRIED CASHEW PASTE
Makes about 300g/11oz
200g/7oz cashew nuts
2 tablespoons vegetable or corn oil
200ml/7fl oz water

Fry the cashew nuts in the oil until golden, then remove from the pan with a slotted spoon. Soak the nuts in the water for 20 minutes, then drain. Blend to a smooth paste in a food processor or blender with 5 tablespoons of water. The paste will keep for 4 days in the fridge.

BOILED CASHEW PASTE
Makes about 400g/14oz
200g/7oz cashew nuts
1 blade of mace
1 green cardamom pod
300ml/½ pint water

Soak the cashew nuts in enough water to cover for 10 minutes, then drain. Put them in a pan with the mace, cardamom and water, bring to the boil and simmer for 25 minutes. Remove from the heat and leave to cool. Blend to a smooth paste in a food processor or blender with 100ml/3½fl oz water. The paste will keep for 4 days in the fridge.

FRIED ONION PASTE
Makes about 150g/5oz
600g/1lb 5oz onions, sliced
oil for frying
200ml/7fl oz water

Deep-fry the onions in medium-hot oil until golden brown, then remove and drain on kitchen paper. Put them in a food processor or blender with the water and process until smooth.

The paste will keep for 1 week in the fridge. For additional flavour, the water can be replaced with yoghurt, in which case it will make about 350g/12oz paste.

BOILED ONION PASTE
Makes about 300g/11oz
1 large onion, cut into 2.5cm/
    1 inch cubes
250ml/8fl oz water

Put the onion and water in a small pan and simmer for 15–20 minutes, until the onion is soft. Purée in a food processor or blender until smooth. The paste will keep for 3 days in the fridge.

BOILED CASHEW NUT –ONION SAUCE BASE

450 g whole onions peeled and diced into I inch cubes
225 g broken cashew nut kernels, washed in warm water
450 ml hot water
2 no green cardamom
I blade of mace
I bay leaf
A pinch of salt

Boil for 15 minutes and remove from heat. Using the liquid that is still remaining, blend the onions and cashew nuts to a fine paste. This may take between 8-10 minutes in a domestic blender. Take care to rest the machine in between to protect from burn out!

You will be left with about 850 gms of sauce base that can be used to thicken various sauces.

GARAM MASALA

There are many versions of garam masala; this is a good basic one. It is generally added to dishes towards the end of cooking to impart flavour, not to add heat as its name might suggest (garam means hot and masala means mix).
I would always recommend making your own garam masala if possible. Commercial blends use a larger proportion of the cheaper spices and less of the more expensive aromatic ones, such as cardamom and cinnamon.

50g/2oz coriander seeds
50g/2oz cumin seeds
20 green cardamom pods
IO cinnamon sticks, about 2.5cm/ I inch long
2 tablespoons cloves
IO blades of mace
IO black cardamom pods
½ nutmeg
I tablespoon black peppercorns
4 bay leaves

Put all the ingredients on a baking tray and place in a low oven (about 110°C/225°F/Gas Mark 1/4) for 3–5 minutes; this intensifies the flavours. You could even dry the spices in a microwave for 20 seconds or so.

Grind everything to a fine powder in a spice grinder, then sieve the mixture to remove any husks or large particles. Store in an airtight container and use within 2 weeks.

Variation:
CINNAMON CLUB GARAM MASALA

In The Cinnamon Club's version of garam masala, these extra spices are added to the mixture above to impart a special flavour. We also use rock moss which, like ajino moto in Chinese cooking, brings out the flavours of other ingredients and is absolutely natural and safe. We fly this special ingredient in from India.

the petals from I pink rose, dried
5 star anise
I tablespoon fennel seeds

SAMBAR MASALA

I tablespoon coriander seeds
2 teaspoons cumin seeds
I tablespoon chana dal
6 dried red chillies
I½ teaspoons black peppercorns
2 tablespoons grated coconut
½ teaspoon fenugreek seeds
I sprig of fresh curry leaves

Grind all the ingredients to a powder in a spice grinder. Store in an airtight container and use within 2 weeks.

MACE AND CARDAMOM POWDER

¼ nutmeg
40g/I½oz blades of mace
50g/2oz green cardamom pods

Grate the nutmeg or pound it with a mortar and pestle to break it up. Dry all the spices in a microwave for 30 seconds, then grind them to a fine powder. Store in an airtight container and use within 3–4 days.

PAO BHAJI MASALA

I teaspoon cloves
I teaspoon black peppercorns
½ teaspoon cumin seeds
I teaspoon ajowan seeds
I teaspoon fennel seeds
2.5cm/I inch piece of cinnamon
½ teaspoon black salt (optional)
½ teaspoon fenugreek seeds (optional)
½ teaspoon dried mango powder (optional)
I blade of mace
¼ nutmeg

Dry all the ingredients in a microwave for 30 seconds, then grind to a fine powder in a spice grinder. Store in an airtight container and use within 2 weeks.

RAJASTHANI SPICE PASTE

This is sometimes known as soola masala, as it is used to make soola kebabs. It can also be used with game, chicken or any other kind of meat, and even some types of fish – red snapper is particularly good.

2 tablespoons mustard oil or sunflower oil
2 tablespoons ghee or clarified butter
I large onion, sliced
6 garlic cloves, chopped
20 cloves
I0 green cardamom pods
I tablespoon coriander seeds
I teaspoon black peppercorns
I tablespoon fennel seeds
I50g/5oz fresh coriander leaves, chopped
I teaspoon salt
I50g/5oz plain yoghurt

Heat the mustard or sunflower oil in a heavy-based frying pan until smoking, then add the ghee or clarified butter. Add the sliced onion and cook until softened but not coloured. Add the garlic and cook for a few minutes, until it starts to brown. Add the cloves, cardamom, coriander seeds, peppercorns and fennel seeds in that order and stir quickly over a high heat for a couple of minutes, taking care that the spices do not burn. Stir in the coriander and salt, then remove from the heat and leave to cool. Transfer the mixture to a food processor or blender, add the yoghurt and blend to a paste.

BOILED RICE

Serves 6–8

500g/1lb 2oz basmati rice
a large pinch of salt
2 tablespoons vegetable or corn oil

Soak the rice in cold water for about 10 minutes, then drain. Bring a large pan of water to the boil with the oil and add the salt. Add the rice and simmer, uncovered, for 9–12 minutes, until the grains give way when you press them between your fingertips but are still slightly firm in the centre (al dente).

Remove from the heat and drain through a large colander. To prevent further cooking, you could pour cold water over the rice, or simply spread it out in a large baking tray and leave to cool.

GHEE OR CLARIFIED BUTTER

Cooking butter like this stops it going rancid and also enables it to withstand high temperatures and constant reheating. Correctly made, ghee will keep in the fridge for several years.

Place 250g/9oz unsalted butter in a heavy-based pan and heat gently until it melts. Bring to the boil, then reduce the heat and simmer for 20–30 minutes, skimming off the froth from the surface, until the sediment has settled at the bottom and separated from the clear, golden ghee.

The sediment is the cooked milk solids and should be carefully removed and discarded. The golden liquid solidifies when cool but should stay creamy, like soft margarine. Store in the fridge.

ROASTING (AND CRUSHING) SEEDS

Put the seeds in a moderately hot frying pan or under the grill and roast for a minute or two, until they are just dried but not coloured. Remove from the heat and pound together in a mortar and pestle, until the seeds are crushed but still coarse enough to be identified separately. If you want to grind the seeds to a powder, the best way to do this is in a spice grinder.

MANGO PURÉE

At The Cinnamon Club we use mango purée a lot to decorate plates and for dips, sauces and chutneys. Unsweetened canned mango purée works very well for these purposes and is available in most supermarkets. Alternatively, to make your own, peel a slightly overripe mango and cut the flesh off the stone. Blend it to a fine purée in a blender or food processor and then pass through a sieve to remove any fibres.

STARTERS

FISH

Tandoori-style Seared Tuna, Punjabi Spiced Cod, Swordfish with Mustard and Honey, Swordfish Stir-fry with Green Chillies and Curry Leaves, Steamed Halibut in Banana Leaf, Chargrilled Sea Bream with Pomegranate Extract, Tandoori-style Salmon with Rice Pancakes, Deep-fried Skate Wings with Chilli, Garlic and Vinegar

SEAFOOD

Crab and Cod Cakes, Parsee Spiced Stir-fried Squid, Mussels in Tomato and Curry Leaf Broth, Bengali-style Grilled Lobster

CHICKEN

Minced Chicken Kebabs with Corn, Tandoori-style Chicken Thighs with Green Spices and Mustard, Chicken with Mace and Cardamom, Stir-fried Chicken with Dried Chillies, Tandoori-style Sandalwood Chicken Breasts

GAME

Tandoori-style Pigeon Breasts, Breast of Guinea Fowl with Fennel and Coriander, Rabbit Tikka, Loin of Rabbit Stuffed with Dried Fruit and Paneer

LAMB

Home-smoked Lamb Kebabs, Lamb Kebab Wraps

BEEF

Clove-smoked Tender Beef Kebabs, Minced Veal Kebabs with Mango and Pineapple Salad

VEGETARIAN

Sweet Potato Cakes with Ginger, Fennel and Chilli, Courgette Flowers Stuffed with Corn and Mushrooms, Bengali Spiced Vegetable Cakes, Cheese and Chilli Melt on Naan Bread, Aubergine Caviar with Smoked Cucumber Yoghurt, Asparagus Stir-fry with Bengali Roasted Aubergine, Tapioca and Cumin Fritters with Green Coconut Chutney

TANDOORI-STYLE SEARED TUNA

SERVES 4

I once saw Gordon Ramsay cook seared tuna on British television, and it occurred to me that the tandoor would be an ideal vehicle for searing, given its intense heat. When I suggested it to Vivek, he came up with a tamarind coating for the tuna, which caramelises quickly on the surface and gives the fish a wonderfully deep, glossy colour. The recipe below has been adapted for grilling the tuna at home. Serve with Cucumber Yoghurt (see page 163).

Wine to accompany this recipe
FRENCH SEMILLON
A fresh, crisp, citrus style of wine, such as a *French Semillon*, will balance the natural sweetness of the tamarind and complement the slight dryness of seared tuna.

Put the tamarind paste in a small pan and bring to the boil. Add the sugar and stir until dissolved, then add the chilli powder and salt. Cook over a low heat for about 15 minutes, stirring occasionally, until the mixture is thick and glossy – it will become liquid at first, then gradually thicken. Remove from the heat and leave to cool. Then add the oil, crushed coriander and cumin and mix well.

Coat the tuna thoroughly in the tamarind mixture, then cook under a very hot grill for 1 minute on each side, so it is nicely caramelised on the outside but still rare in the centre. Serve immediately.

4 x 100g/4oz pieces of fresh tuna loin, about 2.5cm/1 inch thick

For the tamarind mixture:
150g/5oz/^{2}/3 cup tamarind paste
100g/4oz/^{1}/2 cup granulated sugar
¼ teaspoon red chilli powder
1 teaspoon salt
1 tablespoon vegetable or corn oil
1 teaspoon coriander seeds, roasted and crushed (see page 33)
1 teaspoon cumin seeds, roasted and crushed (see page 33)

PUNJABI SPICED COD

SERVES 4

It's not only the British who love to eat fish deep-fried in batter. The Punjabis have a similar dish but before frying the fish they rub it with pungent herbs and spices, such as ajowan and chilli powder. Here we have used a more subtle combination of flavours. As long as you don't mind deep-frying, it is very easy to prepare and wonderful to eat.

Pat dry the cod fillet. Mix together the ginger and garlic pastes, salt, chilli powder and lemon juice. Rub this mixture over the fish and set aside for 15 minutes.

Mix all the ingredients for the batter together until smooth and thick. Heat some oil in a deep-fat fryer or a large, deep saucepan. Dip the cod in the batter and fry for about 5 minutes, until golden and crisp. Drain on kitchen paper and serve straight away, with Mango and Mint Chutney and lemon wedges.

Wine to accompany this recipe
VOUVRAY
The soft spicing will suit the delicate acidity of a *Vouvray* and will also lift the fruit element of the wine.

4 x 125g/4½oz pieces of cod fillet
I teaspoon Ginger Paste (see page 30)
I teaspoon Garlic Paste (see page 30)
I teaspoon salt
½ teaspoon red chilli powder
juice of ½ lemon
oil for deep-frying
Mango and Mint Chutney (see page 162) and lemon wedges, to serve

For the batter:
2 tablespoons gram (chickpea) flour
I tablespoon cornflour
½ teaspoon salt
I teaspoon red chilli powder
½ teaspoon ajowan seeds
¼ teaspoon garam masala
Icm/½ inch piece of fresh ginger, finely chopped
I tablespoon chopped fresh coriander
juice of I lemon
3 tablespoons water

SWORDFISH WITH MUSTARD AND HONEY

SERVES 4

At the restaurant we cook this in a tandoor oven but it is also an ideal dish for the barbecue. The firm flesh of swordfish lends itself perfectly to the fierce heat of white hot coals and is complemented by the sweet–sharp elements of the honey and mustard. Serve with Spiced Onion Yoghurt (see page 163).

Mix together all the ingredients for the first marinade and rub them into the fish. Set aside for 30 minutes.

Heat the oil in a large ovenproof frying pan, add the swordfish and sear for 1 minute on each side, until well browned. Mix together all the ingredients for the second marinade, spread them over the fish and transfer to an oven preheated to 240°C/475°F/Gas Mark 9. Cook for 8–10 minutes, then place under a hot grill for 3 minutes. (If you are cooking the fish on a barbecue, simply apply the second marinade immediately after the first marinating period and set aside for another 15 minutes, then place on a barbecue.)

Serve immediately, garnished with a few salad leaves.

SWORDFISH STIR-FRY WITH GREEN CHILLIES AND CURRY LEAVES

SERVES 4

Wine to accompany this recipe
VIOGNIER
The pungent character of the mustard will
be matched by the intense white fruit of a
Viognier, while the sweetness of the honey will
complement the fruit character of the wine.

*This style of stir-fry cooking originates
in the southern state of Karanthaka,
home to Bangalore, and is also a
popular way of preparing chicken.*

Wine to accompany this recipe
VIOGNIER
An unoaked ripe *Viognier* from the
northern Rhône or the *Languedoc Roussillon*
region of France will match the heat of the
green chillies.

4 x 150g/5oz pieces of swordfish fillet
I tablespoon vegetable or corn oil
a few salad leaves, to garnish

For the first marinade:
I teaspoon Ginger Paste (see page 30)
I teaspoon Garlic Paste (see page 30)
1½ teaspoons salt
juice of ½ lemon

For the second marinade:
100g/4oz Greek yoghurt/½ cup
2½ tablespoons mustard seeds, soaked in
   3 tablespoons white vinegar overnight
   and ground to a paste (or use 2
   tablespoons wholegrain mustard)
½ teaspoon ground turmeric
I teaspoon finely ground white pepper
2.5cm/I inch piece of fresh ginger,
   finely chopped
2 green chillies, finely chopped
3 tablespoons chopped fresh coriander
I tablespoon honey
2 tablespoons mustard oil
   (or sunflower oil)

To make the batter, put the cornflour,
chilli powder and salt in a bowl and
mix in the vinegar and water until
smooth. Coat the swordfish in the
batter and deep-fry in hot oil for about
2 minutes, until the batter is crisp but
the fish is still succulent. Drain on
kitchen paper and set aside.

Heat the 2 teaspoons of oil in a wok or
large frying pan and add the curry
leaves. When they crackle, add the
garlic and sauté briskly. Add the onion
and diced pepper and sauté for a
couple of minutes over maximum
heat. While the onion and pepper are
still crunchy, add the green chillies
and the fried swordfish. Stir quickly to
mix all the ingredients well, then add
the yoghurt, making sure that it gets
evenly absorbed and doesn't separate.
Sprinkle with the salt and sugar,
squeeze in the lemon juice and
serve immediately.

500g/1lb 2oz swordfish, cut into
   2.5cm/I inch dice
oil for deep-frying
2 teaspoons vegetable or corn oil
10 fresh curry leaves
2 garlic cloves, crushed
I red onion, cut into 2.5cm/I inch dice
½ red pepper, cut into 2.5cm/
   I inch dice
4 green chillies, cut lengthways in half
2 tablespoons plain yoghurt
I teaspoon salt
½ teaspoon sugar
juice of I lemon

For the batter:
4 tablespoons cornflour
2 teaspoons mild red chilli powder
I teaspoon salt
2 tablespoons white vinegar
I tablespoon water

STEAMED HALIBUT IN BANANA LEAF

Put all the marinade ingredients in a blender or food processor and blend to a smooth paste. Pat dry the pieces of halibut and coat them thoroughly with the paste. Set aside to marinate for 30 minutes.

Wrap each fillet in a piece of banana leaf, taking care that it is well secured so the marinade and juices can't ooze out during cooking (dipping the leaf in hot water for a few seconds softens it and makes it easier to fold). Place the parcels in a steamer and steam for 10–15 minutes. Open up the parcels a little and serve immediately.

SERVES 4

This is an adaptation of a dish called patrani macchi, *cooked by the Parsee community in Bombay, where the fish used is pomfret. We prefer halibut because its firm texture lends itself well to both marinating and steaming. Banana leaves, available from some Indian, Thai and Caribbean food shops, add their subtle flavour, but if you cannot find any, just wrap the halibut in foil instead. Serve with Curried Yoghurt Dip (see page 162).*

4 x 125g/4½oz pieces of halibut fillet, skinned
1 banana leaf, cut into 4 pieces

For the marinade:
50g/2oz/1 cup fresh coriander leaves
20g/¾oz/½ cup fresh mint leaves
3cm/1¼ inch piece of fresh ginger, roughly chopped
4 large garlic cloves, roughly chopped
4 green chillies, roughly chopped
2 tablespoons grated fresh coconut (or 1 tablespoon desiccated coconut and 2 tablespoons coconut milk)
½ teaspoon cumin seeds, roasted (see page 33)
2 tablespoons vegetable or corn oil
juice of 1 lemon
1 teaspoon salt

Wine to accompany this recipe
ARGENTINIAN TORRONTES
An *Argentinian Torrontes* grape will balance the garlic and coriander.

CHARGRILLED SEA BREAM WITH POMEGRANATE EXTRACT

SERVES 4

This is a unique creation of Vivek's and makes an ideal summer starter cooked to perfection on a barbecue. The pomegranate lifts the delicate flavour of the sea bream and also looks stunning on the plate. Serve with a leafy green salad.

Wine to accompany this recipe
AUSTRALIAN SEMILLON
A non-barrel-fermented *Semillon* from *Australia* will have intense citrus flavours to complement the acidity of the pomegranate extract, leaving a complex finish with honey elements.

Mix together all the ingredients for the first marinade, rub them over the bream fillets and leave to marinate for 30 minutes.

For the second marinade, put the cheese in a small bowl and rub it to a paste with your fingers (a teaspoon of flour could be added to help prevent lumps forming). Add the yoghurt and mix until smooth, then mix in the remaining ingredients. Spread this mixture over the fillets and leave for another 10 minutes.

Meanwhile, make the dressing. Pour the pomegranate juice into a small pan, bring to the boil and simmer until reduced by half its volume. Remove from the heat, stir in the sugar and leave to cool. Whisk in the olive oil.

Place the fish skin-side down on a hot barbecue and cook for 5–6 minutes, turning half way through. (Alternatively, place the fish on a baking tray, cover with foil and place under a very hot grill for about 5 minutes, depending upon the thickness of the fish. Then remove the foil and grill for a further 5 minutes, turning the fillets skin-side up towards the end to give a nice, crisp skin.) Place the fish on 4 serving plates, quickly whisk up the dressing again and drizzle it to the side of the fish. Sprinkle over the reserved pomegranate seeds and serve.

4 black sea bream fillets, scaled

For the first marinade:
½ teaspoon Ginger Paste (see page 30)
½ teaspoon Garlic Paste (see page 30)
½ teaspoon salt
juice of ½ lemon
½ teaspoon finely ground white pepper

For the second marinade:
1 tablespoon grated processed
    Cheddar cheese
2 tablespoons Greek yoghurt
1 tablespoon chopped fresh coriander
1 teaspoon Mace and Cardamom
    Powder (see page 32)
¼ teaspoon salt

For the dressing:
2 pomegranates, deseeded (squeeze
    the juice from most of the seeds and
    set aside the rest for garnish)
½ teaspoon sugar
3 tablespoons olive oil

TANDOORI-STYLE SALMON WITH RICE PANCAKES

SERVES 4

Because of its oily texture, salmon works really well in the fierce heat of a tandoor oven. The dual marinade used here means that it can also be cooked in a conventional oven at home retaining all the flavours of a traditional clay oven roasting. Served on a south Indian rice pancake, it's easy to eat with your fingers and makes a great starter or canapé. For canapés, make tiny pancakes about 2.5cm / 1 inch in diameter.

Mix together all the ingredients for the first marinade, combine with the salmon and set aside for 30 minutes.

For the second marinade, put the cheese in a small bowl and rub it to a paste with your fingers (a teaspoon of flour could be added to help prevent lumps forming). Add the yoghurt and mix until smooth, then mix in the remaining ingredients. Spread the marinade over the salmon and set aside for another 30 minutes.

Place the salmon on a baking tray and cook in an oven preheated to 220°C/425°F/Gas Mark 7 for 8–10 minutes, turning once. Sprinkle with the chaat masala, if using, and the lemon juice. Place the salmon on the rice pancakes and serve immediately.

Wine to accompany this recipe
PINOT NOIR FROM BURGUNDY
A light *Pinot Noir* from *Burgundy* or from the *Mornington Peninsula* in *Australia* will match the delicate earthiness of the salmon.

400g/14oz salmon fillet,
    cut into 4 portions
½ teaspoon chaat masala (optional)
a squeeze of lemon juice
4 rice pancakes (see Uttapam on page
    203, including the diced peppers for
    extra colour, if you like)

For the first marinade:
1½ teaspoons Ginger Paste (see page 30)
1½ teaspoons Garlic Paste (see page 30)
1 teaspoon salt
juice of ½ lemon

For the second marinade:
1 tablespoon grated processed
    Cheddar cheese
1 tablespoon Greek yoghurt
½ teaspoon Mace and Cardamom
    Powder (see page 32)
½ teaspoon chopped fresh dill
1 tablespoon single cream

DEEP-FRIED SKATE WINGS WITH CHILLI, GARLIC AND VINEGAR

SERVES 4

This way of cooking fish is very popular among the fishing community. If you can't obtain skate wings, use any firm fleshed fish fillets, such as tilapia. If you are going to use skate, though, make sure it is absolutely fresh, otherwise it will give off an unpleasant ammonia-like smell. Serve with salad leaves and Spiced Onion Yoghurt (see page 163).

Pat the skate wings dry. Mix together all the marinade ingredients and rub them over the fish. Leave to marinate for 15 minutes.

For the batter, mix the garlic paste, egg, cornflour and gram flour together, then stir in the vinegar to give a thick coating consistency. Mix in the chilli powder, salt and onion seeds. Apply the batter to the skate and set aside for 10 minutes.

Heat some oil in a deep-fat fryer or a large, deep saucepan. Fry the fish for about 5 minutes, until crisp and golden, then drain on kitchen paper and serve immediately.

Wine to accompany this recipe
AUSTRALIAN RIESLING
The heat of the chilli will match the mineral, very dry style of an *Australian Riesling*, while the vinegar will balance the dryness of this wine.

2 skate wings, trimmed and cut in half
  oil for deep-frying

For the marinade:
½ teaspoon salt
½ teaspoon red chilli powder
1 tablespoon vegetable or corn oil

For the batter:
1 tablespoon Garlic Paste (see page 30)
1 egg
1½ tablespoons cornflour
1½ tablespoons gram (chickpea) flour
2 tablespoons white vinegar
1 teaspoon red chilli powder
½ teaspoon salt
½ teaspoon black onion seeds

CRAB AND COD CAKES

SERVES 4

The Americans, the British and even the Thais love fishcakes and now they're becoming increasingly popular in India, too. Bengalis traditionally make fish kofta – little balls of flaked fish, cooked in a light sauce. They also make fishcakes called macher chop, *which are fried and served as a starter. This recipe takes inspiration from both Western and Eastern varieties. Serve with a mustardy mayonnaise.*

Wine to accompany this recipe
ALSACE GEWÜRZTRAMINER
The intense flavours of an *Alsace Gewürztraminer* will suit the natural sweetness of the potato and crab.

First cook the cod. Mix together the oil, salt, onion seeds and fennel seeds and rub them over the fish. Place on a baking tray and cook for 15 minutes in an oven preheated to 180°C/ 350°F/ Gas Mark 4. Leave to cool, reserving the juices in the baking tray.

For the crab, heat the oil in a pan and add the cumin seeds. When they crackle, add the onion and sauté until golden, then add the chillies and ginger and sauté for another minute. Add the crab meat and toss well, mixing in the salt. Cook until the liquid evaporates, then remove from the heat and leave to cool.

Put the flour, ajowan seeds and black onion seeds in a dry pan and place over a very low heat. Once the flour has warmed through, add the butter and cook gently, stirring, until it has blended with the flour to form a smooth, thick mixture. Stir in the ginger. Now slowly whisk in the juices from the baked cod, followed by the milk. Sprinkle in the garam masala and mix well. It should look like a very thick béchamel sauce. Remove from the heat and leave to cool.

Put the crab mixture in a large bowl, flake in the cod and gently mix in the sauce. Divide the mixture into 4 portions and shape into balls. Pour the beaten eggs into a shallow dish and put the breadcrumbs in another dish. Dip the fishcakes in the egg and then roll them in the breadcrumbs until thoroughly coated. Flatten slightly and deep-fry in a deep-fat fryer or a large, deep saucepan for 2 minutes or until golden. Drain on kitchen paper and serve straight away.

50g/2oz/½ cup plain flour
½ teaspoon ajowan seeds
¼ teaspoon black onion seeds
75g/3oz/⅓ cup butter
Icm/½ inch piece of fresh ginger, finely chopped
I50ml/¼ pint/²⁄3 cup milk
I teaspoon garam masala
2 eggs, beaten
dried breadcrumbs for coating
oil for deep-frying

For the cod:
I tablespoon vegetable or corn oil
I teaspoon salt
½ teaspoon black onion seeds
I teaspoon fennel seeds
200g/7oz cod fillet

For the crab:
2 tablespoons vegetable or corn oil
I teaspoon cumin seeds
I large onion, finely chopped
2 green chillies, finely chopped
Icm/½ inch piece of fresh ginger, finely chopped
200g/7oz/⁷⁄8 cup fresh white crab meat
½ teaspoon salt

PARSEE SPICED STIR-FRIED SQUID

SERVES 4

In this dish, we have taken the keynote flavours of Parsee cooking – sweet and hot – but instead of making a traditional thin sauce we have reduced the spice paste to a glaze, which seals in all the succulent juices of the squid.

Wine to accompany this recipe
AUSTRALIAN RIESLING
The tropical style of an *Australian Riesling* will complement the sweetness of the spice paste.

For the spice paste, put the cloves, peppercorns, coriander seeds, cumin seeds and cinnamon stick on a baking sheet and dry under a hot grill for a few minutes to remove any moisture. Grind the spices to a powder in a spice grinder.

Heat the oil in a small pan, add the onion and sauté until golden brown. Add the garlic and sauté for a couple of minutes, then stir in the ground spices and chilli powder. Stir briskly for a few seconds, then add the tomato purée, apricot purée, salt and sugar. Cook for 3–4 minutes, until the mixture takes on a jammy consistency. It should taste sweet and spicy.

To cook the squid, heat the oil in a large, heavy-based frying pan until it starts to smoke. Add the squid rings and stir quickly until they begin to sear and colour in parts. Add the spice paste and stir-fry for a few seconds, until it coats the squid evenly. Sprinkle in the fresh coriander and squeeze over the lemon juice. Toss well, check the seasoning and serve immediately.

I tablespoon vegetable or corn oil
500g/Ilb 2oz squid, cleaned and
    cut into Icm/½ inch rings
50g/2oz/I cup fresh coriander,
    chopped
juice of I lemon

For the spice paste:
IO cloves
½ teaspoon black peppercorns
½ teaspoon coriander seeds
½ teaspoon cumin seeds
I cinnamon stick
I tablespoon vegetable or corn oil
½ onion, finely chopped
I garlic clove, finely chopped
I teaspoon red chilli powder
I tablespoon tomato purée
I tablespoon puréed dried apricots
I teaspoon salt
½ teaspoon sugar

MUSSELS IN TOMATO AND CURRY LEAF BROTH

SERVES 4

In southern India the Tamils make a thin soup called rasam, *which is usually served poured over rice. The British turned this into what became known as mulligatawny. Seafood rasam is a modern Indian adaptation and in this recipe we have used mussels. It's a wonderfully simple, quick and inexpensive dish, and can be prepared in advance right up to the point where you add the mussels.*

Wine to accompany this recipe
AMERICAN PINOT BLANC
The citrus flavours of curry leaves, combined with the natural sweetness of the seafood, will be enhanced by the ripe white fruit character of an *American Pinot Blanc*.

Heat the oil in a large saucepan, add the crushed garlic and ginger and sauté for 1 minute. Add the curry leaves and halved tomatoes and cook until the tomatoes are soft. Stir in the turmeric, chilli powder and tamarind and cook for 2 minutes. Pour in the stock and bring to a simmer. Meanwhile, coarsely crush the peppercorns and cumin seeds together in a pestle and mortar. Add them to the simmering stock with the coriander roots and cook for 20 minutes. Strain the broth through a fine sieve into another pan, pressing down on the mixture to extract all the liquid. Stir in the salt and sugar.

Clean the mussels under cold running water, pulling out the beards and discarding any open mussels that don't close when tapped on the work surface. Bring the soup back to the boil, add the mussels, then cover and simmer for about 2 minutes, until they open. Remove from the heat and stir in the diced tomato and chopped coriander

Now quickly temper the soup. Heat the oil in a small pan until very hot, then add the mustard seeds. They should crackle immediately. Add the red chillies next, followed by the curry leaves and the asafoetida, if using, then quickly plunge the mixture into the hot soup. Serve immediately.

2 tablespoons vegetable or corn oil
4 garlic cloves, crushed
2.5cm/1 inch piece of fresh ginger, crushed
1 sprig of fresh curry leaves
12 tomatoes, cut in half
¼ teaspoon ground turmeric
¼ teaspoon red chilli powder
1½ teaspoons tamarind paste
800ml/27fl oz/3 cups fish stock (or water)
1 teaspoon black peppercorns
1 teaspoon cumin seeds
50g/2oz/¾ cup fresh coriander roots, washed
1 teaspoon salt
½ teaspoon sugar
400g/14oz fresh mussels

To garnish:
1 tomato, deseeded and cut into 5mm/¼ inch dice
1 tablespoon chopped fresh coriander

For tempering:
1 tablespoon vegetable or corn oil
¼ teaspoon mustard seeds
2 dried red chillies, split in half
10 fresh curry leaves
a small pinch of asafoetida (optional)

BENGALI-STYLE GRILLED LOBSTER

SERVES 4

Lobster is a treat in any country and for the Bengalis it's certainly no different. If you ask your fishmonger to prepare the lobsters for you, this dish is very easy to make and is bound to impress even the most seasoned of guests. A mustardy mayonnaise makes an excellent accompaniment.

Wine to accompany this recipe
ITALIAN SAUVIGNON BLANC
The dry heat of the Bengali spices and the sweetness of the lobster will be balanced by the slightly ripe citrus element of an *Italian Sauvignon Blanc.*

Twist the claws off the prepared lobsters, crack them open and remove the meat. Set aside. Pat dry the lobster halves. Heat the oil in a large, heavy-based frying pan, add the lobsters, flesh-side down, and sear for a couple of minutes, until the meat starts to colour. Remove the lobsters from the pan and sprinkle with the salt, ground cardamom, sugar and coriander. Drizzle with the coconut milk and lemon juice, then cook under a hot grill for 8–10 minutes.

Meanwhile, cook the claw meat. Heat the oil in a small pan, add the onion and sauté until golden brown. Add the claw meat and stir-fry quickly on a high heat for 1–2 minutes. Add the ginger and chilli powder and sauté for a couple of minutes more, then add the tomato and cook until the liquid has evaporated and the mixture is dry. Season with the salt, then pile up the mixture on the lobster halves and serve at once.

2 live lobsters, cut in half lengthways and cleaned (you can ask your fishmonger to do this, as long as you cook the lobsters on the same day)
1 tablespoon vegetable or corn oil
1 teaspoon salt
1 teaspoon ground cardamom
½ teaspoon sugar
20g/¾oz/½ cup fresh coriander, chopped
1 tablespoon coconut milk
juice of 1 lemon

For the claw meat:
1 teaspoon vegetable or corn oil
½ onion, finely chopped
1cm/½ inch piece of fresh ginger, finely chopped
½ teaspoon red chilli powder
1 tomato, finely chopped
½ teaspoon salt

MINCED CHICKEN KEBABS WITH CORN

SERVES 4

In India a minced chicken kebab is known as a reshmi kebab. We have adapted this classic by simply adding sweetcorn to give a more interesting texture. These kebabs work wonderfully on the barbecue.

Wine to accompany this recipe
NEW ZEALAND RIESLING
The heat of the kebab will lift the fruit of a mineral *Riesling* from *New Zealand*, leaving a pleasant, delicate tropical finish.

600g/1lb 5oz/2½ cups minced chicken
2.5cm/1 inch piece of fresh ginger, chopped
2 garlic cloves, chopped
3 green chillies, chopped
50g/2oz/1 cup fresh coriander, chopped
40g/1½oz/⅓ cup processed Cheddar cheese, grated
½ teaspoon crushed black peppercorns
1 teaspoon Mace and Cardamom Powder (see page 32)
1 teaspoon salt
100g/4oz/1 cup canned sweetcorn
melted butter or oil for basting
juice of ½ lemon
½ teaspoon chaat masala (optional)
a few salad leaves, to garnish

Put the minced chicken in a bowl and mix with the ginger, garlic, chillies, coriander, cheese, black pepper, mace and cardamom powder and salt. Pass through the mincer once again, or use your hands and give the mixture a good squeeze! Chill for 2–3 hours, then mix in the sweetcorn and divide the mixture into 4 portions. Shape each one round a skewer, squeezing the meat gently with wet hands so it adheres to the skewer.

Cook under a very hot grill or on a ridged grill pan for 10–12 minutes, turning constantly to ensure that the kebabs cook evenly and brushing regularly with butter or oil. Sprinkle with the lemon juice and the chaat masala, if using, then serve immediately, garnished with some salad leaves.

TANDOORI-STYLE CHICKEN THIGHS WITH GREEN SPICES AND MUSTARD

Traditionally this dish is made with a Bengali mustard called kasundi. We have substituted the kasundi for wholegrain mustard but you can easily make kasundi at home by soaking mustard seeds in white wine vinegar overnight in a ratio of 4:3 and then blending them to a paste.

4 corn-fed chicken thighs,
    skinned and boned

For the marinade:
I teaspoon Garlic Paste (see page 30)
I teaspoon Ginger Paste (see page 30)
I teaspoon finely ground white pepper
I teaspoon salt
juice of I lemon

For the green spice mix:
100g/4oz/3 cups fresh coriander
    (roots, stalks and leaves)
50g/2oz/2½ cups fresh mint leaves
100g/4oz/3 cups fresh mustard leaves
    (if you can't find these, use double
    the amount of English mustard
    given below)
6 green chillies, chopped
3 tablespoons vegetable or corn oil
I teaspoon English mustard
2 tablespoons wholegrain mustard
I teaspoon salt
¼ teaspoon ground turmeric
I teaspoon garam masala
50g/2oz/¼ cup Greek yoghurt

Put the chicken in a bowl, add all the marinade ingredients and mix well. Set aside for 30 minutes.

Put all the spice mix ingredients except the yoghurt in a food processor or blender and mix to a smooth paste. Check the seasoning; it should taste quite pungent, as its strength decreases during cooking. Rub the paste on to the chicken, add the yoghurt and mix well. Leave to marinate for another 30 minutes.

Place the chicken on a baking tray and cook in an oven preheated to 200°C/400°F/Gas Mark 6 for 20 minutes, turning once. If the meat starts to dry out, pour over some of the marinade.

Wine to accompany this recipe
NEW ZEALAND OR FRENCH SYRAH
A medium-ripe *New Zealand* or *French Syrah* from gravelly soil on hills with sufficient minerality will complement the pungent mustard flavour, while the delicate heat of the green spices will be matched by the wine's fruit.

CHICKEN WITH MACE AND CARDAMOM

SERVES 4

This subtly flavoured dish is simple to prepare and will do full justice to the best chicken you can afford. Sometimes organic, corn-fed birds lose their distinctive flavour when given the spice treatment but subtle, aromatic spices like mace and cardamom allow the quality of the meat to shine through.

Mix the ingredients for the first marinade and rub all over the chicken. Leave for 20 minutes. For the second marinade, put the cheese in a bowl and rub to a paste (a little flour could be added to help prevent lumps forming). Add the yoghurt and mix until smooth. Add the remaining spices and then fold in the cream carefully, as the mixture might separate if mixed too vigorously.

Heat the oil in a large ovenproof frying pan, add the chicken and sear for 3 minutes on each side, until nicely coloured. Remove from the heat. Spread the second marinade on top and transfer to an oven, preheated to 200°C/400°F/Gas Mark 6. Bake for about 15 minutes, until the chicken is cooked through, then serve immediately.

Wine to accompany this recipe
ALSACE RIESLING
The sharp citrus notes of the mace will be matched by the minerality and citrus elements of a dry *Alsace Riesling*, leaving pleasant floral notes on the palate.

4 boneless, skinless chicken breasts
1 tablespoon vegetable or corn oil

For the first marinade:
1 teaspoon Ginger Paste (see page 30)
1 teaspoon Garlic Paste (see page 30)
1 teaspoon salt

For the second marinade:
2 teaspoons grated processed
    Cheddar cheese
3 tablespoons Greek yoghurt
1cm/½ inch piece of fresh ginger,
    finely chopped
2 green chillies, finely chopped
½ teaspoon salt
¼ teaspoon finely ground white pepper
½ teaspoon Mace and Cardamom
Powder (see page 32)
1 tablespoon single cream

STIR-FRIED CHICKEN WITH DRIED CHILLIES

SERVES 4

There has been a sizeable Chinese population in India for centuries, which has resulted in a fascinating crossover of the two cuisines, known as Indo-Chinese. Vivek is a big fan of this style of cooking and we sometimes have an Indo-Chinese dish on our menu at the restaurant. In India you can find this chicken stir-fry in both Chinese and Indian restaurants. The secret of cooking it at home is never to let the heat in the pan reduce. Your burner should be on high throughout and you should only add an ingredient to the pan when you are sure it is hot enough.

Mix the chicken with all the marinade ingredients and set aside for 30 minutes.

Deep-fry the chicken in hot oil for about 5 minutes, until it is golden brown, crisp and cooked through. Drain on kitchen paper and set aside.

For the stir-fry, heat the 2 tablespoons of oil in a wok until smoking. Add the dried red chillies and move them quickly as they start to burn. Add the garlic and stir quickly. Almost immediately, as the garlic starts to change colour, add the diced onion and the fried chicken and stir-fry for 2 minutes. Add the red or green pepper and cook for another couple of minutes. Add the salt, sugar, red chilli powder and cumin and stir-fry for another minute. Finally add the soy sauce and chicken stock cube and mix well.

When the chicken is dark and shiny, add the cornflour paste and stir quickly to mix evenly. This gives the dish an attractive glaze and also thickens the juices. Squeeze in the lemon juice, add the chives or spring onions and serve immediately, as a snack with drinks or as a starter.

Wine to accompany this recipe
GEWÜRZTRAMINER FROM ALSACE
A rich *Gewürztraminer* from *Alsace* or *Germany* will balance the dried heat of the chillies, leaving an intense fruit on the palate.

500g/1lb 2oz chicken thighs, skinned, boned and cut in half
oil for deep-frying
2 tablespoons vegetable or corn oil
2 dried red chillies, broken into pieces
3 garlic cloves, chopped
1 red onion, cut into 1cm/½ inch dice
½ red or green pepper, cut into 2.5cm/1 inch dice
1 teaspoon salt
1½ teaspoons sugar
½ teaspoon red chilli powder
1 teaspoon ground cumin
2 teaspoons dark soy sauce
5mm/¼ inch piece of chicken stock cube
1 tablespoon cornflour, mixed to a paste with a little water
juice of ½ lemon
2 tablespoons chopped fresh chives or spring onions

For the marinade:
2 tablespoons cornflour
1 egg, lightly beaten
1 teaspoon light soy sauce
1 teaspoon dark soy sauce
1 tablespoon white vinegar or rice vinegar
5mm/¼ inch piece of chicken stock cube
1 garlic clove, chopped
1 teaspoon salt

TANDOORI-STYLE SANDALWOOD CHICKEN BREASTS

SERVES 4

Tandoori chicken is a noble dish and one we wanted to include on our opening menu at The Cinnamon Club but we refused to serve it 'straight up'. So Vivek set to work to devise this variation, which instead of relying on the pungency of fenugreek uses aromatic sandalwood and rosewater. Sandalwood is common in India as an ingredient in incense and soap but not in cooking. A pity, as its subtle flavour and fragrance brings a subtle note to a dish. Rosewater, too, is a great thing to have in your kitchen. Just a few drops add life to many delicately flavoured dishes. It's worth a trip to an Asian grocery shop for this and for kewra, the water of another delicate and fragrant flower.

Wine to accompany this recipe
ALSACE GEWÜRZTRAMINER
The delicate, subtle spicing of the sandalwood will match the gentle acidity of an *Alsace Gewürztraminer*, while the rose petal notes of the wine will complement the tandoor flavours of the cooking process.

Mix together all the ingredients for the first marinade and rub them over the chicken breasts. Set aside for 30 minutes.

Mix together all the ingredients for the second marinade, then add the chicken and leave to marinate for 15 minutes.

Heat the oil in a large frying pan or a wok and add the cumin seeds. When they start to crackle, gradually add the gram flour, stirring over a low heat to prevent lumps forming. When the flour has turned golden, raise the heat, add the chicken breasts and cook for about 5 minutes, until the flour has formed a coating. Sprinkle the chicken with the rosewater and kewra water, transfer to a baking tray and leave to cool.

Cook the cooled chicken breasts in an oven preheated to 200°C/400°F/Gas Mark 6 for 10–12 minutes. Serve with a spoonful of Cucumber Yoghurt.

2 skinless, boneless chicken breasts
3 tablespoons vegetable or corn oil
½ teaspoon royal cumin or black cumin seeds
25g/1oz/¼ cup gram (chickpea) flour
½ teaspoon rosewater
½ teaspoon kewra water
Cucumber Yoghurt, to serve (see page 163)

For the first marinade:
1 teaspoon Ginger Paste (see page 30)
1 teaspoon Garlic Paste (see page 30)
½ teaspoon yellow chilli powder (if unavailable, substitute finely ground white pepper)
¼ teaspoon ground turmeric
juice of ½ lemon

For the second marinade:
4 tablespoons Greek yoghurt
3 tablespoons single cream
1 teaspoon Mace and Cardamom Powder
1 teaspoon ground sandalwood
¼ teaspoon saffron strands, infused in 2 tablespoons warm milk for 5 minutes

TANDOORI-STYLE PIGEON BREASTS

SERVES 4

Pigeons are eaten and enjoyed through-out the subcontinent and contributed to one of my most memorable teenage meals. We were visiting relatives in Bangladesh and found ourselves waiting for the ferry on the banks of a muddy river when I noticed a small restaurant nearby (actually more of a roadside hut). Led by the smells from within, I discovered that they were cooking recently shot pigeons and despite warnings from my companions about the dangers of the unkempt kitchen, I knew that I just had to try them. I wasn't disappointed, they were quite wonderful, though the kitchen eventually wreaked its revenge over the following days. With Vivek's recipe, the pigeon breast gets the tandoor treatment, while the rest of the bird is minced to make a a stunning kebab. This is a very simple way of serving a small bird that can otherwise be really fiddly to eat. Ask you butcher to take the pain out of the preparation for you by getting him to bone the breasts and mince the legs, liver and heart.

Wine to accompany this recipe
NEW ZEALAND SYRAH
The gamy character of the pigeon will match the intense blackberry fruit of a mineral *New Zealand Syrah*, while the freshness of this wine will balance the natural sweet notes of the meat.

If preparing the pigeons yourself, cut off the breasts and legs and bone them. Set the breasts aside. Mince the leg meat with the livers and hearts, if you have them, then set aside.

For the kebabs, heat the oil in a pan and add the cumin seeds. When they start to crackle, add the onion and sauté until golden brown. Add the minced pigeon and the beetroot and sauté for 3 minutes, then add the chilli powder and ground cumin and cook until the mixture is almost dry. Stir in the ginger, chillies, mint, salt and garam masala, then remove from the heat and leave to cool. Shape into 4 cakes.

Pat dry the pigeon breasts. Mix together the ingredients for the first marinade and rub over the breasts. Set aside for 20 minutes. Heat the oil in an ovenproof frying pan, add the breasts and sear for 2 minutes on each side, skin-side first. Remove from heat. Mix the ingredients for the second marinade, spread over the breasts and transfer to an oven preheated to 200°C/400°F/Gas Mark 6. Cook for 3–5 minutes. The breasts should still be succulent and slightly pink inside.

Dip the kebabs in the beaten egg, roll in breadcrumbs and deep-fry in hot oil until golden brown. Drain on kitchen paper and accompany with the pigeon breasts and the Cucumber Yoghurt.

4 pigeons
I tablespoon vegetable or corn oil
Cucumber Yoghurt (see page 163),
   to serve

For the minced kebabs:
I tablespoon vegetable or corn oil
¼ teaspoon royal cumin seeds
   (or black cumin seeds)
I onion, finely chopped
½ small beetroot, finely chopped
¼ teaspoon red chilli powder
¼ teaspoon cumin seeds, roasted
   and ground (see page 33)
Icm/½ inch piece of fresh ginger,
   finely chopped
2 green chillies, chopped
leaves from I sprig of fresh mint, shredded
I teaspoon salt
¼ teaspoon garam masala
I egg, beaten
dried breadcrumbs for coating
oil for deep-frying

For the first marinade:
I teaspoon Ginger Paste (see page 30)
I teaspoon Garlic Paste (see page 30)
I teaspoon salt
I teaspoon red chilli powder
juice of ½ lemon

For the second marinade:
I tablespoon Fried Onion Paste
I tablespoon Greek yoghurt
½ teaspoon garam masala
½ teaspoon salt
I tablespoon vegetable or corn oil

BREAST OF GUINEA FOWL WITH FENNEL AND CORIANDER

SERVES 4

This is a tandoori rendition of guinea fowl flavoured with liberal quantities of fennel seeds, coriander seeds and coriander leaves. In India it is referred to as pahadi kebab, *meaning kebab from the hills. Serve with a salad of your choice or with Cucumber Yoghurt (see page 163).*

Wine to accompany this recipe
ALSACE GEWÜRZTRAMINER
An *Alsace Gewürztraminer* will balance the dried heat of the marinade and the pungent flavours of the fennel and coriander.

Mix together all the ingredients for the first marinade, rub them over the guinea fowl breasts and set aside for 20 minutes. Meanwhile, make the second marinade. Put the yoghurt in a bowl and whisk until smooth, then mix in all the ingredients except the cream. Now fold in the cream carefully, otherwise the mixture may separate.

Heat the oil in a large ovenproof frying pan, add the guinea fowl breasts and sear for 1–2 minutes on each side. Remove from the heat, spread the second marinade on top and place in an oven preheated to 200°C/400°F/Gas Mark 6. Cook for 8–10 minutes, then serve.

4 guinea fowl breasts, skinned
I tablespoon vegetable or corn oil

For the first marinade:
I teaspoon Ginger Paste (see page 30)
I teaspoon Garlic Paste (see page 30
I teaspoon salt

For the second marinade:
I tablespoon Greek yoghurt
Icm/½ inch piece of fresh ginger, finely chopped
2 green chillies, finely chopped
½ teaspoon salt
½ teaspoon Mace and Cardamom Powder (see page 32
¼ teaspoon finely ground white pepper
I teaspoon fennel seeds, lightly roasted (see page 33)
½ teaspoon coriander seeds, roasted and coarsely crushed (see page 33)
I tablespoon chopped fresh coriander
I tablespoon single cream

RABBIT TIKKA

SERVES 4

Rabbit and hare are rightly considered delicacies in India. Rabbit tikka makes an ideal barbecue dish, as the charcoal smoke brings out the best in the mustard and honey marinade. Papaya is used in the first marinade as a tenderiser. Serve with Missi Roti (see page 157) and Spiced Onion Yoghurt (see page 163). This dish also works well as a canapé with drinks.

Wine to accompany this recipe
FRENCH SYRAH
The gentle, supple tannins and silky blackberry fruit of a *French Syrah* from the *Languedoc Roussillon* or *southern Rhône* will match the heat of the chilli marinade.

Combine all the ingredients for the first marinade, mix thoroughly with the rabbit and leave to marinate for 1 hour. Then mix together all the ingredients for the second marinade and apply to the rabbit. Leave to marinate for another hour or so.

Thread the meat on to skewers and cook on a barbecue. Alternatively, place on a baking tray and cook in an oven preheated to 200°C/400°F/ Gas Mark 6 for 20 minutes, turning regularly. If the rabbit cooks but does not colour, place under a very hot grill for a couple of minutes.

500g/1lb 2oz boned rabbit legs, cut into 2.5cm/1 inch dice

For the first marinade:
1½ teaspoons Garlic Paste (see page 30)
1½ teaspoons Ginger Paste (see page 30)
½ teaspoon red chilli powder
1 teaspoon ground turmeric
2 teaspoons salt
juice of 1 lemon
2.5cm/1 inch piece of green papaya, grated (or use 2 tablespoons fresh pineapple juice)

For the second marinade:
100g/4oz/½ cup Greek yoghurt
2 tablespoons wholegrain mustard
1 tablespoon honey
1 teaspoon garam masala
1 tablespoon chopped fresh coriander
2 tablespoons mustard oil (or vegetable oil mixed with 1 teaspoon English mustard)

LOIN OF RABBIT STUFFED WITH DRIED FRUIT AND PANEER

SERVES 4

This dish may sound complex but is easier to prepare than it first seems, and looks absolutely stunning. It makes a spectacular starter for a dinner party.

Wine to accompany this recipe
ALSACE GEWÜRZTRAMINER
An *Alsace Gewürztraminer* has weight and rose petal flavours that will complement the dried fruit and balance the pungent spice of the mustard.

Lay the saddle out flat on a large sheet of clingfilm and run your fingers over it to check for any small bones. Cover the saddle with another piece of clingfilm and flatten it to an even layer, using a meat mallet or a wooden rolling pin. Remove the top sheet of clingfilm, then spread the ginger and garlic pastes over the meat and sprinkle with the salt.

For the stuffing, fry the onion in the oil, stirring constantly, until it is an even golden brown colour. Lift out with a slotted spoon and drain on kitchen paper. Place in a bowl, add all the remaining stuffing ingredients and mix well. Place the stuffing in the centre of the saddle and roll up the saddle, using the clingfilm to help keep the roll tight. Chill in the fridge for a few hours (or in the freezer for 20–30 minutes) so that it retains its shape. Then remove the clingfilm, spread the marinade all over the roll and place on a baking tray, with the fold underneath so it stays rolled up. Set aside for about 10 minutes.

Cook the roll for 20 minutes in an oven preheated to 200°C/400°F/Gas Mark 6. Remove from the oven and leave to cool to room temperature, then wrap it in the roomali bread or tortilla, taking care to include as much of the marinade as possible. Leave to stand for 20 minutes, then cut the roll into 6 thick slices. Lay them flat on a baking tray and place in a moderate oven or under the grill until thoroughly heated through. Meanwhile, whisk together all the ingredients for the mustard vinaigrette.

Serve the rabbit with the dressing drizzled round.

I saddle of rabbit, boned
I teaspoon Ginger Paste (see page 30)
I teaspoon Garlic Paste (see page 30)
I teaspoon salt
I large roomali bread (follow the recipe on page 64 but make a 30cm/ I2 inch bread) or I large tortilla

For the stuffing:
I large onion, finely sliced
3 tablespoons vegetable or corn oil
250g/9oz/2¼ cups paneer cheese, grated
I½ tablespoons raisins
I tablespoon salted roasted pistachio nuts, coarsely crushed
2 tablespoons salted roasted cashew nuts, coarsely crushed

For the marinade:
4 tablespoons wholegrain mustard
3 tablespoons Greek yoghurt
I teaspoon salt
2 tablespoons mustard oil (or use vegetable oil mixed with I teaspoon English mustard)

For the mustard vinaigrette:
6 tablespoons mustard oil
4 tablespoons lemon juice
a pinch of salt
½ teaspoon sugar
½ teaspoon black onion seeds

LAMB KEBAB WRAPS

SERVES 4

Seekh kebabs are sometimes served wrapped in roomali bread which gets its name from the Hindi word for handkerchief, as it is made by cooking a large, thin sheet of dough on a huge, hot dome like an upside-down wok and then folding it many times. It's virtually impossible to make roomali at home in this way, so we have adapted the recipe to a more chapati-like style of bread. Alternatively, you could wrap the kebabs in tortillas rather than making your own bread.

Wine to accompany this recipe
ALSACE GEWÜRZTRAMINER
An *Alsace Gewürztraminer* with plenty of fruit flavours will complement the spice mix in the kebabs.

For the bread, mix together the flour, water, salt and sugar to give a smooth, firm dough. Cover and leave to rest for 20 minutes. Meanwhile, shape and cook the seekh kebabs as described on page 65. Mix together the red onion and lemon juice and set aside.

Divide the bread dough into 4 portions and roll each one out into a thin round about 20cm/8 inches in diameter. Heat a large, heavy-based frying pan or a flat griddle over a high heat and place one of the breads in it. Cook for 2 minutes on each side, until dry and just starting to colour. Brush the top with oil, turn the bread over and cook for a minute, then brush with oil again and turn again. As the bread starts to colour underneath, reduce the heat, flip the bread over and pour a quarter of the beaten egg on to it. Let the egg congeal for a minute or so, then turn the bread over again to cook the side with the egg on it. Remove from the pan and set aside. Repeat with the remaining breads.

Once the breads are all cooked, lay them out egg-side upwards, spread them with butter and top with the red onion mixture. Remove the lamb kebabs from the skewers, place a kebab in the centre of each bread and drizzle with Mango and Mint Chutney. Roll up the bread so the kebab is completely covered. Secure with toothpicks to prevent the bread opening, trim off the ends, then cut in half – or into smaller piece for cocktail snacks.

I quantity of Seekh Kebab Mixture
  (see page 65)
I red onion, sliced
juice of ½ lemon
Mango and Mint Chutney (see page 162)

For the bread:
100g/4oz/I cup plain flour
4 tablespoons water
a pinch of salt
a pinch of sugar
oil for brushing
2 eggs, lightly beaten
butter for spreading

HOME-SMOKED LAMB KEBABS

SERVES 6

India's kebabs are loved the world over and this recipe is a winning combination of two styles – the popular seekh kebab, made of minced lamb, and the lesser-known soola. Soola are eaten primarily in princely states such as Rajasthan where it is said that when princes and warriors returned with their spoils from hunting they would have the flesh sliced thinly and smoked over charcoal infused with spices. Wild boar or venison were probably used originally but lamb works just as well. Ideally the kebabs should be cooked on a barbecue to get that smokiness, but the double marinade that Vivek has devised means that they work almost as well in the kitchen. Serve with Cucumber Yoghurt (see page 163).

Wine to accompany this recipe
NAPA VALLEY CABERNET FRANC
The ripeness of a *Napa Valley Cabernet Franc* with notes of eucalyptus and tobacco leaves will complement the smoky notes and the heat of the marinade.

For the soola, pat dry the lamb and mix together the ginger and garlic pastes, salt, chilli powder and lemon juice. Rub this mixture over the meat and leave to marinate for 15–20 minutes.

Heat the ghee or oil in a large, heavy-based frying pan, drop in the cloves and then remove them from the pan when they puff up. Add the meat to the pan and sear for 3 minutes on each side, until well browned, then remove from the heat.

Now mix the yoghurt, Rajasthani spice paste and oil together to form the second marinade. Spread it over the lamb and set aside for 20 minutes. Place under a hot grill and cook for 8 minutes, until well coloured, turning once.

For the seekh kebabs, mix all the ingredients together and divide into 4 portions. Shape each one round a skewer, squeezing the meat gently with wet hands so it adheres to the skewer. Place under a medium-hot grill for 8 minutes, turning regularly, until the kebabs are dark brown all over. Serve with the soola.

For the soola:
400g/14oz lamb fillet, cut into
    6 thin slices
1 teaspoon Ginger Paste (see page 30)
1 teaspoon Garlic Paste (see page 30)
½ teaspoon salt
1 teaspoon red chilli powder
juice of ½ lemon
1 tablespoon ghee or oil
3 cloves
1 tablespoon Greek yoghurt
1 tablespoon Rajasthani Spice Paste
    (see page 32)
1 teaspoon vegetable or corn oil

For the seekh kebabs:
500g/1lb 2oz/2 cups minced lamb
¼ teaspoon cumin seeds
2 green chillies, finely chopped
8 sprigs of fresh coriander,
    finely chopped
3 garlic cloves, finely chopped
1cm/½ inch piece of fresh ginger,
    finely chopped
3 tablespoons grated processed
    Cheddar cheese
½ teaspoon red chilli powder
1 teaspoon salt

CLOVE-SMOKED TENDER BEEF KEBABS

SERVES 4

These fabulous kebabs originate from Lucknow, where they are called galouti. *They are meant to be tender enough to melt in your mouth. These days they are most often made with lamb but originally beef was used. Traditionally the kebabs are prepared by putting a pile of smoking coals in the centre of a pot containing the meat. Some cloves are placed on the coals and the pot is covered so the meat becomes infused, which makes for an aromatic and distinctive dish. We have devised an alternative method to achieve that smoky flavour.*

Wine to accompany this recipe
CALIFORNIAN ZINFANDEL
The powerful aromas of ripe berries and tobacco leaves from a *Californian Zinfandel* will balance the heat of the cloves and chilli.

Fry the onion in 3 tablespoons of the oil, stirring constantly, until it is an even golden brown colour. Lift out with a slotted spoon and drain on kitchen paper. Add the cashew nuts to the pan and fry until golden, then drain.

Mix together the fried onion, cashews, beef, spices, salt, garlic, ginger, green chilli, mint, ghee and rosewater, if using. Pass through a mincer 3 or 4 times, or blend in a food processor for 7–8 minutes (do this in several 2–3 minute bursts), until you get a very smooth mixture – the fibres of the meat should have completely broken down. Place in the fridge to chill.

For the smoking, heat the ghee or oil in a small pan or a ladle and when it is very hot, add the cloves. Once they start to smoke, remove from the heat and add the oil (but not the cloves) to the beef mixture.

Divide the mixture into 4 and shape into patties. Heat the remaining vegetable oil in a frying pan, add the kebabs and fry over a medium heat for 3 minutes on each side. Serve with red onions and a bread of your choice.

1 onion, finely sliced
5 tablespoons vegetable oil
25g/1oz/¼ cup cashew nuts
400g/14oz/1²/3 cups minced beef (don't buy extra-lean mince, as it needs some fat content to retain the moisture)
½ teaspoon red chilli powder
1 teaspoon Mace and Cardamom Powder (see page 32)
6 cloves, roasted and ground
1 teaspoon salt
2 garlic cloves, chopped
1cm/½ inch piece of fresh ginger, finely chopped
1 green chilli, chopped
1 tablespoon finely shredded fresh mint
2 tablespoons ghee or clarified butter
3 drops of rosewater (optional)
chopped red onions, to serve

For smoking:
1 tablespoon ghee or vegetable oil
4 cloves

MINCED VEAL KEBABS WITH MANGO AND PINEAPPLE SALAD

SERVES 4

This exotic starter is simple to prepare and carries an abundance of sophisticated and subtle flavours. Kebabs like this are more commonly made with lamb, but veal adds a lightness of touch, while a little cream cheese helps keep the kebabs moist.

Wine to accompany this recipe
ALSACE PINOT GRIS
Veal works well with wines made from grapes that grow on hills, where more minerals and acidity lift the flavours. Try a fresh *Alsace Pinot Gris*, or one from the north-east of Italy.

400g/14oz/1²/3 cups lean minced veal
1½ teaspoons salt
½ teaspoon finely ground white pepper
25g/1oz/¼ cup processed Cheddar cheese, grated
2.5cm/1 inch piece of fresh ginger, finely chopped
1 green chilli, finely chopped
2 garlic cloves, finely chopped
1 tablespoon finely chopped fresh coriander
1 teaspoon Mace and Cardamom Powder (see page 32)

For the salad:
1 ripe mango, peeled, stoned and cut into 2cm/¾ inch dice
150g/5oz/⁷/8 cup ripe pineapple, cut into 2cm/¾ inch dice
50g/2oz/4 cups mixed salad leaves
juice of ½ lemon
½ teaspoon chaat masala (optional)

Mix together all the ingredients for the kebabs, either by passing them once through a mincer or by blitzing briefly in a food processor. Set aside in the fridge for 30 minutes.

Mix together the mango, pineapple and green leaves for the salad (don't add the lemon and chaat masala until just before serving, otherwise the leaves will become limp and lifeless).

Mould the kebab mixture into 4 sausage shapes and place on a baking tray. Cook for 10 minutes in an oven preheated to 200°C/400°F/Gas Mark 6, turning them regularly. When the kebabs are ready, toss the salad with the lemon juice and the chaat masala, if using. Serve with the kebabs on top.

SWEET POTATO CAKES WITH GINGER, FENNEL AND CHILLI

SERVES 4

Potato cakes are made throughout India in many shapes and forms – flavoured with onion, chilli and fresh coriander, for example, or stuffed with lamb. Here we have brought together Desiree and sweet potatoes, along with carrot and celery, for a more rounded flavour and texture. Ginger, fennel and chilli add excitement to what might otherwise be a fairly conservative layer of tastes. Serve with Tamarind Chutney (see page 161) and a dollop of plain or spiced yoghurt.

Wine to accompany this recipe
PINOT GRIGIO
The natural sweetness of the potato will complement the subtle fruit of a young *Pinot Grigio*, while the delicate heat of the potato stuffing will lift the fruit flavours of the wine.

Heat 1 tablespoon of the oil in a pan, add the cumin seeds and let them crackle. Add the fennel seeds, followed by the diced carrot, celery and sweet potato, and sauté very quickly on a high heat for 2–3 minutes, until softened. Add the salt and leave to cool. Mix the sautéed vegetables with the grated potatoes, then stir in the chopped coriander and the cornflour. Divide the mixture into 4 and shape into balls.

For the filling, coarsely pound together the ginger, chillies and fennel seeds in a pestle and mortar. Peel the roasted sweet potato, mash the flesh with a fork and mix in the pounded spice mixture. Season with the salt and sugar.

Take each potato ball, make an indentation in the centre with your thumb and fill it with a teaspoon of the sweet potato filling. Shape it back into a ball, making sure the filling is completely covered, and flatten it into a cake. Shallow-fry the potato cakes in the remaining oil until golden and crisp on both sides.

3 tablespoons vegetable or corn oil
½ teaspoon cumin seeds
½ teaspoon fennel seeds
I small carrot, finely diced
50g/2oz/¼ cup celery, finely diced
75g/3oz/²/3 cup sweet potato, cut into 5mm/
    ¼ inch dice
I teaspoon salt
3 medium-sized Desiree potatoes, boiled until tender, then peeled and grated
a small handful of chopped fresh coriander
25g/Ioz/¼ cup cornflour

For the filling:
Icm/½ inch piece of fresh ginger, chopped
5 green chillies (fewer if you prefer), chopped
I teaspoon fennel seeds
I very small sweet potato, baked until tender, then left to cool
½ teaspoon salt
I teaspoon sugar

COURGETTE FLOWERS STUFFED WITH CORN AND MUSHROOMS

SERVES 4

'What have courgette flowers got to do with Indian cooking?' you might ask. Well, not a lot, but we have given this fashionable ingredient the Indian treatment and it has proved a big hit whenever we have served it in the restaurant. You might be lucky enough to find courgette flowers in a greengrocer's or market during the summer, otherwise, if you grow your own, or you know someone who does, use the flowers for this dish. Serve with Tamarind Chutney (see page 161) and mango purée.

Wine to accompany this recipe
GERMAN RIESLING
The natural sweetness of corn and mushrooms will complement the delicate fruit of a *German Riesling* from the *Rheingau* without overpowering it.

Gently open up the courgette flowers a little, taking care not to tear the petals. Remove the stigma from the inside.

For the stuffing, heat the oil in a small pan, add the onion and sauté until softened and starting to colour. Add the sweetcorn and green chilli and sauté for 2–3 minutes. Add the mushrooms and cook until softened, then add the turmeric and sauté for a minute. Stir in the salt, coriander and lemon juice, then finish with the garam masala.

Stuff the courgette flowers with this mixture, folding the petals back over to enclose it completely. If the stuffing does not bind together properly, then let it cool first and mix in the grated boiled potato.

Heat some oil in a deep-fat fryer or a large, deep saucepan. Mix together all the ingredients for the batter until smooth. Dip the flowers in the batter so they are lightly coated, then fry in the hot oil for a few minutes until crisp. Drain on kitchen paper and serve immediately.

4 courgette flowers
oil for deep-frying

For the stuffing:
1 tablespoon vegetable or corn oil
1 tablespoon finely chopped red onion
1 tablespoon sweetcorn (canned will do)
½ green chilli, finely chopped
100g/4oz/1 cup assorted mushrooms, finely chopped
½ teaspoon ground turmeric
½ teaspoon salt
1 tablespoon chopped fresh coriander
juice of ½ lemon
½ teaspoon garam masala
2 tablespoons grated boiled potato (optional)

For the batter:
2 tablespoons cornflour
½ teaspoon salt
½ teaspoon black cumin seeds
juice of ½ lemon
1 tablespoon water

BENGALI SPICED VEGETABLE CAKES

SERVES 4

The Bengalis love savoury cakes – they make them with potatoes and fish but call them 'chops'. Here, a mixture of vegetables is given the same treatment, with beetroot adding its distinctive pinkish hue. Serve with Mustard and Tomato Sauce (see page 162).

Wine to accompany this recipe
ITALIAN GEWÜRZTRAMINER
The delicate dried heat of the Bengali spices and the neutral flavours of the potato will enhance the fresh fruit of an *Italian Gewürztraminer* from the *Trentino Alto Adige* region of *Italy*.

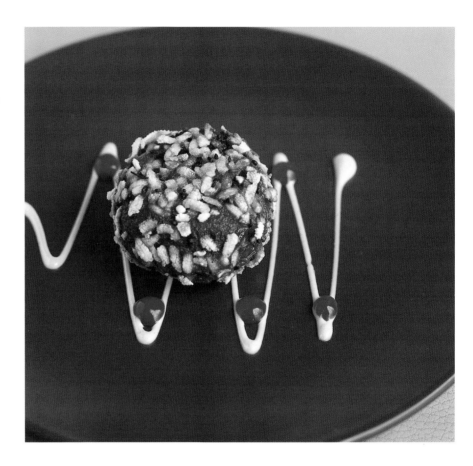

Coarsely pound together all the ingredients for the spice mix in a pestle and mortar, then set aside.

Heat the ghee or clarified butter in a wok or large frying pan and add the onion seeds, fennel seeds, cumin and bay leaves. When they begin to crackle, add the onion and sauté until golden. Now add the carrots, cauliflower and French beans, in that order, sautéing each vegetable until slightly softened before adding the next. Add the chilli powder, cumin and spice mix and stir-fry for 2–3 minutes. Add the raisins and beetroot and cook for 1 minute. Stir in the salt and sugar, then add the grated potatoes and cook for 3–4 minutes, until everything is well combined and has turned a shiny, reddish colour.

Remove from the heat and leave to cool.

Divide the mixture into 8 portions and shape into balls. Dip them in the beaten egg and coat in breadcrumbs. Chill until firm. Heat some oil in a deep-fat fryer or a large, deep saucepan and fry the vegetable cakes until golden brown. Drain on kitchen paper and serve.

CHEESE AND CHILLI MELT ON NAAN BREAD

SERVES 4

Vivek calls this Indian pizza, whereas I think of it as Indian cheese on toast. Either way, we have given the usually bland paneer cheese some crunch and colour with peppers and a bit of bite with green chillies. You could try your hand at making the naan bread (see page 155), or simply use bought naan. This dish is well suited to serving as a canapé if you cut the bread into small squares.

(see page 155)

50g/2oz/¼ cup ghee or clarified butter
½ teaspoon black onion seeds
½ teaspoon fennel seeds
½ teaspoon cumin seeds
2 bay leaves
I onion, finely chopped
2 carrots, finely chopped
¼ cauliflower, finely chopped
125g/4½oz/½ cup green beans, finely chopped
½ teaspoon red chilli powder
I teaspoon ground cumin
I tablespoon raisins
2 beetroot, boiled, peeled and finely chopped
I teaspoon salt
½ teaspoon sugar
2 medium potatoes, boiled until tender, then peeled and grated
oil for deep-frying

For the spice mix:
I teaspoon coriander seeds, roasted (see page 33)
2 dried red chillies
I teaspoon cumin seeds
2 green cardamom pods

For coating:
2 eggs, beaten
150g/5oz dried breadcrumbs

Heat the oil, ghee or butter in a frying pan and add the cumin seeds. When they start to crackle, add the garlic and sauté until golden. Add the onion and sauté until it starts to colour. Then add the turmeric, salt and diced peppers and sauté for 5 minutes, until the peppers have softened. Add the green chillies and cook for 2 minutes, then add the grated paneer and mix well. Stir in the cream, followed by the coriander and lemon juice. Remove from the heat and leave to cool.

Mix in the grated Cheddar and spread the mixture on the naan breads (cutting them in half, if you are using bought ones). Place under a hot grill, until the topping has softened and heated through. Serve immediately.

Wine to accompany this recipe
BAROSSA VALLEY CABERNET SAUVIGNON
A rich *Cabernet Sauvignon* from the *Barossa Valley* in *Australia* will complement the melted cheese, while the neutral flavour of the bread will allow the palate to appreciate the intensity of this wine.

2 tablespoons oil, ghee or clarified butter
½ teaspoon cumin seeds
½ teaspoon finely chopped garlic
I onion, finely chopped
½ teaspoon ground turmeric
1½ teaspoons salt
½ red pepper, finely diced
½ yellow pepper, finely diced
½ green pepper, finely diced
2 green chillies, finely chopped
125g/4½oz/I cup paneer cheese, grated
2 tablespoons single cream
I tablespoon chopped fresh coriander
juice of I lemon
2 tablespoons grated Cheddar cheese
4 home-made naan breads (see page 155) or 2 bought ones

AUBERGINE CAVIAR WITH SMOKED CUCUMBER YOGHURT

SERVES 4

This is a hugely popular dish at The Cinnamon Club, with the smoked cucumber yoghurt lending a subtle but distinctive flavour.

Wine to accompany this recipe
SOUTH AFRICAN SAUVIGNON BLANC
Mustard is the dominant flavour of this dish and requires the freshness of a *Sauvignon*, such as a *South African Sauvignon Blanc*.

Brush the aubergines with oil, then place on a baking tray and roast in an oven preheated to 200°C/400°F/ Gas Mark 6 for 25–30 minutes, until very tender. Leave until cool enough to handle, then peel off the skin. Finely chop the flesh.

Fry the onion in the tablespoon of oil, stirring constantly, until it is an even golden-brown colour. Lift out with a slotted spoon and drain on kitchen paper. Put the aubergine and fried onion in a bowl and mix in the garlic, red onion, chillies, herbs, ginger, salt, sugar and lemon juice. Shape the mixture into 4 balls and place in the freezer until frozen (this helps them keep their shape during frying).

Meanwhile, for the cucumber yoghurt, heat the ghee to smoking point in a small pan and add the cloves. Let them crackle and smoke, then add to the cucumber yoghurt, cover and set aside.

Remove the aubergine balls from the freezer and dip in seasoned flour, the beaten eggs and finally the rice flakes to form a crust. Deep-fry in hot oil for 2–3 minutes, until crisp and golden. Drain on kitchen paper and place in a preheated oven, 180°C/350°F/Gas Mark 4, for 2–3 minutes to thaw the inside. Place each crisp ball on a bed of smoked cucumber and yoghurt and serve immediately.

2 large aubergines
½ onion, finely sliced
I tablespoon vegetable or corn oil
I tablespoon chopped garlic
I red onion, finely chopped
2 green chillies, finely chopped
I5 fresh basil leaves, finely chopped
50g/2oz/I cup fresh coriander, finely chopped
2.5cm/I inch piece of fresh ginger, finely chopped
½ teaspoon salt
½ teaspoon sugar
juice of ½ lemon
oil for deep-frying

For the crust:
2 tablespoons plain flour, seasoned with salt and pepper
2 eggs, lightly beaten
I00g/4oz/I¼ cups pressed rice flakes (pawa)

For the smoked cucumber yoghurt:
I tablespoon ghee
6 cloves
4 tablespoons Cucumber Yoghurt (see page I63)

ASPARAGUS STIR-FRY WITH BENGALI ROASTED AUBERGINE

Although asparagus is not exactly on the must-have section of the Indian house-wife's shopping list, it works beautifully in this dish. We have retained the vegetable's distinctive firmness and given it a cumin and tomato coating to bring out the best of its flavour. Balancing it with a very traditional aubergine crush gives a stark balance of textures.

2 tablespoons vegetable or corn oil
1 teaspoon cumin seeds
1 onion, finely chopped
1 teaspoon red chilli powder
2 tomatoes, roughly chopped
20 asparagus spears, trimmed
   and peeled
1 teaspoon salt
2.5cm/1 inch piece of fresh ginger,
   finely chopped
1 tablespoon chopped fresh coriander
2 teaspoons lemon juice
¼ teaspoon garam masala

For the roasted aubergine:
1 aubergine
a little oil for brushing
1 red onion, finely chopped
1 green chilli, finely chopped
1cm/½ inch piece of fresh ginger,
   finely chopped
1 tablespoon mustard oil
   (or vegetable oil)
½ teaspoon salt
1 tablespoon chopped fresh coriander

First prepare the aubergine. Brush it with oil, place on a baking tray and roast in an oven preheated to 200°C/400°F/Gas Mark 6 for about 20 minutes, until soft. Leave until cool enough to handle, then peel off the skin and chop up the pulp very finely. Mix in all the remaining ingredients and set aside.

For the stir-fry, heat the oil in a large wok or frying pan and add the cumin seeds. When they crackle, add the onion and sauté until golden brown. Then add the chilli powder and sauté for 30 seconds. Add the tomatoes and cook until soft. Add the asparagus and toss well, adding the salt as you do so. Cook for 2–3 minutes, until the asparagus is just tender, then sprinkle over the ginger and coriander, followed by the lemon juice and garam masala. Serve the asparagus immediately, on a bed of the roasted aubergine.

Wine to accompany this recipe
NEW ZEALAND SAUVIGNON BLANC
A fresh *New Zealand Sauvignon Blanc*, with gooseberry and citrus fruit , will complement the delicate, grassy element of the asparagus.

TAPIOCA AND CUMIN FRITTERS WITH GREEN COCONUT CHUTNEY

SERVES 4

This recipe from Maharashtra is one of India's lesser-known street snacks and is often served at teatime. We think it makes an ideal canapé.

Mix together all the ingredients except the oil and chutney and leave to stand for 1 hour. The tapioca will soak up some of the moisture from the potatoes and soften a little.

Grease the palms of your hands with a little oil and divide the mixture into 8 balls. Flatten each ball with the palm of your hand to shape it into a mini burger. Deep-fry in hot oil for 3–4 minutes, until crisp and golden on the outside. Drain on kitchen paper and serve immediately, accompanied by the chutney.

Wine to accompany this recipe
CLARE VALLEY AUSTRALIAN RIESLING.
The warmth of the cumin and the sweetness of the chutney require a fresh, crisp *Riesling* from the *Clare Valley* in *Australia* to balance the spice mix.

100g/4oz/½ cup tapioca
75g/3oz/½ cup boiled potato, broken
    into pieces
1 teaspoon cumin seeds, roasted
    (see page 33)
2.5cm/1 inch piece of fresh ginger,
    finely chopped
4 green chillies, chopped
1½ teaspoons salt
2 tablespoons finely chopped fresh
    coriander
½ teaspoon garam masala
oil for deep-frying
Green Coconut Chutney (see page 161),
    to serve

MAIN COURSES

FISH
Tandoori-style Halibut with
Coconut and Ginger Sauce
Seared Sea Bass with
Green Spices
Seared Wild Bass with
Bottle Gourd Stir-fry and
Fenugreek Sauce
Spice-crusted Monkfish with
Tomato and Lemon Sauce
Seared Black Cod with
Coconut and Lemon Sauce
Mackerel in Hot South
Indian Sauce
Mullet in a Bengali
Vegetable Broth
Wild Salmon with Dill
and Mustard
Rice-crusted Sea Bream with
Kerala Curry Sauce
Parsee-style Roast Sea Bass
Goan Spiced Trout with
Bean Salad

SEAFOOD
King Prawns in Saffron
Almond Sauce
Mustard-flavoured Tandoori-
style King Prawns with Saffron
Kedgeree
Kerala-style Seafood Curry

CHICKEN/FOWL
Old Delhi-style Chicken Curry
Hot South Indian
Chicken Curry
Chicken Breasts Stuffed with
Spinach and Apricot in a
Korma Sauce
Seared Duck Breasts with
Sesame Tamarind Sauce

LAMB/PORK
Rack of Lamb with Mint
and Onion Sauce
Lamb Shank Rogan Josh
Rajasthani Roast Rump of
Lamb with Corn Sauce
Hyderabadi-style Biryani
of Lamb
Tandoori-style Lamb with
Masala Spinach
Vindaloo of Pork Shoulder

BEEF/GAME
Spice-crusted Rib Eye of
Beef with Masala Sautéed
Potatoes
Calf's Liver with Masala
Mashed Potatoes and
Stir-fried Okra
Hot and Sour Wild Boar
Chops with South Indian
Rice Vermicelli
Rajasthani Roast Venison
Saddle with Ginger and
Onion Sauce
Tandoori Grouse with
Aubergine Crush and
Layered Bread

VEGETARIAN
Potatoes Stuffed with Paneer
in a Sweet and Sour Sauce
Baby Aubergines in Pickling
Spices with Curry Leaf
Semolina
Hyderabadi-style
Aubergine Steaks
Green Pea and Corn Parcels
with Cauliflower and Potato
Stir-fry
Spinach Dumplings with
Tomato and Fenugreek
Sauce

TANDOORI-STYLE HALIBUT WITH COCONUT AND GINGER SAUCE

SERVES 4

Halibut is a great fish for the tandoor treatment but works just as well at home with a combination of searing and roasting. This is a recipe that would also suit a barbecue very well, in which case do not sear the fish after the first marinating period. Serve with basmati rice and lightly cooked spinach.

Wine to accompany this recipe
ITALIAN WHITE
The coconut and ginger base of the sauce will be balanced by the freshness of a white wine from *north-eastern Italy.*

Pat the halibut dry on kitchen paper. Mix together all the ingredients for the first marinade, rub them over the fish and leave to marinate for 1 hour. Meanwhile, for the second marinade, put the cheese in a small bowl and rub it to a paste with your fingers (a teaspoon of flour could be added to prevent lumps forming). Add the yoghurt and mix until smooth, then beat in all the remaining ingredients.

Heat the oil in a large, ovenproof frying pan, add the fish and sear on both sides. Pour the second marinade over the fish and set aside for 30 minutes. Then place in an oven preheated to 180°C/350°F/Gas Mark 4 and roast for 20 minutes.

Meanwhile, make the sauce. Heat the oil in a pan, add the curry leaves and onion and fry until the onion is soft. Add the chillies, ginger and turmeric and fry for 1 minute. Pour in the coconut milk, bring to the boil and simmer for about 5 minutes, until the sauce thickens slightly. Season with the salt.

Divide the sauce between 4 serving plates, place the fish on top and serve at once.

4 x 200g/7oz pieces of halibut fillet
I tablespoon vegetable or corn oil

For the first marinade:
I teaspoon Ginger Paste (see page 30)
I teaspoon Garlic Paste (see page 30)
2 teaspoons salt
I teaspoon finely ground white pepper

For the second marinade:
2 teaspoons grated processed
    Cheddar cheese
2 tablespoons Greek yoghurt
I teaspoon salt
I green chilli, finely chopped
Icm/½ inch piece of fresh ginger,
    finely chopped
I teaspoon Mace and Cardamom
    Powder (see page 32)
½ tablespoon chopped fresh coriander
2 tablespoons single cream

For the coconut and ginger sauce:
2 tablespoons vegetable or corn oil
I sprig of fresh curry leaves
I onion, sliced
5 green chillies, slit open lengthways
2.5cm/I inch piece of fresh ginger,
    cut into fine strips
½ teaspoon ground turmeric
500ml/I8fl oz/2¼ cups coconut milk
I teaspoon salt

SEARED SEA BASS WITH GREEN SPICES

SERVES 4

This is a very quick and easy recipe given wonderfully fresh, zesty flavours from the spice paste, which is really a sort of Indian pesto, made with coriander, mint, garlic and cashew nuts. Serve with a crisp green salad.

Wine to accompany this recipe
ALSACE RIESLING
The upfront fruits of an *Alsace Riesling* will balance the powerful herbal and garlic flavours of the spice paste.

Pat the bass fillets dry on kitchen paper. Mix together the salt, onion seeds. lemon juice and 1 tablespoon of the oil. Dip the fillets in this mixture and set aside for 10 minutes.

Meanwhile, prepare the green spice paste. Heat the oil in a small frying pan, add the cashew nuts and fry until golden. Drain on kitchen paper and set aside. Wash the mint and coriander and pat dry. Put the herbs in a food processor with the garlic, chillies and fried cashew nuts and process to a coarse paste, adding just enough of the olive oil and lemon juice to give the correct consistency. Mix in the salt and sugar.

To cook the fish, heat the remaining oil in a large frying pan, add the bass fillets, skin-side down, and fry for 2–3 minutes on each side, until crisp. Spoon over the green spice paste and serve immediately.

4 x 175g/6oz sea bass fillets.
   cut lengthways in half
½ teaspoon salt
¼ teaspoon black onion seeds
juice of 1 lemon
4 tablespoons vegetable or corn oil

For the green spice paste:
1 tablespoon vegetable or corn oil
50g/2oz/½ cup cashew nuts
100g/4oz/5 cups fresh mint
50g/2oz/1 cup fresh coriander
6 garlic cloves. roughly chopped
2 green chillies. roughly chopped
about 3 tablespoons olive oil
juice of 1 lemon
1 teaspoon salt
½ teaspoon sugar

SEARED WILD BASS WITH BOTTLE GOURD STIR-FRY AND FENUGREEK SAUCE

SERVES 4

This is a dish that we created in the restaurant to go with a specific wine (a 2001 Australian Sauvignon Blanc) – it is a real showpiece dish that deserves the best and freshest wild sea bass. If you can't find wild bass though, you will still get a very fine result using farmed fish. Bottle gourd is a popular vegetable throughout the Subcontinent and is available in Asian shops, where it is called potol. If you can't obtain any, French beans make a good alternative. You will need about 200g/7oz.

Wine to accompany this recipe
AUSTRALIAN SAUVIGNON BLANC
The citrus element of an *Australian Sauvignon Blanc* will go well with the onion seeds on the fish. The grassy tones of the wine will complement the mineral element of the bottle gourd and the fenugreek sauce.

First make the sauce. Heat the oil in a heavy-based pan, add the onion and sauté until golden brown. Stir in the turmeric, followed by the cashew paste, and cook on a low heat until thickened. The cashew paste might stick to the pan, or alternatively might splatter if there is too much water in it, so stir it constantly. When it begins to thicken, add the yoghurt and cook over a moderate heat for 2 minutes. Add the fish stock and cook for 3 minutes. Now add the ginger, soaked fenugreek leaves, salt and sugar and simmer for 3 minutes, or until the oil starts to separate from the sauce around the edge of the pan. Stir in the lemon juice, then set aside and keep warm.

For the sea bass, mix together the salt, black onion seeds and 1 tablespoon of the oil. Coat the fish with this mixture and set aside for 20 minutes. Meanwhile, make the stir-fry. Heat the oil in a pan and add the cumin seeds. When they begin to crackle, add the potato and turmeric and toss over a medium heat for a minute or two. Cover the pan and cook for about 5 minutes, then add the bottle gourds and salt and toss well. Add the ginger, lemon juice and coriander, stir in the tomato and cook for 2 minutes, until the vegetables are just tender.

To cook the fish, heat the remaining oil in a large frying pan over a high heat, add the bass, skin-side down, and cook for about 4 minutes, until crisp. Flip it over and cook the other side.

Divide the sauce between 4 serving plates, then put the fish on top and the stir-fry to the side.

½ teaspoon salt
¼ teaspoon black onion seeds
4 tablespoons vegetable or corn oil
4 x 200g/7oz wild sea bass fillets

For the fenugreek sauce:
3 tablespoons vegetable or corn oil
I onion, finely chopped
¼ teaspoon ground turmeric
300g/IIoz/I¾ cups Boiled Cashew Paste (see page 30)
I00g/4oz/½ cup plain yoghurt
4 tablespoons fish stock
2.5cm/I inch piece of fresh ginger, finely chopped
2 teaspoons dried fenugreek leaves, soaked in water for 5 minutes, then drained
I teaspoon salt
I teaspoon sugar
juice of ½ lemon

For the bottle gourd stir-fry:
2 tablespoons vegetable or corn oil
¼ teaspoon cumin seeds
I large potato, peeled and cut into Icm/½ inch dice
¼ teaspoon ground turmeric
6 bottle gourds, scraped, deseeded and cut into Icm/½ inch dice
¾ teaspoon salt
Icm/½ inch piece of fresh ginger, finely chopped
juice of ½ lemon
½ tablespoon chopped fresh coriander
I tomato, deseeded and cut into Icm/½ inch dice

SPICE-CRUSTED MONKFISH
WITH TOMATO AND LEMON SAUCE

SERVES 4

Monkfish has a firm texture and can become dry during cooking so we have devised a marinade of cheese and yoghurt to keep it succulent, accompanying it with a sauce that has a clean, light feel that manages to lift the meatiness of the fish.

Wine to accompany this recipe
NEW ZEALAND PINOT GRIS
The acidity of a *New Zealand Pinot Gris* will balance the lemon and allow the fruit to lift the spices and tomato.

Mix together all the ingredients for the first marinade, rub them over the monkfish and set aside for 20 minutes. Meanwhile, roast all the ingredients for the spice mix in a dry frying pan and crush them coarsely with a pestle and mortar. For the second marinade, put the cheese in a small bowl and rub it to a paste with your fingers (a teaspoon of flour could be added to help prevent lumps forming). Add the yoghurt and mix to a smooth paste, then mix in all the other ingredients, adding the cream last.

Heat the oil in a large ovenproof frying pan, add the fish and sear on both sides. Spread the second marinade over the fish, then sprinkle over the roasted spice mix. Transfer to an oven preheated to 200°C/400°F/Gas Mark 6 and cook for about 10 minutes, until the fish is done.

Meanwhile, for the sauce, heat the ghee or butter in a pan, add the bay leaf and sieved tomatoes and simmer for 5 minutes. In a bowl, mix the ginger and garlic pastes, red chilli powder and cumin with a little water to make a smooth paste. Add this mixture to the pan and simmer for 5 minutes, stirring to prevent sticking. Stir in the coconut milk and simmer for 3–4 minutes, until the sauce turns glossy. Now add the salt, sugar and lemon leaves (or lemongrass). Simmer for another 3–4 minutes, until the sauce is infused with the lemon flavour. Serve the monkfish with the sauce and some plain rice.

800g/1¾lb monkfish, cut into 4 pieces
1 tablespoon vegetable or corn oil

For the first marinade:
½ teaspoon Ginger Paste (see page 30)
½ teaspoon Garlic Paste (see page 30)
½ teaspoon finely ground white pepper
¼ teaspoon salt

For the spice mix:
½ teaspoon coriander seeds
½ teaspoon cumin seeds
½ teaspoon black peppercorns
1 dried red chilli

For the second marinade:
1 tablespoon grated processed
   Cheddar cheese
2 tablespoons Greek yoghurt
2.5cm/1 inch piece of fresh ginger,
   finely chopped
2 green chillies, finely chopped
½ tablespoon chopped fresh coriander
½ teaspoon salt
1 tablespoon single cream

For the tomato and lemon sauce:
100g/4oz/½ cup ghee or clarified butter
1 bay leaf
6 ripe tomatoes, boiled in a little water
   until tender, then pushed through a
   sieve to make a purée
1 teaspoon Ginger Paste (see page 30)
1 teaspoon Garlic Paste (see page 30)
1 teaspoon red chilli powder
1 teaspoon ground cumin
300ml/½ pint/1¼ cups coconut milk
1¼ teaspoons salt
½ teaspoon sugar
4 fresh lemon leaves (or 2 lemongrass
   stalks, lightly crushed)

SEARED BLACK COD WITH COCONUT AND LEMON SAUCE

SERVES 4

If you have trouble getting hold of black cod, and you probably will, subsitute with ordinary cod, though you will be missing out on the very singular and special flavour of the black variety. It is an exceptionally moist fish with a fine buttery texture.

Wine to accompany this recipe
VOUVRAY
A demi-sec *Vouvray* from the *Loire Valley* will cut through the richness of the coconut to bring out the lemon.

First make the sauce. Heat the oil in a pan, add the onion and sauté until soft. Add the lemongrass, lemon leaves, chillies and ginger and sauté for 1 minute. Then add the turmeric and stir for a minute. Pour in the coconut milk, bring to the boil and simmer for 6–8 minutes, until the sauce thickens. Stir in the salt and set aside.

Rub 1 tablespoon of the oil, the black onion seeds and salt into the cod. Heat the remaining oil in a large frying pan, add the cod, skin-side down, and sear for 2–3 minutes, until crisp. Turn and cook the other side. Depending on the thickness of the fillet, you might need to finish the cod in a moderately hot oven for 5–6 minutes, but be careful not to cook it for too long or the flakes of flesh will start to separate and the fish will disintegrate.

Mix together the chilli flakes and rice flakes and press them on top of the fish to form a crust. Place under a hot grill for a minute or two, until golden. To serve, pour the sauce on to 4 plates and place the fish on top.

2 tablespoons vegetable or corn oil
1 teaspoon black onion seeds
1 teaspoon salt
4 x 200g/7oz pieces of black cod fillet
½ teaspoon dried red chilli flakes
2 tablespoons pressed rice flakes
  (pawa)

For the coconut and lemon sauce:
2 tablespoons vegetable or corn oil
1 onion, sliced
1 lemongrass stalk, cut into 3 or
  4 pieces
6 lemon leaves (if you cannot find any,
  use 1 extra lemongrass stalk)
5 green chillies, cut lengthways in half
5cm/2 inch piece of fresh ginger,
  cut into fine strips
½ teaspoon ground turmeric
500ml/18fl oz/2¼ cups coconut milk
1 teaspoon salt

MACKEREL IN HOT SOUTH INDIAN SAUCE

SERVES 4

Although mackerel is caught off India's coasts it is nowhere near as popular as it is in many parts of Europe. In an attempt to try and redress this imbalance we have given it the south Indian treatment – which if you're been to Kerala you may well have experienced on the trawlers where fishermen cook part of their catch on board driven by the fact that they are away for a whole day or more and simply have to eat.

Wine to accompany this recipe
AUSTRALIAN RIESLING
The heat of this dish will require a certain amount of freshness from a wine such as an aged *Australian Riesling* to tone it. The heat will lift the fruit of the wine, leaving a pleasant tropical finish.

Wash and pat dry the mackerel fillets, then cut them in half. Mix together the salt, turmeric and chilli powder, rub them over the mackerel and set aside for 20 minutes.

Heat the oil in a large frying pan, add the mackerel fillets skin-side down and fry for 2 minutes on each side (do this in batches if necessary). Remove from the heat and set aside.

For the sauce, place a large pan over a low heat, add the ground coriander, chilli powder and curry leaves and dry-roast them for 2–3 minutes. Add the fish stock or water and simmer for 2 minutes, then add the tomatoes and cook gently until soft. Add the chillies and salt and stir well. Then add the coconut milk and bring to the boil. Place the fillets in the sauce, add the sugar and simmer for 2 minutes. Serve garnished with curry leaves and accompanied by plain rice.

8 mackerel fillets
½ teaspoon salt
½ teaspoon ground turmeric
1 teaspoon red chilli powder
3 tablespoons vegetable or corn oil

For the sauce:
2 tablespoons ground coriander
1½ teaspoons mild red chilli powder
2 sprigs of fresh curry leaves,
   plus a few leaves to garnish
5 tablespoons fish stock or water
2 tomatoes, chopped
2 green chillies, cut lengthways in half
1 teaspoon salt
150ml/¼ pint/ ²/3 cup coconut milk
¼ teaspoon sugar

MULLET IN A BENGALI VEGETABLE BROTH

SERVES 4

The Bengalis are noted for having spawned more intellectuals than any other part of India and this is often ascribed to the fact that they eat so much fish. Across the rest of the country, mothers tell their children at dinnertime, 'Eat your fish and be as brainy as the Bengalis.' This is a classic Bengali dish called macher johl, meaning fish with sauce. Bengalis prefer their sauces thinner than other regions and this one brings out the traditional flavour of mustard.

Wine to accompany this recipe
PINOT BLANC FROM ALSACE
The natural sweetness of the shellfish broth will be balanced by a fresh and crisp *Pinot Blanc* from *Alsace*.

Wash the red mullet fillets and pat them dry with kitchen paper. Rub them with the salt, turmeric and chilli powder and set aside while you made the broth.

If you are using mustard oil, heat it in a pan over a high heat. When it smokes, remove from the heat and leave to cool, then heat it again (this is to get rid of the pungent raw flavour of the mustard).

When the oil is hot, add the cardamom pods, peppercorns, bay leaves, onion seeds and fennel seeds and let them crackle. Add the onions and sauté until golden brown. Add the turmeric, chilli powder and ground cumin and sauté for a minute. Add the aubergines and potatoes and sauté for 3 minutes, then add the fish stock or water and the salt and simmer for 15 minutes, to give a thin broth.

Heat the oil in a large frying pan, add the mullet fillets and fry over a high heat until browned on both sides. Remove from the heat and add to the pan with the tomatoes. Simmer for 3 minutes, then stir in the sugar, green chillies and fresh coriander. Cover the pan and cook for 2 minutes longer.

Pour the broth into 4 deep bowls and place the red mullet fillets on top in a criss-cross fashion. Serve with plain rice.

8 red mullet fillets, scaled
1 teaspoon salt
¼ teaspoon ground turmeric
1 teaspoon red chilli powder
3 tablespoons vegetable or corn oil

For the broth:
2 tablespoons mustard oil (or use 2 tablespoons vegetable oil mixed with 1 teaspoon English mustard)
4 green cardamom pods, crushed
6 black peppercorns
2 bay leaves
½ teaspoon black onion seeds
½ teaspoon fennel seeds
2 red onions, chopped
¼ teaspoon ground turmeric
1 teaspoon red chilli powder
1 teaspoon cumin seeds, roasted and ground (see page 30)
2 small aubergines, cut into quarters
2 small potatoes, peeled and cut into quarters
500ml/18fl oz/2¼ cups fish stock or water
1¼ teaspoons salt
2 tomatoes, cut into quarters
½ teaspoon sugar
2 green chillies, cut lengthways in half
1 tablespoon chopped fresh coriander

WILD SALMON WITH DILL AND MUSTARD

SERVES 4

Bengalis often cook fish with mustard. Here we have adapted the idea to salmon. Wild salmon is preferable to farmed for this dish, as the firmer flesh holds the creamy yoghurt marinade better and stands up to the robustness of the mustard. Plain rice or coriander mash makes a good accompaniment, together with some wilted spinach.

Wine to accompany this recipe
AMERICAN PINOT BLANC
The persistent flavours of dill and mustard will match the fruit intensity of an *American Pinot Blanc*.

Wash the salmon fillets and pat them dry on kitchen paper. Mix together all the ingredients for the first marinade, rub them over the fish and set aside for 15 minutes. Meanwhile, make the second marinade. Put the cheese in a small bowl and rub it to a paste with your fingers (a teaspoon of flour could be added to help prevent lumps forming). Add the yoghurt and mix to a smooth paste, then add the mustard seeds, wholegrain mustard and chillies and finally mix in the cream.

Heat the oil in a large ovenproof frying pan, add the salmon and sear for about 1½ minutes on each side. Remove from the heat and spread the second marinade over the fish. Transfer to an oven preheated to 180°C/350°F/ Gas Mark 4 and cook for 10 minutes.

Meanwhile, make the sauce. Heat the ghee in a heavy-based pan, then add the cashew and onion pastes. Cook over a low heat, stirring frequently to prevent sticking, until you can see specks of ghee on top of the cashew paste and a sheen appears. Now stir in the wholegrain mustard and cream, followed by the salt and dill.

Pour some of the sauce on to 4 serving plates, place the salmon on top, then drizzle with the remaining sauce.

4 x 175g/6oz wild salmon fillets
1 tablespoon vegetable or corn oil

For the first marinade:
½ teaspoon Ginger Paste (see page 30)
½ teaspoon Garlic Paste (see page 30)
1 teaspoon salt
1 teaspoon finely ground white pepper
1 tablespoon vegetable or corn oil

For the second marinade:
2 tablespoons grated processed
    Cheddar cheese grated
2 tablespoons Greek yoghurt
1 teaspoon mustard seeds, ground
1 tablespoon wholegrain mustard
2 green chillies, finely chopped
1 tablespoon single cream

For the sauce:
2 teaspoons ghee
300g/11oz of Boiled Cashew Paste
    (see page 30)
300g/11oz of Boiled Onion Paste
    (see page 30)
1 tablespoon wholegrain mustard
1 tablespoon single cream
1 teaspoon salt
1 teaspoon chopped fresh dill

RICE-CRUSTED SEA BREAM WITH KERALA CURRY SAUCE

SERVES 4

The Keralans love their fish. Boatmen trawl the waters for many types of seafood and often cook the best part of their catch on the boat. If you ever go to Kerala, make sure you take a trip on one of these. On the boats, the fish is rubbed with spices and fried. Once the boatmen come home, however, this is the kind of sauce they cook their fish in. The rice crust adds texture to this delicate fish. If you can't find rice flakes, use bread-crumbs, but make your own rather than buying the packet variety.

Wine to accompany this recipe

CLARE VALLEY AUSTRALIAN RIESLING
The very dry, mineral style of a *Clare Valley Australian Riesling* will cut through the sweetness of the coconut sauce, while the delicate heat will lift the wine's floral element.

Mix together all the marinade ingredients, rub them over the sea bream and set aside for 20 minutes.

Meanwhile, make the sauce. Heat the oil in a pan, add the curry leaves and onion and sauté until the onion is brown. Add the chilli powder and tomatoes and cook until the tomatoes are soft. Add the kokum berries and fish stock and simmer for 2–3 minutes. Stir in the coconut milk and simmer for 2–3 minutes longer, until the sauce has a creamy consistency. Season with the salt.

To cook the fish, heat the oil in a large frying pan, add the fish fillets, skin-side down, and cook for about 2 minutes on each side. Press the rice flakes on top of the fish to form a crust and place under a hot grill for a minute or two, until golden. Pour the sauce on to 4 serving plates, place the fish on top and serve.

4 sea bream, filleted
1 tablespoon vegetable or corn oil
2 tablespoons pressed rice flakes
    (pawa)

For the marinade:

1 tablespoon vegetable or corn oil
1 teaspoon black onion seeds
1 teaspoon salt

For the sauce:

3 tablespoons vegetable or corn oil
10 fresh curry leaves
1 large onion, chopped
2 teaspoons mild red chilli powder
2 tomatoes, finely chopped
2 kokum berries (or 2 teaspoons
    tamarind paste)
3 tablespoons fish stock
250ml/8fl oz/1 cup coconut milk
1 teaspoon salt

PARSEE-STYLE ROAST SEA BASS

The Parsees are very partial to some sweetness. Followers of the ancient religion of Zoroastrianism, they were originally from Persia. Their cuisine retains much from their roots, in particular a sweetness in their cooking taken from dried fruits – mainly raisins, sultanas and apricots. Parsee cuisine remains largely unexplored primarily because there are reputed to be less that 100,000 of them left. They are blessed with one notable ambassador in London in the form of the irrepressible Cyrus Todiwala, the chef owner of Café Spice Namaste and a more recent restaurant called The Parsee. Here the sweetness in the spice paste comes from dried apricots. Serve with Masala Mashed Potatoes on page 140.

Wine to accompany this recipe
AUSTRALIAN OR TASMANIAN RIESLING
The heat of this dish will be balanced by the acidity of an *Australian* or *Tasmanian Riesling* and will also enhance the wine's tropical flavours.

For the spice paste, spread the cloves, peppercorns, coriander seeds, cumin seeds and cinnamon stick out on a baking tray and dry them under the grill on a low heat for a few minutes. Transfer to a spice grinder and grind to a powder. Heat the oil in a pan, add the onion and sauté until golden brown. Add the chopped garlic and sauté for a couple more minutes, until it starts changing colour, then add the ground spices and the chilli powder. Stir briskly for a few seconds, then add the tomato purée, puréed apricots, salt and sugar. Cook over a medium heat until the mixture has a jammy consistency. It should taste sweet and spicy. Remove from the heat and set aside.

Wash the sea bass and pat dry on kitchen paper. Mix together the ingredients for the marinade and rub them over the fish, then set aside for 30 minutes.

Heat a large non-stick frying pan and add the oil. When the oil is hot, add the fish and sear for 3 minutes on each side or until the skin is evenly coloured and crisp (you may have to do this in batches, depending on the size of your pan). Arrange the fish on a baking tray, spread the spice paste on both sides of the fish and place in an oven preheated to 200°C/400°F/Gas Mark 6. Roast for 6 minutes, until the fish is just cooked. Remove from the oven, sprinkle with the fresh coriander and lemon juice and serve immediately.

4 x 350–400g/12–14oz sea bass, cleaned
2 tablespoons vegetable or corn oil
2 tablespoons chopped fresh coriander
juice of I lemon

For the marinade:
I½ teaspoons salt
I teaspoon red chilli powder
I tablespoon vegetable or corn oil

For the spice paste:
I5 cloves
½ teaspoon black peppercorns
I teaspoon coriander seeds
I teaspoon cumin seeds
I cinnamon stick
I tablespoon vegetable or corn oil
I onion, finely chopped
2 garlic cloves, finely chopped
I½ teaspoons mild red chilli powder
I½ tablespoons tomato purée
I½ tablespoons puréed dried apricots
I½ teaspoons salt
I teaspoon sugar

GOAN SPICED TROUT WITH BEAN SALAD

SERVES 4

This is an ideal summer dish that is well suited to barbecue cooking. The Goan spice mix is robust yet doesn't overpower the fish and the use of vinegar helps lift the flavours. The bean salad (see page 147) makes a perfect accompaniment.

Wine to accompany this recipe
ITALIAN SAUVIGNON BLANC
The dry heat of the spice mix will be balanced by the acidity of an *Italian Sauvignon Blanc*, while the mineral and citrus elements of the wine will remain.

Slash the trout 2 or 3 times on each side with a sharp knife. Mix together all the ingredients for the marinade and rub them into the fish, then set aside to marinate for 1 hour. Meanwhile, make the Goan spice mix. Dry-roast the whole spices one by one in a frying pan, then put them in a blender or food processor with the garlic, vinegar, salt and sugar and blend to a paste.

Heat the oil in a large frying pan, add the fish (you may have to cook them in 2 batches) and sear over a high heat for 2 minutes on each side. Remove from the heat and spread the Goan spice mix on top. Place the fish on a baking tray and cook in an oven preheated to 180°C/350°F/Gas Mark 4 for 10 minutes.

Serve the trout alongside the Lentil Bean Salad, accompanied by lemon wedges.

4 trout, cleaned
2 tablespoons vegetable or corn oil
lemon wedges, to serve

For the marinade:
1½ teaspoons salt
1 teaspoon Ginger Paste (see page 30)
1 teaspoon Garlic Paste (see page 30)
1 teaspoon red chilli powder

For the Goan spice mix:
20 cloves
1 tablespoon coriander seeds
1½ tablespoons black peppercorns
3 black cardamom pods
5 star anise
10 dried red chillies
5 garlic cloves, peeled
3 tablespoons white vinegar
1 teaspoon salt
1 tablespoon sugar

KING PRAWNS IN SAFFRON ALMOND SAUCE

SERVES 4

This dish as served in the restaurant is rather more complicated than the one below, involving as it does an extra shrimp sauce and delicate rice pancakes. This version however, is no less brilliant.

Wine to accompany this recipe
ALSACE GEWÜRZTRAMINER
The natural sweetness of the almonds combined with the delicate saffron will enhance the rich flavour of an *Alsace Gewürztraminer.*

800g/1¾lb raw, headless king prawns, shell on
1 tablespoon vegetable or corn oil

For the first marinade:
1 teaspoon Ginger Paste (see page 30)
1 teaspoon Garlic Paste (see page 30)
¼ teaspoon ground turmeric
1 teaspoon salt
½ teaspoon finely ground white pepper

For the saffron almond sauce:
75g/3oz/¾ cup blanched almonds
100g/4oz/1 cup cashew nuts
2 tablespoons ghee or clarified butter
1 bay leaf
2 green cardamom pods, crushed
1 onion, finely chopped
1cm/½ inch piece of fresh ginger, finely chopped
1 green chilli, finely chopped
¼ teaspoon ground turmeric

4 tablespoons fish stock or water
a small pinch of saffron strands, infused in 2 tablespoons warm milk
1 teaspoon salt
½ teaspoon sugar
2 tablespoons single cream
a pinch of garam masala

For the second marinade:
2 tablespoons Greek yoghurt
2 tablespoons single cream
a pinch of saffron strands, infused in 2 tablespoons warm milk
1 teaspoon Mace and Cardamom Powder (see page 32)
½ teaspoon salt
¼ teaspoon royal cumin seeds (or black cumin seeds)

Peel the prawns, leaving the tail shell intact, then de-vein them by making a shallow cut along the back and lifting out the dark intestinal vein with the point of a sharp knife. Place the prawns in a bowl, mix in all the ingredients for the first marinade and set aside for 10 minutes.

Heat the oil in a large, heavy-based frying pan, add the prawns and sear quickly so that they curl up. Remove from the heat immediately and set aside to cool.

For the sauce, put the almonds and cashew nuts in a pan, add enough water to cover and bring to the boil. Simmer until soft, then drain. Blend to a smooth purée with a little water in a food processor or blender.

Heat the ghee or clarified butter in a heavy-based pan, add the bay leaf, crushed cardamom and onion and sauté until the onion is golden. Add the ginger and green chilli and sauté for 1 minute, then add the turmeric and sauté for about a minute longer, until everything becomes bright yellow. Add the almond and cashew purée and cook, stirring frequently, for 3–5 minutes. Add the fish stock or water and simmer for 2–3 minutes, until the sauce turns glossy. Stir in the saffron infusion and

cook for 1 minute. Stir in the salt and sugar, followed by the cream and garam masala. If the sauce is too thick, dilute it with a little more fish stock or water. Remove from the heat and keep warm.

Mix together all the ingredients for the second marinade and dip the prawns in it. Thread the prawns on bamboo skewers, piercing the skewer through the tail of each prawn and taking it out through the tip of the head. Cook for 5–6 minutes in an oven preheated to 200°C/400°F/ Gas Mark 6. Divide the sauce between 4 serving plates. Remove the prawns from the skewers, place on top of the sauce and serve.

MUSTARD-FLAVOURED TANDOORI-STYLE KING PRAWNS WITH SAFFRON KEDGEREE

SERVES 4

Prawns are immensely popular throughout Bengal and neighbouring Bangladesh, where kasundi is the preferred cooking style. Kasundi is a type of mustard that is as fragrant as it is pungent (page 230). Typically, prawns would be cooked in a sauce where kasundi mustard was the overwhelming flavour, but in our recipe they are grilled and served with a separate sauce, in the French style.

Wine to accompany this recipe
NEW ZEALAND SYRAH
The pungent mustard flavour will be balanced by the freshness of a mineral *New Zealand Syrah*, while the prawns' sweetness and the subtle character of the saffron kedgeree will support the blackberry fruit of the wine.

800g/1¾lb raw, headless king prawns, shell on
I tablespoon vegetable or corn oil

For the saffron kedgeree:
100g/4oz/²⁄3 cup split yellow mung beans
250ml/8fl oz/I cup water
a pinch of ground turmeric
2 tablespoons ghee or clarified butter
½ teaspoon cumin seeds
I large onion, chopped
Icm/½ inch piece of fresh ginger, finely chopped
2 green chillies, finely chopped
a pinch of saffron strands, infused in 2 teaspoons warm water
I teaspoon salt

75g/3oz/½ cup basmati rice, cooked (see page 33)
I tomato, deseeded and cut into Icm/½ inch dice
2 tablespoons chopped fresh coriander

For the first marinade:
I teaspoon Ginger Paste (see page 30)
I teaspoon Garlic Paste (see page 30)
I teaspoon salt
juice of ½ lemon

For the second marinade:
I tablespoon Greek yoghurt
I tablespoon kasundi mustard (or wholegrain Dijon mustard)
25g/Ioz/¾ cup fresh mustard leaves, whizzed to a paste in a blender with a

First prepare the kedgeree. Wash the mung beans, put them in a pan with the water and turmeric and bring to the boil. Simmer until the beans are tender and all the water has evaporated, then remove from the heat and set aside.

Heat the ghee or butter in a pan and add the cumin seeds. When they crackle, add the onion and sauté until it begins to colour. Add the ginger, green chillies and saffron infusion and cook for 2 minutes. Stir in the mung beans and salt, then fold in the rice. Mix in the tomato and coriander and stir over a low heat for 3–4 minutes. Remove from the heat and keep warm.

Peel the prawns, then de-vein them by making a shallow cut along the back and lifting out the dark intestinal vein with the point of a sharp knife. Put the prawns in a bowl, add all the ingredients for the first marinade and mix well. Leave to marinate for 20 minutes. Meanwhile, mix together all the ingredients for the second marinade.

Heat the oil in a large ovenproof frying pan, add the prawns and sear briefly over a high heat. Remove from the heat and immediately spread the second marinade on top of the prawns. Transfer to an oven preheated to 200°C/400°F/ Gas Mark 6 and cook for 5–6 minutes.

KERALA-STYLE SEAFOOD CURRY

SERVES 4

little oil (or use I teaspoon English
mustard)
2 green chillies, finely chopped
5mm/¼ inch piece of fresh ginger,
finely chopped

For the mustard sauce:
3 tablespoons kasundi mustard
(or wholegrain Dijon mustard)
I50ml/¼/²/3 cup pint coconut milk
2 tablespoons plain yoghurt
4 tablespoons shellfish stock or water
½ teaspoon salt
¼ teaspoon ground turmeric
a little sugar (optional)

*This simple and very colourful dish is
packed with flavour. The Keralans love
to cook fish in coconut milk with a
mixture of hot and sour tastes.*

Wine to accompany this recipe
VOUVRAY
The soft spicing and sourness of the sauce
will be matched by the delicate acidity of a
Vouvray from the *Loire Valley* or *South Africa*.
This acidity will also cut through the coconut
element of the sauce.

For the sauce, put the mustard, coconut milk, yoghurt, stock or water, salt and turmeric in a small pan and heat slowly, stirring constantly, until the mixture comes to the boil. Simmer for 5–6 minutes, until thickened, then taste and check the seasoning. You might need a little sugar to balance the sourness.

To serve, divide the kedgeree between 4 plates, place the prawns on top and drizzle the sauce around.

Heat the oil in a deep pan and add the mustard seeds. When they crackle, add the curry leaves, then the onion, and sauté until the onion is about to turn brown. Add the chilli powder and cook for 30 seconds. Add the tomatoes and tamarind paste and cook until the tomatoes begin to dry out.

Now pour in the fish stock or water and bring to a simmer. Add the salt, followed by the salmon and white fish. Let them cook for a minute, then pour in the coconut milk and simmer for 1–2 minutes. As the sauce slowly thickens, add the prawns, squid and mussels. Simmer for 2 minutes, then serve with plain rice.

3 tablespoons vegetable or corn oil
½ teaspoon mustard seeds
2 sprigs of fresh curry leaves
I onion, chopped
2 teaspoons mild red chilli powder
3 tomatoes, chopped
2 tablespoons tamarind paste
200ml/7fl oz/⁷/8 cup fish stock or water
I teaspoon salt
200g/7oz salmon fillet, cut into 2.5cm/
I inch dice
200g/7oz white fish fillet, such as
halibut, cod or pollock, cut into
2.5cm/I inch dice
250ml/8fl oz/I cup coconut milk
I00g/4oz/I cup shelled raw prawns
I00g/4oz/I cup squid, cleaned and cut
into rings
200g/7oz fresh mussels, cleaned

OLD DELHI-STYLE CHICKEN CURRY

SERVES 4

In Old Delhi Vivek and I visited the legendary Moti Mahal restaurant, which in the 1950s created the dish that now defines Indian food for millions of people around the world. Murgh makhani (butter chicken), as Moti Mahal calls it, is the original chicken tikka masala. Outside of India this a dish that has been much interpreted (or rather misinterpreted), and has been rendered pink, red, orange – you name it. When I ran an Indian restaurant trade magazine, I became so tired of answering media enquiries about this dish that I made up a tale of an Englishman in the 1970s going to a curry house and asking for chicken tikka, a dry dish served straight from the tandoor oven. When his meal arrived, he realised to his horror that he was being deprived of an Englishman's fundamental culinary right – a sauce. The dish was sent back to the kitchen with the instruction, 'Add sauce.' Bemused, the chef looked around his larder, spotted a can of tomato soup, chucked it in a pan with a dash of cream and added the chicken tikka, thus creating what has virtually become Britain's national dish.

Wine to accompany this recipe
ALSACE GEWÜRZTRAMINER
The rich sauce will complement an equally rich *Gewürztraminer* from *Alsace*, while the smoky flavours and the fenugreek will enhance the wine's fruit.

Mix together all the ingredients for the first marinade, add the chicken and toss well. Set aside for 20 minutes.

Mix together the yoghurt and garam masala for the second marinade, pour over the chicken and set aside for 20 minutes. Ideally the chicken should be cooked in a tandoor oven to give it a smoky flavour, otherwise put it in a roasting tin and place in an oven pre-heated to 220°C/425°F/Gas Mark 7 for 12–15 minutes, until not quite cooked through. (Alternatively thread the meat on skewers and cook on a barbecue.) Remove from oven and set aside. Pour off the juices from the tin and reserve.

For the sauce, put the tomatoes in a large saucepan with the crushed ginger, garlic, whole spices, bay leaf and water. Bring to the boil and simmer until the tomatoes have completely broken down. Purée in a blender and strain through a fine sieve into a clean pan. Bring to the boil, add the chilli powder and simmer until the sauce begins to thicken. Whisk in the butter a little at a time to give a glossy sauce. Add the chicken and the reserved juices and simmer for 5 minutes. Add the ginger and the cream and simmer until red spots of fat appear on the surface of the sauce. Stir in the salt, fenugreek leaves and garam masala, check seasoning and add sugar if necessary. Serve with naan bread or Star Anise Pilau Rice (see page 132).

800g/1¾lb chicken thighs, skinned, boned and cut in half

For the first marinade:
1 teaspoon Ginger Paste (see page 30)
1 teaspoon Garlic Paste (see page 30)
1½ teaspoons salt
1½ teaspoons mild red chilli powder
juice of ½ lemon

For the second marinade:
100g/4oz/½ cup Greek yoghurt
¼ teaspoon garam masala

For the sauce:
800g/13/4lb tomatoes, cut in half
1cm/½ inch piece of fresh ginger, crushed, plus a 2.5cm/1 inch piece of fresh ginger, finely chopped
2 garlic cloves, peeled
2 green cardamom pods
2 cloves
1 bay leaf
125ml/4fl oz/1 cup water
1 tablespoon mild red chilli powder
50g/2oz/¼ cup butter, diced
5 tablespoons single cream
1 teaspoon salt
2 teaspoons dried fenugreek leaves, crushed between your fingers
¼ teaspoon garam masala
2 teaspoons sugar (optional)

HOT SOUTH INDIAN CHICKEN CURRY

SERVES 4

South Indians like their curries very spicy and flavoured with coconut. Curry houses across Britain serve a dish called chicken Madras, which is code for 'hot curry but not quite as hot as a vindaloo'. If you went to Madras (in any case now called Chennai) and asked for chicken Madras you would receive quizzical looks. But presumably it originated from this curry. Traditionally this dish is prepared with unskinned pieces of chicken on the bone, which are fried first for extra crispness. We prefer to use skinned boned chicken thighs, which look more attractive and are easier to eat. We have also increased the amount of coconut milk in order to tone down the spiciness of the sauce. If you prefer it less spicy still, you could reduce the quantity of dried chillies and peppercorns and increase the coconut milk further.

Wine to accompany this recipe
AUSTRALIAN RIESLING
The hot spicing in this dish will require a certain amount of freshness from the wine. The heat will lift the fruit of a young *Australian Riesling.*

First prepare the spice paste. Heat the oil in a pan, add the onions and sauté until translucent. Now add the remaining ingredients one by one, cooking them in turn for 30 seconds each. When all the ingredients have been added, sauté for a minute longer, then remove from the heat and leave to cool. Blitz the mixture in a food processor or blender, adding just enough water to make a smooth paste. Set aside.

To make the curry, heat the oil in a deep, heavy-based pan, add the onions and half the curry leaves and cook until the onions are golden. Add the spice paste and cook on a low heat, stirring constantly, until the mixture has formed a mass and the oil has begun to separate out round the sides. Add the tomato purée and cook for 1 minute, then add the chicken and salt. If the sauce thickens too much, add a little water. Stir in the tomatoes and cook for 5 minutes. Pour in the coconut milk, bring to the boil and add the sugar. Simmer for 20 minutes, until the chicken is tender.

Sprinkle the remaining curry leaves on top, cover the pan and leave to stand for a few minutes. Serve with plain rice.

3 tablespoons vegetable or corn oil
2 red onions, finely chopped
1 sprig of fresh curry leaves
1 tablespoon tomato purée
800g/1¾lb chicken thighs, skinned, boned and each cut into 2–3 pieces
1½ teaspoons salt
3 tomatoes, finely chopped
250ml/8fl oz/1 cup coconut milk
½ teaspoon sugar

For the spice paste:
2 tablespoons vegetable or corn oil
2 red onions, roughly chopped
5 green cardamom pods
2 black cardamom pods
15 cloves
1½ tablespoons black peppercorns
5 star anise
4 garlic cloves, peeled
4 tablespoons coriander seeds
1 tablespoon fennel seeds
5 dried red chillies
3 blades of mace
1 tablespoon cumin seeds
1 tablespoon white poppy seeds
100g/4oz/1 cup fresh coconut, grated
2 sprigs of fresh curry leaves

CHICKEN BREASTS STUFFED WITH SPINACH AND APRICOT IN A KORMA SAUCE

SERVES 4

Chicken korma is Britain's second most popular Indian restaurant dish after chicken tikka masala. Whereas it used to be dismissed as a bland entry point into Indian food, it is now much more likely to be cooked properly and appreciated as a subtly aromatic and creamy dish. There are many local variations across the Subcontinent – some regions use rosewater, others keep the sauce very dry. Here we retain the characteristic aromas and flavours but roll the chicken breasts up round a filling of spinach and apricot. It looks complicated, but in fact is quite a straightforward dish to prepare and is quite wonderful.

Wine to accompany this recipe
VIOGNIER
The mineral flavour of the spinach will cut through a rich wine such as a *Viognier*, while the apricots will support its fruit character.

First prepare the filling. Heat a heavy-based pan and add the oil. When hot, add the cumin seeds and let them crackle. Add garlic and onion and sauté until they start to colour. Add the ginger and green chilli, followed by the spinach, and cook on a high heat for 5 minutes or so, stirring constantly. Add salt and garam masala, stir in the apricots and remove from the heat. Leave to cool, then stir in the grated cheese.

Slice each chicken breast horizontally

in half with a very sharp knife, leaving it joined at one side, then open it out flat like a book. Flatten it slightly with a meat mallet or rolling pin, so it is an even thickness and place on a piece of clingfilm that is more than large enough to wrap around it. Sprinkle with the salt, mace and cardamom. Divide the filling into 4 portions and place one portion on top of each chicken breast. Fold the chicken in from both sides, then roll up. Wrap the clingfilm round tightly, using it to give the chicken roll a more even shape. Poach the wrapped chicken in simmering water for 5–7 minutes, then drain. Heat the oil in a large frying pan, remove the clingfilm from the chicken and add to the pan. Cook until seared on all sides, turning frequently to give an even colour.

For the sauce, heat the ghee or butter in a pan and add the bay leaf and cardamom pods. When they crackle, add the cashew paste and cook for 5 minutes. Whisk in the yoghurt and cook for 6–8 minutes, until the fat rises on the side of the pan. Add some water if the sauce gets very thick. Add salt and cream and finally the lemon juice.

Cut the chicken breasts in half to reveal the colourful filling inside, then serve with the sauce and a bread or rice of your choice.

4 skinless, boneless corn-fed
   chicken breasts
½ teaspoon salt
½ teaspoon Mace and Cardamom
   Powder (see page 30)
I tablespoon vegetable or corn oil

For the filling:
2 tablespoons vegetable or corn oil
½ teaspoon cumin seeds
4 garlic cloves, finely chopped
I large onion, finely chopped
2.5cm/I inch piece of fresh ginger,
   finely chopped
I green chilli, finely chopped
300g/IIoz fresh spinach,
   finely shredded
½ teaspoon salt
½ teaspoon garam masala
75g/3oz/½ cup dried apricots,
   finely chopped
75g/3oz/¾ cup paneer cheese, grated

For the korma sauce:
2 tablespoons ghee or clarified butter
I bay leaf
2 green cardamom pods
250g/9oz/I¼ cups Boiled Cashew
   Paste (see page 30)
50g/2oz/¼ cup plain yoghurt
I teaspoon salt
I tablespoon single cream
juice of ½ lemon

SEARED DUCK BREASTS WITH SESAME TAMARIND SAUCE

SERVES 4

Together with Halibut with Coconut and Ginger Sauce (see page 78), this could claim to be The Cinnamon Club's signature dish, and is certainly one of the most popular choices on our menu. Vivek created it with a bottle of wine in his hand. He and our wine buyer, Laurent Chaniac, were trying to devise a recipe to go with a St Joseph Les Pierres Sèches Domaine Combier 1997. Inventing a dish to suit a wine is not the usual way of doing things and it caused quite a stir when we first opened - but it worked. In the restaurant, we serve this with Wild Mushroom and Spinach Stir-fry (see page 147). A Californian Pinot Noir as recommended below will go just as well with this spectacular duck dish.

Wine to accompany this recipe
CALIFORNIAN PINOT NOIR
The earthy character of the tamarind will complement the terroir elements of a *Californian Pinot Noir*. The dry tannins and the raspberry fruit of the wine will also complement the duck.

Mix together all the ingredients for the marinade and rub them over the duck breasts. Set aside for 30 minutes.

Make the sauce by mixing together the sesame, coriander, cumin and fenugreek seeds and roasting them in a dry frying pan over a moderate heat until they begin to colour. Set aside. Roast the coconut in the same pan until golden, then add to the seeds. Heat a teaspoon of the oil to the pan, add the cashew nuts and fry until golden. Place in a food processor with the roasted seeds and coconut and blend to a smooth paste with a little water. Heat the remaining oil in a large pan until very hot. Add the mustard seeds, followed by the black onion seeds and curry leaves. Reduce the heat, add the onion paste and cook, stirring, until it thickens. Then stir in the chilli powder, turmeric and tamarind and bring to a simmer. Add the nut and seed paste and cook for 3–4 minutes, until the oil begins to separate out at the side of the pan. It is important to stir constantly, as the sauce has a tendency to stick. If it becomes too thick, add enough duck stock or water to give the consistency of thin cream. Stir in the salt and the jaggery or sugar, remove from the heat and keep warm.

Heat the oil in an ovenproof frying pan, add the breasts, skin-side down, and sear until well browned. Turn the breasts over and transfer the pan to an oven preheated to 180°C/350°F/Gas Mark 4. Roast for 15 minutes; the duck should still be pink inside. Leave to rest for 5 minutes, then slice neatly. Divide the sauce between 4 serving plates and arrange the duck on top.

4 duck breasts, preferably
  Cressingham duck
I tablespoon vegetable or corn oil

For the marinade:
I tablespoon vegetable or corn oil
I teaspoon salt
I teaspoon red chilli powder

For the sesame tamarind sauce:
I tablespoon sesame seeds
I tablespoon coriander seeds
I teaspoon cumin seeds
½ teaspoon fenugreek seeds
I tablespoon desiccated coconut
I00ml/3½fl oz/scant ½ cup vegetable or
  corn oil
I tablespoon cashew nuts
I teaspoon mustard seeds
½ teaspoon black onion seeds
I0 fresh curry leaves
I quantity of Boiled Onion Paste
  (see page 30)
2 teaspoons mild red chilli powder
½ teaspoon ground turmeric
50g/2oz/¼ cup tamarind paste
up to I50ml/¼ pint/²/3 cup duck stock
  or water (optional)
I teaspoon salt
I tablespoon jaggery or
  molasses sugar

RACK OF LAMB WITH MINT AND ONION SAUCE

SERVES 4

Rack of lamb is not usually served in India, as the lamb reared there tends to be pretty lean and tough. In Britain, however, the lamb is so tender that it lends itself perfectly to this quick and simple cooking method. The two marinades used in this recipe give a subtle flavour that manages not to overwhelm the quality of the meat. Serve with Masala Mashed Potatoes (see page 140).

Wine to accompany this recipe
CALIFORNIAN PINOT NOIR
The powerful fresh fruit and integrated tannins of a *Californian Pinot Noir* will balance the sweetness of the meat and onions.

If the racks haven't already been prepared, trim off the skin and fat, leaving just a thin layer of fat on the meat. Mix together all the ingredients for the first marinade, rub them over the lamb and set aside for 30 minutes. Then mix together the ingredients for the second marinade and apply to the racks. Leave for another 15 minutes.

Meanwhile, make the sauce. Put the whole mint leaves, coriander and green chillies in a food processor and blend to a paste. Heat the ghee or butter in a pan, add the cashew paste and cook for 5 minutes. Whisk in the yoghurt and cook until the fat begins to separate out at the side of the pan. You might need to add a little water if the mixture is very thick. Stir in the diced red onion and the herb and chilli paste and simmer for 1 minute. Stir in the salt and cream, then season with the lemon juice and sprinkle in the shredded mint. Keep warm.

In a large, heavy-based frying pan, heat the oil and sear the lamb racks over a high heat until browned all over. Transfer to a roasting tin and place in an oven preheated to 200°C/400°F/Gas Mark 6. Roast for 10–15 minutes, depending on how well done you like your meat, then remove from the oven and leave to rest in a warm place for 5 minutes.

Divide the sauce between 4 serving plates, place the lamb racks on top and serve immediately.

2 racks of lamb, cut in half
I tablespoon vegetable or corn oil

For the first marinade:
I tablespoon Ginger Paste (see page 30)
I tablespoon Garlic Paste (see page 30)
I teaspoon red chilli powder
I teaspoon salt
juice of I lemon
½ teaspoon garam masala

For the second marinade:
I tablespoon Fried Cashew Paste
    (see page 30)
2 tablespoons Fried Onion Paste
    (see page 30)
2 tablespoons Greek yoghurt

For the mint and onion sauce:
2 tablespoons fresh mint leaves, plus I
    tablespoon finely shredded fresh mint
4 tablespoons fresh coriander leaves
3 green chillies, roughly chopped
2 tablespoons ghee or clarified butter
250g/9oz/I¼ cups Boiled Cashew
    Paste (see page 30)
4 tablespoons plain yoghurt
I red onion, cut into Icm/½ inch dice
I teaspoon salt
I tablespoon single cream
juice of I lemon

LAMB SHANK ROGAN JOSH

SERVES 4

The name may sound exotic to the Western ear but sadly Rogan Josh means nothing more than 'red juice'. It is a wonderful Kashmiri dish, in which the redness comes from the bark of a local tree called a rattan jyoth. *It is very difficult to find outside India, even in Asian shops, so we suggest that you use crushed beetroot instead.*

First blanch the lamb shanks. Bring a large pan of water to the boil, add the shanks, then cover and simmer for 20 minutes. Drain well and trim off any gristle and excess fat.

Heat the oil in a large pan and add the crushed cardamom and the cinnamon sticks. When they crackle, add the onions and cook until golden brown. Add the ginger and garlic pastes and cook for 2 minutes, stirring constantly to prevent the mixture sticking to the pan. Add the ground spices and cook for 3 minutes, then slowly whisk in the yoghurt, being careful not to add it all at once or it will lower the temperature of the sauce. Stir until the sauce comes to simmering point. Now add the puréed tomatoes and the salt and return the sauce to the boil. Add the lamb shanks, cover with a tight-fitting lid and cook very gently for about 1 hour, until the shanks are tender, adding the stock if the sauce is too thick.

Heat the ghee in a small pan, tie up the rattan jyoth or beetroot in a square of muslin and add to the ghee. Leave it to infuse for 1 minute. Add the infused ghee, the muslin bag and the garam masala to the lamb shanks and simmer for 2 minutes, until the sauce has turned dark red. Remove the muslin bag. Serve the lamb with rice or bread.

4 lamb shanks
3 tablespoons vegetable or corn oil
2 black cardamom pods, crushed
2 cinnamon sticks
2 large onions, chopped
1 teaspoon Ginger Paste (see page 30)
1 teaspoon Garlic Paste (see page 30)
1½ teaspoons red chilli powder
½ teaspoon ground fennel seeds
½ teaspoon ground coriander
1 teaspoon ground ginger
4 tablespoons plain yoghurt
5 tomatoes, puréed in a blender
1½ teaspoons salt
about 500ml/18fl oz lamb stock (optional)
¼ teaspoon garam masala

For tempering:
2 tablespoons ghee or clarified butter
2 sticks of rattan jyoth
(or ½ raw beetroot, roughly crushed with a rolling pin or meat mallet)

Wine to accompany this recipe
ALSACE RIESLING
The delicate heat of this dish will lift the fruit of an *Alsace Riesling*, while bringing the fruit closer to the natural sweetness of the lamb.

RAJASTHANI ROAST RUMP OF LAMB WITH CORN SAUCE

SERVES 4

Though this dish is full of Indian flavours the technique of searing the meat and then reducing the sauce is distinctly French in style. The silky corn sauce is common to much of Rajasthani cuisine but we like to use a mixture of mashed and whole corn kernels to give a more interesting texture. Serve with Star Anise Pilau Rice (see page 132).

Wine to accompany this recipe
AUSTRALIAN PINOT NOIR
The ripeness and freshness of a western *Australian Pinot Noir* will balance the natural sweetness of the lamb, while the corn will complement the oaky flavour of the wine.

Mix together all the ingredients for the marinade and rub them over the lamb. Set aside to marinate for 20–30 minutes.

Meanwhile, make the sauce. Heat the ghee or clarified butter in a heavy-based pan and add the cloves, cardamom and bay leaf. When they start to crackle, add the onions and cook on a medium heat until golden. Add the chillies and cook for 1–2 minutes. Then add the turmeric and salt and sauté briskly for a minute, taking care that the dry spices do not start to burn. Add the garlic paste and cook, stirring, for a couple of minutes. As soon as the fat starts to separate out at the side of the mixture, stir in the diced lamb. Cook for 4–5 minutes, until browned, then add three-quarters of the corn and all the yoghurt. Cook gently for about 30 minutes, stirring occasionally, until the corn is nearly mashed and the sauce is becoming very thick. Add the lamb stock or water, bring back to the boil, then add the ginger, coriander and the remaining corn. Reduce heat to medium and simmer for 10 minutes. Check seasoning and add lemon juice.

Heat the oil in a large ovenproof frying pan over a medium heat, add the lamb and sear for 4 minutes on each side. Transfer to an oven preheated to 180°C/350°F/Gas Mark 4 and roast for 6–7 minutes. Leave the meat to rest for 3–4 minutes, then cut into slices. Divide the sauce between 4 serving plates, place the lamb on top and serve.

4 x 175–200g/6–7oz lamb chump chops
   or saddle steaks, fat trimmed off
1 tablespoon vegetable or corn oil

For the marinade:
½ teaspoon red chilli powder
½ teaspoon salt
1 tablespoon vegetable or corn oil

For the corn sauce:
100g/4oz/½ cup ghee or clarified butter
8 cloves
2 black cardamom pods
1 bay leaf
2 onions, finely chopped
3 green chillies, chopped
½ teaspoon ground turmeric
1 teaspoon salt
1 tablespoon Garlic Paste
   (see page 30)
100g/4oz/½ cup lamb, finely diced
200g/7oz/1¾ cups sweetcorn (canned
   is fine)
4 tablespoons plain yoghurt
150ml/¼/²⁄₃ cup pint lamb stock or water
6cm/2½ inch piece of fresh ginger,
   finely chopped
50g/2oz/1 cup fresh coriander,
   chopped
juice of 1 lemon

HYDERABADI-STYLE BIRYANI OF LAMB

SERVES 4-6

Biryani is often called the king of dishes. It's much more than just 'meat downstairs, rice upstairs', as I once heard an East London waiter describe it to an American tourist. Most curry house renditions involve stir-frying pre-cooked lamb with pilau rice. Throughout the Subcontinent there are inumerable regional variations, some more aromatic, others spicier. In Hyderabad they follow the traditional route of making kacchi biryani, where the rice is cooked in the juices of the lamb and the lid of the cooking pot is sealed with dough so that none of the aromas escape during cooking. It is then cracked open just before serving, with great ceremony, thrilling the waiting diners with the sensational aromas that immediately fill the room.

Wine to accompany this recipe
CALIFORNIAN ZINFANDEL
The dry heat of the Hyderabadi spicing will be matched by the intense fruits of a *Californian Zinfandel*, with notes of tobacco leaves and liquorice.

For the marinade, fry the onions in 4 tablespoons of the oil, stirring constantly, until they are an even golden-brown colour. Lift out with a slotted spoon and drain on kitchen paper. Put the lamb in a bowl, add the remaining oil, the fried onions and all the other ingredients for the marinade and mix well. Set aside for 4 hours.

Wash the basmati rice in one or two changes of water, then cover with fresh water and leave to soak for 30 minutes. Put 2.5 litres/4½ pints of water in a large pan with the whole spices and salt and bring to the boil. Drain the rice, add to the pan and cook, uncovered, for about 10 minutes, until the water has reduced to the level of the rice.

Place the marinated meat in a large, heavy-based casserole (choose one with a tight-fitting lid). Drain the half-boiled rice and spread it over the meat. Sprinkle the ghee or butter and the saffron mixture on to the rice, then cover the casserole with the lid. Seal the sides with aluminium foil, leaving a small gap for steam to escape. Put the casserole on a high heat for 8–10 minutes. When you see the steam through the gap, reduce the heat to as low as possible and cook the biryani for 25 minutes. Remove from the heat and leave to stand, undisturbed, for 5 minutes. Then take off the lid. Serve the aromatic biryani immediately, with Spiced Onion Yoghurt.

1kg/2¼lb boned leg of lamb, cut into 2.5cm/1 inch cubes
50g/2oz/¼ cup ghee or clarified butter
a generous pinch of saffron strands, infused in 3 tablespoons warm milk
Spiced Onion Yoghurt (see page 163), to serve

For the marinade:
2 onions, sliced
6 tablespoons vegetable or corn oil
1 teaspoon Ginger Paste (see page 30)
1 teaspoon Garlic Paste (see page 30)
1 tablespoon mild red chilli powder
1 teaspoon garam masala
1 teaspoon ground turmeric
1 small bunch of fresh mint, chopped
3 green chillies, cut lengthways in half
¼ nutmeg, grated
juice of ½ lemon
1 tablespoon salt
100g/4oz/½ cup Greek yoghurt

For the rice:
400g/14oz/2 cups basmati rice
3 green cardamom pods
2 black cardamom pods
4 cloves
2 blades of mace
1 tablespoon cumin seeds
2 bay leaves
2 tablespoons salt

TANDOORI-STYLE LAMB WITH MASALA SPINACH

SERVES 4

A year or so after The Cinnamon Club opened, I visited a very decent Indian restaurant in London and was reacquainted with saag gosht – a dish of curried diced lamb and puréed spinach that is very popular in British curry houses and in Indian homes. The next day I cheekily challenged Vivek to create a Cinnamon Club version of the dish. He came up with this stunning interpretation: a seared lamb steak on a bed of spiced minced lamb and spinach. The best accompaniment is garlic naan bread, which, if you don't fancy making you own, is available in most supermarkets.

Wine to accompany this recipe
AMERICAN MERLOT
The natural sweetness of the lamb will match the gentle raspberry fruit of an *American Merlot.*

Mix together all the ingredients for the first marinade, rub them over the lamb steaks and leave to marinate for 15 minutes. Meanwhile, mix together all the ingredients for the second marinade.

Heat the oil in a large ovenproof frying pan, add the lamb and sear for 5 minutes, until well browned on both sides. Spread the second marinade on top and transfer to an oven preheated to 200°C/400°F/Gas Mark 6. Cook for 4 minutes, then leave to rest in a warm place for 3 minutes.

For the masala spinach, heat the oil in a pan and add the cumin seeds and cloves. When they crackle, add the garlic and cook until golden. Add the onion and sauté until golden brown. Now add the tomatoes and chilli powder and cook until the liquid from the tomatoes has evaporated. Stir in the salt, then add the minced lamb and sauté until browned all over. Stir in the shredded spinach and cook until it has wilted and you get a nice juicy masala mince with spinach. Add the garam masala and ginger and mix well.

Cut each saddle steak in half and serve on a bed of the masala spinach.

4 x 175g/6oz lamb saddle steaks, fat trimmed
I tablespoon vegetable or corn oil

For the first marinade:
I teaspoon Ginger Paste (see page 30)
I teaspoon Garlic Paste (see page 30)
I teaspoon salt
I teaspoon red chilli powder
juice of ½ lemon

For the second marinade:
I tablespoon vegetable or corn oil
1½ tablespoons Greek yoghurt
½ teaspoon garam masala

For the masala spinach:
2 tablespoons vegetable or corn oil
½ teaspoon cumin seeds
2 cloves
2 garlic cloves, chopped
I large onion, finely chopped
3 tomatoes, chopped
I teaspoon red chilli powder
I teaspoon salt
250g/9oz/I cup minced lamb
100g/4oz/2 cups fresh spinach leaves, shredded
¼ teaspoon garam masala
Icm/½ inch piece of fresh ginger, finely chopped

VINDALOO OF PORK SHOULDER

SERVES 4

It is said that when the Portuguese set sail to colonise India they first pickled pork in vinegar, garlic and chillies. After they landed in Goa, they cooked up their concoction and called it vindalho – from vinho for wine vinegar and ahlos for garlic – a dish that eventually became known as vindaloo and a byword for 'bloody hot curry'. The sauce for this dish is indeed spiked with chilli but it also has a distinctive flavour from the sourness of the vinegar. We have given the dish an extra new twist by using a rolled pork shoulder. Serve with basmati rice or crusty bread.

Wine to accompany this recipe
ITALIAN SAUVIGNON BLANC
The mix of heat and acidity from the vinegar requires the delicate acidity of a wine such as an *Italian Sauvignon Blanc* to balance it.

Mix together all the ingredients for the first marinade, rub them over the pork shoulder and set aside for 20 minutes. Heat 3 tablespoons of the oil in a large frying pan and sear the meat until evenly coloured on all sides. Remove from the pan and set aside.

Blend all the ingredients for the vindaloo spice mix to a smooth paste in a food processor or blender and apply it all over the meat. Place in a roasting tin and roast for 20 minutes in an oven preheated to 180°C/350°F/Gas Mark 4, turning the meat regularly to prevent the spice mix burning. Pour the stock in around the meat and stir well to deglaze the roasting tin. Cook for another 25 minutes, turning the meat occasionally so it cooks evenly.

Meanwhile, heat the remaining oil in a large frying pan, add the potatoes and sauté quickly until browned all over. Place them in the roasting tin with the pork shoulder and cook for about 20 minutes longer, until both pork and potatoes are tender. Remove the meat and potatoes from the liquid and keep warm.

Place the tin on the hob and simmer until the sauce becomes thick enough to coat the meat and develops a nice shine. Check the seasoning and sprinkle in fresh coriander. Slice the meat and serve with the potatoes and sauce.

I pork shoulder, weighing
   1-1.25kg/2¼-2½lb, boned and rolled
5 tablespoons vegetable or corn oil
1.2 litres/2 pints/5 cups stock or water
8 medium-sized Charlotte potatoes,
   peeled and cut in half
2 tablespoons chopped fresh
   coriander

For the first marinade:
I tablespoon vegetable or corn oil
2 teaspoons mild red chilli powder
I teaspoon salt
I teaspoon finely ground black pepper
I teaspoon sugar
3 tablespoons malt vinegar

For the vindaloo spice mix:
8 green cardamom pods
5 cloves
8 dried red chillies
5 x 2.5cm/I inch pieces of
   cinnamon stick
I teaspoon cumin seeds
I tablespoon coriander seeds
½ teaspoon ground turmeric
5 garlic cloves, peeled
I0cm/4 inch piece of fresh ginger
I00ml/3½fl oz/scant ½ cup malt vinegar
3 tablespoons vegetable or corn oil

SPICE-CRUSTED RIB EYE OF BEEF
WITH MASALA SAUTÉED POTATOES

SERVES 4

A sort of steak and chips Indian style! The roughly ground spice crust on the beef gives a balance of texture but doesn't overpower the quality of the steak and neither does the delicate sauce.

Wine to accompany this recipe
PORTUGUESE DOURO VALLEY
The fresh heat from the crust of the beef will match the port fruit character of a wine from the *Douro Valley* in *Portugal*.

Coarsely crush together all the ingredients for the spice crust in a pestle and mortar, then set aside. Mix together all the ingredients for the marinade, rub them over the steaks and leave to marinate while you make the sauce.

For the sauce, heat the ghee or butter in a pan and add the cloves and bay leaf. When the cloves puff up, add the onion paste and cook over a low heat until the ghee separates out at the side of the pan. If the paste gets too thick, you might have to add a little stock or water. Stir in the ginger and chilli powder and cook for 5 minutes. Now whisk in the yoghurt and cook gently for 10 minutes. Add the tomato purée and salt and cook for 3–5 minutes or until the fat starts to separate from the sauce. The sauce will slowly turn glossy and should be thick enough to coat the back of a spoon; if it is too thick, add a little more stock or water.

To cook the steaks, heat the oil in a large, heavy-based frying pan, add the steaks and sear for about 2 minutes on each side for medium rare. If you prefer medium or well done, transfer them to an oven preheated to 200°C/400°F/Gas Mark 6 and cook for a further 6–8 minutes. Leave the steaks to rest for 2–3 minutes. Press the spice crust on top and place under a hot grill for a minute or two, until the crust begins to colour.

Divide the sauce between 4 serving plates, place the steaks on top and serve immediately, accompanied by the Masala Sautéed Potatoes.

4 x 200g/7oz rib eye steaks
I tablespoon vegetable or corn oil
Masala Sautéed Potatoes (see page 140), to serve

For the spice crust:
I tablespoon coriander seeds, roasted (see page 33)
I teaspoon cumin seeds, roasted (see page 33)
2 dried red chillies

For the marinade:
I teaspoon salt
I teaspoon red chilli powder
I tablespoon vegetable or corn oil

For the sauce:
I tablespoon ghee or clarified butter
2 cloves
I bay leaf
I quantity of Fried Onion Paste (see page 30)
150ml/¼ pint/²/₃ cup beef stock or water (optional)
2.5cm/I inch piece of fresh ginger, finely chopped
I½ teaspoons mild red chilli powder
2 tablespoons Greek yoghurt
2 tablespoons tomato purée
I teaspoon salt

CALF'S LIVER WITH MASALA MASHED POTATOES AND STIR-FRIED OKRA

SERVES 4

One of my favourite dishes in European restaurants is grilled calf's liver. This is not part of the Indian repertoire, primarily because cows are sacred animals for Hindus. However, Pakistanis and Sikhs make a dish call gurde kaleji, *which is a dry, spicy mixture of lamb's liver and kidneys while in Bangladesh lamb's liver is cooked with diced potatoes. This is a much more subtle dish reflecting the delicacy of the liver. Serving it with masala mash and crunchy okra gives a spectacular combination of colours, textures and flavours.*

Wine to accompany this recipe
GERMAN SPÄTLESE RIESLING
The natural sweetness of the liver combined with the delicate heat of the chilli will be complemented by the powerful fruit of a *German Spätlese Riesling* from the *Rheingau*, while the heat of the chilli will lift the fruit of the wine on the palate.

Sprinkle half the salt and half the chilli powder over the calf's liver and set aside for 10 minutes.

Mix together the gram flour, ginger and garlic pastes, ajowan seeds, lemon juice and the remaining salt and chilli powder to give a smooth, thick, spoonable batter. If it is too thick, add a little water to correct the consistency. Apply the batter to the liver and set aside for 10 minutes before cooking.

Heat the oil in a large frying pan, add the liver and sear for 4 minutes on each side, until golden and crisp. Serve immediately, with the Masala Mashed Potatoes and Stir-fried Okra.

I teaspoon salt
I teaspoon red chilli powder
4 x 150g/5oz slices of calf's liver
50g/2oz/½ cup gram (chickpea) flour
I teaspoon Ginger Paste (see page 30)
I teaspoon Garlic Paste (see page 30)
½ teaspoon ajowan seeds
juice of I lemon
2 tablespoons vegetable or corn oil
Masala Mashed Potatoes (see page 140)
Stir-fried Okra with Dried Mango
  (see page 143)

HOT AND SOUR WILD BOAR CHOPS WITH SOUTH INDIAN RICE VERMICELLI

SERVES 4

This dish picks up various elements from different regions of southern India. Wild boar is hunted and cooked in parts of India and its meat takes extremely well to the type of hot and sour cooking that is most commonly found in Goa. The vermicelli accompaniment derives from the Tamil Nadu dish, iddiappam, where a rice flour dough is rolled into noodles in a similar fashion to that found in Chinese cooking.

Wine to accompany this recipe
ALSACE RIESLING.
The sharp, dry heat and the sour elements of this dish need a wine with very little residual sugar, such as an *Alsace Riesling,* to balance them. The fruity parts of the wine then remain on the palate.

Mix together all the marinade ingredients, rub them over the wild boar chops and set aside for 30 minutes.

Meanwhile, for the sauce, mix together the dry spices and roast them in a dry frying pan over a moderate heat until they begin to colour. Tip them out and grind to a fine powder. Heat the oil in a pan, add the garlic and sauté until it starts to turn golden. Add the onion and sauté until softened, then add the ground spices, stirring briskly to prevent them burning. Add the tomato purée and cook for 2 minutes. Finally, stir in the stock or water and check the seasoning.

Heat the oil in a pan and sear the chops until brown on the outside but still raw inside. Transfer to a baking tray, cover with the sauce and place in an oven preheated to 180°C/350°F/Gas Mark 4 for about 18 minutes, until cooked through. Set aside and keep warm.

Place the vermicelli in a colander and pour some boiling water over. Heat the oil in a large pan and add the mustard seeds and curry leaves. When they start to crackle, add the onion and sauté until soft. Add the chillies and turmeric and sauté briskly for 1 minute. Drain the vermicelli, add to the pan and mix well. Add the red pepper and salt and move briskly around the pan until the ingredients are mixed but the red pepper retains its crunch. Serve with the chops.

4 x 175g/6oz wild boar chops
  (if you can't get wild boar, use
  good-quality pork chops)
1 tablespoon vegetable or corn oil

For the marinade:
2 teaspoons mild red chilli powder
1 teaspoon salt
½ teaspoon sugar
1 teaspoon Ginger Paste (see page 30)
1 teaspoon Garlic Paste (see page 30)
2 tablespoons malt vinegar

For the sauce:
6 cloves
2.5cm/1 inch piece of cinnamon stick
½ teaspoon black peppercorns
½ teaspoon fennel seeds
½ teaspoon cumin seeds
½ teaspoon coriander seeds
1 tablespoon vegetable or corn oil
2 garlic cloves, finely chopped
1 onion, finely chopped
1 tablespoon tomato purée
3 tablespoons stock or water

For the rice vermicelli:
100g/4oz/3 cups dried rice vermicelli
  (a Chinese variety will do)
2 tablespoons vegetable or corn oil
1 teaspoon mustard seeds
10 fresh curry leaves
½ onion, sliced
2 green chillies, cut lengthways in half
¼ teaspoon ground turmeric
½ red pepper, cut into thin strips
½ teaspoon salt

RAJASTHANI ROAST VENISON SADDLE WITH GINGER AND ONION SAUCE

SERVES 4

The noblemen of princely states such as Rajasthan would often go out hunting for game. They pursued four-legged varieties such as boar and deer, unlike their British counterparts who preferred to shoot birds. Latter-day Indian aristocrats have to sneak out in the middle of the night to avoid the wrath of the police, since shooting deer is strictly illegal. This dish captures Rajasthani flavours but is cooked European style – searing the meat, then finishing it off with an aromatic spice paste smeared on top and flashed under the grill. Serve with Star Anise Pilau Rice (see page 132).

Mix together all the ingredients for the marinade, rub them over the venison and set aside to marinate for at least 30 minutes. Meanwhile, prepare the sauce. Heat the ghee or clarified butter in a heavy-based pan and add the cloves. When they puff up, add the fried onion paste and cook until thickened. Then whisk in the yoghurt and cook on a low heat, stirring occasionally to prevent the yoghurt separating. When the sauce comes to the boil, add the venison trimmings, followed by the salt, sugar, ginger and lemon juice. Simmer for 10 minutes, until the sauce becomes glossy and the fat has separated out at the side of the pan. If the sauce is too thick, add a few spoonfuls of lamb stock or water. Set aside and keep warm while you cook the venison.

Heat the oil in a large ovenproof frying pan, add the meat and sear over a medium-high heat for 5–6 minutes, until browned all over. Transfer to an oven preheated to 200°C/400°F/Gas Mark 6 and roast for 12 minutes, if you like your meat pink. Remove from the oven, spread the Rajasthani spice paste on top and place under a hot grill (or return it to the oven) for 1 minute, until the paste is lightly browned.

Divide the sauce between 4 serving plates and place the venison on top.

1 venison saddle, cleaned and cut into 4 steaks (ask your butcher to do this and reserve the trimmings for the sauce)
1 tablespoon vegetable or corn oil
1 quantity of Rajasthani Spice Paste (see page 32)

For the marinade:
½ teaspoon salt
½ teaspoon red chilli powder
1 tablespoon vegetable or corn oil

For the ginger and onion sauce:
50g/2oz/¼ cup ghee or clarified butter
6 cloves
1½ quantities of Fried Onion Paste (see page 30)
4 tablespoons plain yoghurt
50g/2oz/¼ cup venison trimmings, finely diced
¾ teaspoon salt
¼ teaspoon sugar
2.5cm/1 inch piece of fresh ginger, finely chopped
juice of 1 lemon
a little lamb stock or water (optional)

Wine to accompany this recipe
CALIFORNIAN PINOT NOIR
The sweetness of the venison and onion will complement the fruit of a *Californian Pinot Noir*, while the freshness of the wine will be balanced by the acidity of the ginger.

TANDOORI GROUSE WITH AUBERGINE CRUSH AND LAYERED BREAD

SERVES 4

Grouse, of course, do not exist in India: none the less their distinctive flavour stands up well to the mix of pickling spices used for the leg meat in this dish. The breasts are marinated twice; first in salt and lemon juice to open up the meat, so that the clove-scented second marinade can do its work. Ask your butcher to prepare the grouse for you. You will need the breasts boned and the legs and fillets minced. If you are short of time, you can buy Indian breads (or even tortillas) instead of making the layered paratha bread.

Wine to accompany this recipe
AUSTRALIAN OR TASMANIAN RIESLING
The acidity of an *Australian* or *Tasmanian Riesling* will be balanced by the heat of this dish, while the fruit of the wine will remain.

If you are preparing the grouse yourself, cut off the breasts and legs and bone them. Remove the fillet from each breast (the small flap of meat underneath) and set the breasts aside. Coarsely mince the leg meat with the fillets, then set aside.

Mix together all the ingredients for the first marinade, rub them over the grouse breasts and leave to marinate for 30 minutes. Mix together all the ingredients for the second marinade and set aside.

Meanwhile, cook the minced leg meat. Heat the ghee or butter in a pan and add the pickling spice mix. When the spices crackle, add the garlic and sauté until beginning to colour. Then add the onion and cook until golden brown. Stir in the minced grouse and chilli powder and cook for 5 minutes. Add the salt and diced tomato and simmer until all the liquid has evaporated. Add the coriander, check the seasoning and, if necessary, add the jaggery or sugar to balance the flavours. Keep warm.

Heat the oil in an ovenproof frying pan, add the marinated grouse breasts and sear on both sides until well coloured. Spread the second marinade on top, then transfer to an oven preheated to 200°C/400°F/Gas Mark 6 and roast for 4–6 minutes, until cooked medium. The breasts cook quickly, and there is a danger of them ending up quite dry if roasted for too long, so keep an eye on them.

Divide the mince between 4 serving plates and top with the grouse breasts. Fold each bread into a cone shape, place some aubergine crush inside and serve with the grouse.

4 grouse
1 tablespoon vegetable or corn oil
4 Layered Parathas (see page 154)
Roasted Aubergine Crush
   (see page 149), to serve

For the first marinade:
1 teaspoon Ginger Paste (see page 30)
1 teaspoon Garlic Paste (see page 30)
½ teaspoon salt
1 teaspoon lemon juice

For the second marinade:
1 tablespoon vegetable or corn oil
100g/4oz/½ cup
  Fried Cashew Paste
   (see page 30)
½ teaspoon cumin seeds, roasted
   and ground (see page 33)
6 cloves, roasted and ground
   (see page 33)

For the minced leg:
1½ tablespoons ghee or clarified butter
1 teaspoon mixed cumin seeds, black
   onion seeds, fennel seeds and
   mustard seeds (this mixture is
   known as pickling spice)
2 garlic cloves, chopped
1 small onion, chopped
½ teaspoon red chilli powder
¼ teaspoon salt
1 tomato, deseeded and diced
2 tablespoons chopped
   fresh coriander
½ teaspoon sugar or jaggery (optional)

POTATOES STUFFED WITH PANEER IN A SWEET AND SOUR SAUCE

SERVES 4

The individual elements of this dish are all essentially Indian but they are not usually put together in this way. The stuffed potatoes are served on a base made with chickpea flour, which has much in common with Italian gnocchi.

Wine to accompany this recipe
ALSACE GEWÜRZTRAMINER
The fresh elements of an *Alsace Gewürztraminer* will balance the sourness of the sauce, while the spices will enhance the rich fruit of this wine.

With an apple corer or a melon baller, carefully scoop out the centre of each potato to make a hollow shell about 5mm/¼ inch thick. Heat some oil to 170°C/325°F in a deep-fat fryer or a large, deep saucepan and fry the potatoes for 6–8 minutes, until they are soft and cooked through but not coloured. Remove from the oil and drain on kitchen paper. Now heat the oil to 190°C/375°F and fry the potatoes again for 2–3 minutes, until crisp on the outside. Drain on kitchen paper and leave to cool.

Mix together all the ingredients for the stuffing. When the potatoes are cold, fill them with the stuffing and set aside.

For the chickpea base, put all the ingredients in a heavy-based pan and bring to the boil, stirring constantly, as the mixture has a tendency to stick to the bottom of the pan and also to separate. Keep stirring for 5–6 minutes, until it thickens to a semi-solid mass. Spread the mixture in a lightly oiled baking tray in a layer about 1cm/½ inch thick and leave to cool.

Meanwhile, make the sauce. Put the cashew paste, turmeric, salt, sugar, ginger and chilli powder in a pan and bring to the boil. Simmer for 3–4 minutes, adding the water a little at a time and stirring constantly. Add the tomato purée and cook for 2–3 minutes, then stir in the tamarind paste and cook for 2–3 minutes longer, until the sauce turns thick and glossy. Check the seasoning and set aside.

Cut the chickpea base into four 7.5cm/ 3 inch squares and then cut a 2.5cm/ 1 inch circle out of the centre of each one and discard. Deep-fry the squares in hot oil for about 2 minutes, until crisp, then drain on kitchen paper.

Put the stuffed potatoes on a baking tray and heat in a moderate oven for 8–10 minutes. To serve, divide the sauce between 4 serving plates, place a chickpea square on each one and then place a potato on top.

4 medium-sized Desiree potatoes, peeled
oil for deep-frying

For the stuffing:
125g/4l/2oz/1 cup paneer cheese, grated
25g/1oz/¼ cup roasted salted cashew
   nuts, crushed
1½ tablespoons raisins
½ teaspoon salt
1 green chilli, finely chopped
1cm/½ inch piece of fresh ginger,
   finely chopped

For the chickpea base:
50g/2oz/½ cup gram (chickpea) flour
5 tablespoons plain yoghurt
½ teaspoon salt
½ teaspoon sugar
1cm/½ inch piece of fresh ginger,
   finely chopped
25g/1oz/½ cup fresh coriander,
   finely shredded
¼ teaspoon ground turmeric
2 tablespoons vegetable or corn oil

For the sweet and sour sauce:
100g/4oz/²/3 cup Boiled Cashew Paste
   (see page 30)
¼ teaspoon ground turmeric
½ teaspoon salt
½ teaspoon sugar
¼ teaspoon ground ginger
½ teaspoon red chilli powder
150ml/¼ pint/²/3 cup water
50g/2oz/¼ cup tomato purée
50g/2oz/¼ cup tamarind paste

BABY AUBERGINES IN PICKLING SPICES WITH CURRY LEAF SEMOLINA

500g/1lb 2oz baby aubergines
1 teaspoon salt
1 teaspoon red chilli powder
oil for deep-frying

For the pickling spices:
¼ teaspoon black onion seeds
¼ teaspoon mustard seeds
¼ teaspoon cumin seeds
¼ teaspoon fenugreek seeds
¼ teaspoon fennel seeds

For the sauce:
2 tablespoons coriander seeds
1 tablespoon cumin seeds
1 teaspoon sesame seeds
2 tablespoons desiccated coconut
2 tablespoons oil, preferably mustard oil
50g/2oz/½ cup cashew nuts
2 red onions, chopped
3 tablespoons tamarind paste
½ teaspoon ground turmeric
1 teaspoon red chilli powder
1 teaspoon salt
2 tablespoons jaggery or
    molasses sugar
25g/1oz/1 cup fresh mint, finely shredded
a squeeze of lemon juice (optional)

For the curry leaf semolina:
2 tablespoons vegetable or corn oil
¼ teaspoon mustard seeds
1 teaspoon roasted chana dal
1 sprig of fresh curry leaves
1 red onion, chopped
2.5cm/1 inch piece of fresh ginger,
    finely chopped
2 green chillies, finely chopped
½ teaspoon ground turmeric
150g/5oz/¾ cup semolina
1 teaspoon salt
300ml/½ pint/1¼ cups boiling water
15g/½oz/1 tablespoon butter
25g/1oz/½ cup fresh coriander,
    chopped
1 tomato, deseeded and diced

SERVES 4

In the Punjab, large aubergines are cooked to a pulp with pickling spices. We like to use baby aubergines and cook them for less time, so that they retain their shape and texture.

Wine to accompany this recipe
AMERICAN PINOT BLANC
The intensity of the pickling spices will be balanced by the rich fruit of an *American Pinot Blanc*, while the natural sweetness of the aubergine will complement the fruit of the wine.

Using a sharp knife, slit each aubergine in quarters half way through to the centre (be careful not to cut all the way through). Rub the salt and chilli powder into the cuts and set aside for about 15 minutes.

For the sauce, mix together the coriander, cumin and sesame seeds and roast them in a dry frying pan over a moderate heat until they begin to colour. Tip them out on to a plate and set aside. Roast the coconut in the same pan until golden, then add it to the seeds. Heat about a teaspoon of the oil in the pan, add the cashew nuts and fry until golden. Put them in a food processor or blender with the roasted seeds and coconut and blend to a smooth paste with a little water.

Heat the remaining oil in a pan and add the pickling spices. When they crackle, add the red onions and sauté until

brown. Add the blended paste and cook over a low heat, stirring occasionally, for 8–10 minutes. Stir in the tamarind paste, turmeric and chilli powder and cook for 12–15 minutes, until the oil separates out at the side of the pan. Stir in the salt and the jaggery or sugar.

Deep-fry the aubergines in hot oil for 3–4 minutes, until soft, then drain well on kitchen paper. Add them to the sauce and simmer for 3–4 minutes; they should still retain their shape. Stir in the mint, then check the seasoning, adding a squeeze of lemon juice if necessary.

To make the curry leaf semolina, heat the oil in a heavy-based pan and add the mustard seeds. When they crackle, add the roasted chana dal and cook until golden. Add the curry leaves and onion and sauté until the onion is translucent. Now add the ginger, chillies and turmeric and sauté for 1 minute. Add the semolina and salt and cook over a low heat for 3 minutes. Gradually stir in the boiling water. The semolina should form a thick mass as the water is absorbed. Cook for 2 minutes longer, then add the butter, coriander and tomatoes, remove from the heat and mix in gently.

Make a mound of semolina on each plate, pour the sauce around it and place the baby aubergines on top of the sauce.

HYDERABADI-STYLE AUBERGINE STEAKS

SERVES 4

The Hyderabadi inspiration for this dish is evident in the sauce rather than in the very Cinnamon Club presentation. As aubergines can have a slightly gooey consistency, we prefer to give them a crisp coating, balanced with a spicy potato layer. Yoghurt Rice (see page 133) makes a very good accompaniment.

Wine to accompany this recipe
NEW ZEALAND RIESLING
The heat and sweetness present in this dish require a little residual sugar and a touch of freshness to complement them – a *New Zealand Riesling* would be ideal.

Trim off the ends of the aubergines and then slice them into 8 rounds about 2.5cm/1 inch thick. Rub the salt, turmeric and chilli powder into the aubergine slices and set aside.

For the stuffing, heat the oil in a frying pan, add the onion and curry leaves and sauté until the onion is golden. Add the ginger, green chilli, turmeric and salt and sauté for 30 seconds. Mix in the grated potatoes, squeeze in the lemon juice, then set aside to cool.

Pat dry the aubergine slices, place 4 on a work surface and spoon a tablespoon of the potato stuffing on top of each one. Top with the remaining slices to make 4 aubergine sandwiches.

For the coating, mix the breadcrumbs with the poppy seeds and onion seeds.

Make a thick batter with the gram flour, salt and water. Dip the sandwiches into the batter, then into the breadcrumb mixture and chill while you make the sauce.

For the sauce, mix together the coriander, sesame and cumin seeds and roast them in a dry frying pan over a moderate heat until they begin to colour. Tip them out on to a plate and set aside. Roast the coconut in the same pan until golden, then add to the seeds. Heat 1 tablespoon of the oil in the pan, add the peanuts or cashew nuts and fry until golden. Put them in a food processor or blender with the roasted seeds and coconut and blend to a smooth paste with a little water. Heat the remaining oil in a pan and add the dried chillies and mustard seeds. When they crackle, add the onion seeds and curry leaves, followed by the onion paste, and cook for 8–10 minutes, until the moisture has almost all evaporated. Now add the seed and nut paste and sauté on a low heat for a minute or two. Stir in the chilli powder, turmeric and tamarind paste and cook for 15 minutes, until the sauce is thick. Stir in the salt, sugar and coriander.

Heat some oil in a deep-fat fryer or a large, deep saucepan, add the aubergines steaks and deep-fry for 3 minutes, until golden brown and tender (or you can shallow-fry them if you prefer). Divide the sauce between 4 serving plates and place the steaks on top.

2–3 large aubergines
I teaspoon salt
½ teaspoon ground turmeric
½ teaspoon red chilli powder
oil for deep-frying

For the stuffing:
2 tablespoons vegetable or corn oil
I red onion, chopped
I sprig of fresh curry leaves
2.5cm/I inch piece of fresh ginger,
    finely chopped
I green chilli, finely chopped
¼ teaspoon ground turmeric
I teaspoon salt
2 medium-sized potatoes, boiled until
    tender, then peeled and grated
juice of ½ lemon

For the coating:
100g/4oz/I ½ cups dried breadcrumbs
I teaspoon poppy seeds
½ teaspoon black onion seeds
50g/2oz/½ cup gram (chickpea) flour
¼ teaspoon salt
3 tablespoons water

For the sauce:
2 tablespoons coriander seeds
I tablespoon sesame seeds
I teaspoon cumin seeds
100g/4oz/I heaping cup desiccated
    coconut
4 tablespoons vegetable oil
50g/2oz peanuts or cashew nuts
4 dried red chillies
½ teaspoon mustard seeds
½ teaspoon black onion seeds
2 sprigs of fresh curry leaves
2 quantities of Boiled Onion Paste
    (see page 30)
I teaspoon red chilli powder
½ teaspoon ground turmeric
2 tablespoons tamarind paste
I teaspoon salt
½ teaspoon sugar
25g/Ioz/½ cup fresh coriander leaves,
    chopped

GREEN PEA AND CORN PARCELS WITH CAULIFLOWER AND POTATO STIR-FRY

SERVES 4

The flavours in this dish are earthy and thoroughly Indian. The packaging of the peas and corn is similar to that of a samosa, but the overall look of the dish is very European. It tastes wonderful.

Wine to accompany this recipe
ALSACE RIESLING
The pungent flavour of cumin will require a persistent fruit finish in a wine such as an *Alsace Riesling* for balance.

Put the peas, ginger and green chillies in a blender and blitz to a fine paste, adding a little water if necessary. Heat the ghee or clarified butter in a large pan or a wok and add the cumin seeds. As they crackle, add the asafoetida, followed almost immediately by the green pea, ginger and chilli paste. Stir over a low heat until most of the moisture has evaporated and the mixture acquires a soft, doughy consistency. This might take 12–15 minutes of constant stirring.

Add the sweetcorn and cook for another couple of minutes. Then stir in the salt and garam masala and adjust the seasoning if required. Cook for another 3 minutes, stir in the sugar and remove from the heat. Mix in the coriander and leave to cool.

Lay out a sheet of filo pastry on a work surface and brush with melted butter. Cover with the second sheet and then cut the double sheet into quarters. Place a quarter of the cooled pea and corn mixture in the centre of each piece, fold over the top and bottom of the pastry, then tuck the sides underneath to make parcels. Place the filo parcels on a well-greased baking tray, brush with melted butter and place in an oven preheated to 200°C/400°F/Gas Mark 6. Cook for 8–10 minutes, until crisp and golden.

Meanwhile, make the cauliflower and potato stir-fry. Heat the oil in a large pan and add the cumin seeds. When they crackle, add the onion and sauté until golden. Add the potatoes and cook for 3 minutes, covering the pan with a lid to allow the potatoes to cook in their own steam. Add the turmeric, salt, chilli powder and cumin and sauté for a couple of minutes. Add the cauliflower florets and cover the pan again. Reduce the heat to minimum and let the vegetables cook in their own juices for about 5 minutes. If they are not tender after this time, sprinkle with a little water and cook for a couple more minutes. Mix in the tomato, sprinkle in the garam masala and finish with chopped coriander and lemon juice. Serve with the green pea and corn parcels.

350g/12oz/2½ cups frozen peas, thawed
4cm/1½ inch piece of fresh ginger, finely chopped
5 green chillies, chopped
2 tablespoons ghee or clarified butter
1 teaspoon cumin seeds
a pinch of asafoetida
50g/2oz/½ cup canned sweetcorn, drained
1½ teaspoons salt
1 teaspoon garam masala
½ teaspoon sugar
2 tablespoons chopped fresh coriander
2 large sheets of filo pastry
a little melted butter for brushing

For the cauliflower & potato stir-fry:
1 tablespoon vegetable or corn oil
½ teaspoon cumin seeds
½ onion, chopped
2 floury potatoes, such as Desiree, peeled and cut into 1cm/½ inch dice
½ teaspoon ground turmeric
1 teaspoon salt
½ teaspoon red chilli powder
½ teaspoon ground cumin
150g/5oz/2 cups cauliflower, divided into florets roughly the same size as the potato dice
1 tomato, deseeded and finely diced
½ teaspoon garam masala
1 tablespoon finely chopped fresh coriander
juice of ½ lemon

SPINACH DUMPLINGS WITH TOMATO AND FENUGREEK SAUCE

SERVES 4

You certainly won't find spinach dumplings in India. The nearest thing is kofta, which are usually balls of minced lamb but which can be made with mashed vegetables. The tomato and fenugreek sauce, though, is typically Punjabi.

To make the dumplings, put the paneer, grated potato, spinach, ginger, chillies, salt and ajowan seeds in a bowl and mix well with a wooden spoon. Divide the mixture into 12 balls, the size of golf balls.

For the batter, put the flour, ajowan and salt in a bowl and make a well in the centre. Gradually stir in the water until you have a smooth, thick batter. Spread the shredded spinach out on a baking tray. Dip the dumplings in the batter and then roll them in the spinach to form a good coating.

For the sauce, put the tomatoes in a large pan and cook over a medium heat until they begin to soften. Pour in the water, then add the garlic, ginger, cardamom pods, cloves and bay leaf. Bring to the boil and simmer until the tomatoes have completely disintegrated. Pass through a sieve into a clean pan, add the chilli powder and simmer for 10–15 minutes, until slightly thickened. Add the butter a little at a time, stirring constantly. When the sauce turns glossy, add the cream and simmer for 2–3 minutes. Stir in the salt, fenugreek and garam masala, then taste and add the sugar if necessary.

Heat some oil in a deep-fat fryer or a deep saucepan. Add the dumplings and fry for about 1$\frac{1}{2}$ minutes, until crisp and golden. Drain on kitchen paper and serve with the sauce.

Wine to accompany this recipe
AUSTRALIAN SAUVIGNON BLANC
The minerality of the spinach and the grassiness of the fenugreek will be matched by the intense citrus flavours of an *Australian Sauvignon Blanc*.

250g/9oz/2¼ cups paneer cheese, grated
2 large potatoes, boiled until tender, then peeled and grated
100g/4oz/2 cups fresh spinach leaves, finely shredded
2.5cm/1 inch piece of fresh ginger, finely chopped
2 green chillies, chopped
1 teaspoon salt
½ teaspoon ajowan seeds
oil for deep-frying

For the batter:
100g/4oz/1 cup gram (chickpea) flour
¼ teaspoon ajowan seeds
½ teaspoon salt
150ml/¼²/3 cup pint water
150g/5oz/2½ cups fresh spinach leaves, finely shredded

For the tomato and fenugreek sauce:
1kg/2¼lb tomatoes, cut in half
125ml/4fl oz/½ cup water
2 garlic cloves, peeled
2.5cm/1 inch piece of fresh ginger, crushed
3 green cardamom pods
5 cloves
1 bay leaf
2 teaspoons mild red chilli powder
75g/3oz/⅓ cup butter, diced
100ml/3½fl oz/scant ½ cup single cream
1 teaspoon salt
¼ teaspoon crushed dried fenugreek leaves
¼ teaspoon garam masala
a pinch of sugar (optional)

ACCOMPANIMENTS

Pilau Rice, Star Anise Pilau Rice, Yoghurt Rice, Lemon Rice, Black-eyed Beans with Onion and Tomatoes, Punjabi-style Red Kidney Beans, Rajasthani Chickpea Dumplings with Yoghurt, Marrow with Cumin, Masala Mashed Potatoes, Masala Sautéed Potatoes, Stir-fried Green Beans with Coconut, Stir-fried Okra with Dried Mango, Black Lentils with Tomatoes and Cream, Rajasthani Five-Lentil Mix, Wild Mushroom and Spinach Stir-fry, Lentil Bean Salad, Mixed Greens with Mustard, Roasted Aubergine Crush, Rajasthani Sangri Beans, Layered Parathas, Naan Bread, Bakarkhani, Missi Roti.

PILAU RICE

SERVES 6-8

Pilau Rice is made with Basmati and, as with wine, matures with age, taking on a firmer and more consistent character. The fragrance of aged rice (we use two year old in the restaurant) is more distinctive. Basmati on its own is fine, but to add the butter and aromatic spices for a pilau turns rice into a treat.

Wash the rice in cold running water once or twice, then place in a bowl of cold water and leave to soak for 25 minutes (this reduces the cooking time and prevents the grains breaking during cooking).

Heat the ghee or butter in a large, heavy-based casserole and add the whole spices and the bay leaf. When they crackle, add the sliced onion and sauté until golden brown. Now add the water and salt and bring to the boil. Drain the rice and add to the pan. Cover until it returns to the boil, then remove the lid and cook over a medium-high heat for about 6 minutes, stirring occasionally but keeping in mind that too much handling can break the rice grains.

When the water has nearly all been absorbed and you can see small holes on the surface of rice, sprinkle over the mint and coriander. Cover the casserole with a tight-fitting lid, reduce the heat to minimum and cook for 10 minutes (or cook in a very low oven for 10 minutes).

500g/1lb 2oz/2½ cups basmati rice
50g/2oz/¼ cup ghee or clarified butter
I teaspoon cumin seeds
3 cloves
2 green cardamom pods
I cinnamon stick
I bay leaf
I red onion, sliced
I litre/1¾ pints/4 cups water
I teaspoon salt
I teaspoon chopped fresh mint
I teaspoon chopped fresh coriander

STAR ANISE PILAU RICE

SERVES 6-8

The sweet and slightly pungent flavours of the star anise give an extra lift to the pilau and works paticularly well with strong flavoured dishes such as Hot South Indian Chicken Curry on page 99.

Wash the rice in cold running water once or twice, then place in a bowl of cold water and leave to soak for 25 minutes.

Heat the ghee or butter in a large, heavy-based casserole and add the whole spices and the bay leaf. When they crackle, add the sliced onion and sauté until golden brown. Now add the water and salt and bring to the boil. Drain the rice and add to the pan. Cover until it returns to the boil, then remove the lid and cook over a medium-high heat for about 6 minutes, stirring occasionally but keeping in mind that too much handling can break the rice grains.

When the water has nearly all been absorbed and you can see small holes on the surface of rice, cover the casserole with a tight-fitting lid, reduce the heat to minimum and cook for 10 minutes (or cook in a very low oven for 10 minutes).

YOGHURT RICE

SERVES 4

Despite its bold ingredients, this dish has a soothing effect on the stomach, due largely to the alkaline quality of the yoghurt and is especially popular in southern India. You could stir in some pomegranate seeds, diced cucumber, mango or even grated carrot for colour.

Take the covered casserole to the table and then remove the lid, so the wonderful aromas fill the room and wow your guests. The larger spices, such as the star anise and cinnamon, can be picked out before serving.

500g/1lb 2oz/2½ cups basmati rice
50g/2oz/¼ cup ghee or clarified butter
50g/2oz/1 cup star anise
3 cloves
2 green cardamom pods
I cinnamon stick
I bay leaf
I red onion, sliced
I litre/1¾ pints/4 cups water
I tablespoon salt

Wash the rice in cold running water once or twice then place in a bowl of cold water and leave to soak for 25 minutes. Drain well. Bring 500ml/18fl oz/2¼ cups water to the boil in a saucepan and add the rice. Cook, uncovered, for 12–15 minutes, until the rice is very soft; it should be a little overcooked. Drain and leave to cool.

Add the chillies, ginger, salt and curry leaves to the rice and mix in with a wooden spoon, mashing the rice a little with the back of the spoon. Now mix in the milk and yoghurt.

To temper the rice, heat the oil in a pan until very hot and add the mustard seeds. When they crackle, add the roasted chana dal and dried chillies. As soon as the chana dal turns golden, add the curry leaves and onion and sauté until the onion is golden. Pour on to the rice and cool. Chill well and sprinkle with the coriander.

200g/7oz/cup basmati rice
2 green chillies, chopped
2.5cm/I inch piece of fresh ginger, finely chopped
2 teaspoons salt
5 fresh curry leaves, shredded
200ml/7fl oz/⅞ cup milk
250g/9oz/1⅛ cups Greek yoghurt
I tablespoon chopped fresh coriander

For tempering:
2 tablespoons vegetable or corn oil
I teaspoon mustard seeds
2 teaspoons roasted chana dal
2 dried red chillies, broken in half
10 fresh curry leaves
I red onion, chopped

LEMON RICE

SERVES 4-6

A popular dish from the south of India, Lemon Rice has a striking colour and many layers of tastes and is best served with dishes which have light sauces.

Wash the rice in cold running water once or twice. Place in a bowl of cold water and leave to soak for 25 minutes. Drain well. Bring 1 litre/1³/₄ pints/4 cups of water to the boil in a saucepan and add the rice. Cook, uncovered, for 8–10 minutes, until the grains are tender but not mushy. Drain through a sieve and set aside.

Heat the oil in a pan. Add mustard seeds, chana dal and urid lentils and let them crackle. When they start to turn golden, add curry leaves and turmeric. Stir for a minute (sprinkle in some water to prevent the turmeric burning). Add the cooked rice, salt and lemon juice and toss gently to mix well without breaking the rice grains.

400g/14oz/2 cups basmati rice
3 tablespoons vegetable or corn oil
1 tablespoon mustard seeds
1 tablespoon chana dal
   (split yellow chickpeas)
1 teaspoon white urid lentils (optional)
20 fresh curry leaves
1 teaspoon ground turmeric
1½ teaspoons salt
juice of 3 lemons

BLACK-EYED BEANS WITH ONION AND TOMATOES

SERVES 4

Gujaratis love this dish with the wholesome, high protein pulse popular in this largely vegetarian region. The tomato and onion base may encourage your guests to make comparisons to curried baked beans, but this line of discussion is to be discouraged.

Drain the black-eyed beans, put them in a pan with ½ teaspoon of the salt and the water and bring to the boil. Simmer for 45 minutes–1 hour, until the beans are tender and very little liquid remains.

In a separate pan, heat the oil, ghee or butter and add the cumin seeds. When they crackle, add the garlic and sauté until it starts to change colour. Add the onions and sauté until golden brown, then add the ground cumin, coriander, turmeric and chilli powder and cook for a couple of minutes, stirring to prevent the spices burning. Add the chopped tomatoes and cook for about 5 minutes, until the moisture from the tomatoes has evaporated, the mixture has thickened and the oil starts to separate from it. Add the black-eyed beans and mix in thoroughly. Stir in the remaining salt and simmer for 8 minutes. Stir in the ginger, fresh coriander and lemon juice, then taste and adjust the seasoning.

150g/5oz/¾ cup black-eyed beans, soaked in lukewarm water for 3 hours
1½ teaspoons salt
1 litre/1¾ pints/4 cups water
3 tablespoon oil, ghee or clarified butter
1 teaspoon cumin seeds
2 garlic cloves, finely chopped
2 onions, finely chopped
½ teaspoon ground cumin
1 teaspoon ground coriander
1 teaspoon ground turmeric
1½ teaspoons mild red chilli powder
2 large tomatoes, finely chopped
1 teaspoon salt
2.5cm/1 inch piece of fresh ginger, finely chopped
2 tablespoons finely chopped fresh coriander
juice of ½ lemon

PUNJABI-STYLE RED KIDNEY BEANS

SERVES 4

Kidney beans are not indigenous to India but were brought over by French colonialists and cultivated in their settlements. Over the last century this has become a very popular dish in many Punjabi homes.

Drain the kidney beans, put them in a saucepan with the water and bring to the boil. Boil hard for 10 minutes, then reduce the heat and simmer for about 1 hour, until the beans are tender but still hold their shape. Drain, reserving the cooking liquid, and set aside.

Heat the oil in a heavy-based pan, add the cardamom pods, bay leaf and cinnamon stick and let them crackle. Add the cumin seeds, then as soon as they start to change colour, add the onion. Cook, stirring constantly, until the onion turns golden brown.

Add the chilli powder, ground cumin and coriander and salt. Sauté until the fat starts to separate out from the mixture, taking care that the dried spices do not burn. Add the tomatoes and cook until they are soft and the liquid has almost dried up. Add the drained kidney beans and cook for another 10 minutes or so, adding some cooking liquor from the beans, if necessary, to make more sauce.

Add the ginger and green chillies and simmer for a couple of minutes. Check the seasoning, then stir in the garam masala and fresh coriander.

200g/7oz/1 cup red kidney beans, soaked in lukewarm water in a warm place for at least 4 hours, preferably overnight
1 litre/1¾ pints/4 cups water
2 tablespoons vegetable or corn oil
2 black cardamom pods
1 bay leaf
2.5cm/1 inch piece of cinnamon stick
1 teaspoon cumin seeds
1 large onion, chopped
1 teaspoon red chilli powder
1 teaspoon ground cumin
½ teaspoon ground coriander
1 teaspoon salt
2 large tomatoes, chopped
2.5cm/1 inch piece of fresh ginger, finely chopped
2 green chillies, finely chopped
½ teaspoon garam masala
2 tablespoons chopped fresh coriander

RAJASTHANI CHICKPEA DUMPLINGS WITH YOGHURT

SERVES 4

This is a very distinctive side dish found only in Rajasthan, where it is called gatte. Serve as an accompaniment to lighter main courses, as it is really quite substantial.

100g/4oz/1 cup gram (chickpea) flour
½ teaspoon salt
½ teaspoon crushed coriander seeds
½ teaspoon mixed cumin and
    fennel seeds
1 tablespoon vegetable or corn oil
2 tablespoons Greek yoghurt
½ teaspoon sugar
1cm/½ inch piece of fresh ginger,
    finely chopped
2 green chillies, finely chopped
a pinch of garam masala

For the sauce:
2 tablespoons oil, ghee or
    clarified butter
½ teaspoon cumin seeds
a pinch of asafoetida
1 onion, finely chopped
1cm/½ inch piece of fresh ginger,
    finely chopped
1 green chilli, finely chopped
½ teaspoon ground turmeric
½ teaspoon ground coriander
1 teaspoon red chilli powder
1 teaspoon salt
100g/4oz/½ cup plain yoghurt
1 teaspoon dried fenugreek leaves
1 tablespoon finely chopped
    fresh coriander
juice of 1 lemon
a pinch of sugar (optional)

For the dumplings, put all the ingredients except the garam masala into a bowl and mix to a firm dough. Set aside for 20 minutes, then divide into 4 portions and roll them out into sausage shapes.

In a large saucepan, bring just enough water to the boil to cover the dumplings. Turn the heat down to a simmer, then add a pinch of salt and the garam masala. Now add the dumplings and poach for 12 minutes. Remove the dumplings from the pan and leave to cool, reserving the poaching liquid. When the dumplings have cooled down, cut them into bite-sized pieces and set aside.

For the sauce, heat the oil, ghee or butter in a pan and add the cumin seeds. When they crackle, add the asafoetida, followed immediately by the onion. Sauté until the onion just starts to change colour, then add the ginger and green chilli and sauté for another minute or so. Add the turmeric, coriander, chilli powder and salt and sauté for another minute. Add the yoghurt and stir vigorously to prevent it separating. When it starts to boil, reduce the heat and simmer for about 5 minutes, adding a little of the reserved poaching liquid if the sauce starts to thicken too much. Stir in the dried fenugreek leaves and simmer for another 2 minutes.

Add the sliced dumplings and simmer for a further 5–6 minutes, adding more poaching water if necessary. Finish with the chopped fresh coriander and lemon juice, then taste and add the sugar if you like.

MARROW WITH CUMIN

SERVES 4

Marrow can be very bland but here it is perked up with cumin, chillies and coriander and given more texture with the addition of chana dal.

Drain the chana dal, put it in a pan with a pinch of ground turmeric and enough water to cover and bring to the boil. Simmer for 20 minutes, until the chickpeas are just tender but still hold their shape, then drain and set aside.

Blanch the marrow in boiling salted water with 1 teaspoon of the turmeric for a couple of minutes and then drain. Cool it down by plunging it into cold water, then drain again and set aside.

Heat the oil in a large pan and add the cumin seeds, cardamom pods and red chilli. When they crackle, add the onion and sauté until golden. Add the ground coriander, chilli powder and the remaining turmeric and cook for another couple of minutes. Now add the tomatoes and cook for 5 minutes, until the moisture from the tomatoes has evaporated. Add the chana dal and cook for 4 minutes. Add the salt, ginger and green chillies, followed by the blanched marrow, and cook, stirring constantly, for 2 minutes; the chana dal should be cooked but still firm to the bite. Check the seasoning and finish with the fresh coriander and lemon juice.

100g/4oz/½ cup chana dal (split yellow chickpeas), soaked in lukewarm water for 20 minutes
500g/1lb 2oz marrow, peeled, deseeded and cut into 2.5cm/1 inch dice
1½ teaspoons ground turmeric, plus a pinch for cooking the chana dal
3 tablespoons vegetable or corn oil
1½ teaspoons cumin seeds
2 black cardamom pods
1 dried red chilli, broken into 3 pieces
1 large onion, finely chopped
1 teaspoon ground coriander
1 teaspoon red chilli powder
2 large tomatoes, deseeded and chopped
1 teaspoon salt
2.5cm/1 inch piece of fresh ginger, finely chopped
3 green chillies, finely chopped
2 tablespoons finely chopped fresh coriander
juice of 1 lemon

MASALA MASHED POTATOES

SERVES 4

Mashed potato is surprisingly common in India – just not alongside a plate of sausages! The Punjabis stuff parathas with it, while Bengalis eat it spiked with chillies, onion and mustard oil. Our version plays the traditional British role of a starchy accompaniment to meat but is full of Indian spicing.

Cook the potatoes in boiling salted water until tender, then drain. Mash thoroughly and set aside.

Heat the ghee or butter in a saucepan that is large enough to hold the potatoes, then add the cumin seeds. When they start to crackle, add the onion and cook until it colours slightly. Now add the turmeric, ginger and chillies and sauté for 30 seconds. Add the salt and potatoes and mix well over a low heat until the potatoes are heated through and coloured evenly by the turmeric. Add the coriander and tomato and mix well for a couple more minutes. Stir in the butter to give extra shine and richness, then serve immediately.

500g/Ilb 2oz floury potatoes such as
  Desiree, peeled and cut into chunks
2 tablespoons ghee or clarified butter
½ teaspoon cumin seeds
I red onion, finely chopped
¼ teaspoon ground turmeric
Icm/½ inch piece of fresh ginger,
  finely chopped
2 green chillies, finely chopped
I teaspoon salt
I tablespoon chopped fresh coriander
I tomato, deseeded and cut into 5mm/
  ¼ inch dice
20g/¾oz/I½ tablespoons butter

MASALA SAUTÉED POTATOES

SERVES 4

This may sound like a concocted dish but, since potatoes are cheap and easily available, they form part of the staple diet of many Indian families. Often they are sliced much more finely than this and fried with turmeric and fresh chillies. Our version works as an extension of that principle, using two types of onion, plus the staggered addition of ingredients such as ginger, to give a more complex layering of flavours in what is usually a quite simple dish.

Blanch the potatoes by simmering them in a pan of water with the salt and half the turmeric for 5 minutes, then drain well.

Heat the oil in a large frying pan and add the cumin seeds. When they start to crackle, add the chopped onion and sauté until brown. Add the potatoes and the remaining turmeric, sauté for a minute on a medium-high heat, then stir in the chilli powder, ground cumin and salt (you may need to sprinkle in a little water if the ground spices begin to burn). Add the red onion rings and then the tomato. Cook, stirring, for 1–2 minutes, then sprinkle in the ginger, chillies and coriander. Cook for about 3 minutes, until the onion rings are starting to wilt and the potatoes are almost crisp. Serve immediately.

STIR-FRIED GREEN BEANS
WITH COCONUT

SERVES 4

In Tamil Nadu in southern India this dish is called porial. *We like to cook the green beans for slightly less time than usual in order to retain a crunch, which mellows with the grated coconut.*

500g/1lb 2oz large, waxy salad
   potatoes, such as Charlotte, peeled
   and cut into slices 5mm/¼ inch thick
2 teaspoons salt
½ teaspoon ground turmeric
2 tablespoons vegetable or corn oil
1 teaspoon cumin seeds
1 large onion, finely chopped
½ teaspoon red chilli powder
1 teaspoon ground cumin
1 teaspoon salt
1 red onion, sliced into rings
1 tomato, deseeded and diced
1cm/½ inch piece of fresh ginger,
   finely chopped
2 green chillies, finely chopped
1 tablespoon chopped fresh coriander

Heat the oil in a large frying pan, add the red chilli, mustard seeds, chana dal and urid lentils and let them crackle. When the lentils are crisp and starting to colour, add the curry leaves, followed immediately by the onions. Sauté until the onions are softened but not coloured, then add the green chillies, salt and turmeric. Sauté briskly for a minute or two, then add the French beans and stir-fry quickly until they are almost cooked but still crisp and retain their colour.

Add the grated coconut and stir-fry for another couple of minutes. Finally pour in the coconut milk and stir for a few minutes, until it has been absorbed by the beans.

3 tablespoons vegetable or corn oil
1 dried red chilli, broken into pieces
1 teaspoon mustard seeds
1 teaspoon chana dal
   (split yellow chickpeas)
1 teaspoon white urid lentils
1 sprig of fresh curry leaves
2 onions, finely chopped
4 green chillies, finely chopped
1½ teaspoons salt
½ teaspoon ground turmeric
500g/1lb 2oz fine green beans,
   cut into pieces 5mm/¼ inch long
4 tablespoons grated fresh coconut
5 tablespoons coconut milk

STIR-FRIED OKRA WITH DRIED MANGO

SERVES 4

Okra, ladies fingers, bhindi *– there are as many ways of cooking it as there are of naming it. Some make it into a stew, while others cook it with meat. Treated carefully though, okra doesn't always have to end up with a sticky consistency; this Jaipuri version keeps the vegetable crisp whilst lifting its flavours with a light dusting of mango powder.*

Deep-fry the okra for 30 seconds in very hot oil, then drain on kitchen paper and set aside.

Heat the vegetable or corn oil in a pan over a medium heat and add the cumin seeds. When they start to crackle, add the onions and fry until golden brown. Add the tomatoes and cook until they are soft and the juices have evaporated, then add the chilli powder and cook for 2 minutes. Add the fried okra and toss quickly. While stirring briskly over a high heat, add the ginger, salt and dried mango powder. For an extra touch of flavour, add the garam masala. Serve immediately.

800g/1¾lb okra, topped and tailed, then sliced into 1cm/½ inch rounds
oil for deep-frying
4 tablespoons vegetable or corn oil
2 teaspoons cumin seeds
2 onions, finely chopped
2 tomatoes, roughly chopped
1 teaspoon red chilli powder
3cm/1¼ inch piece of fresh ginger, finely chopped
1 teaspoon salt
1 teaspoon dried mango powder (if you cannot find any, use chaat masala instead)
½ teaspoon garam masala (optional)

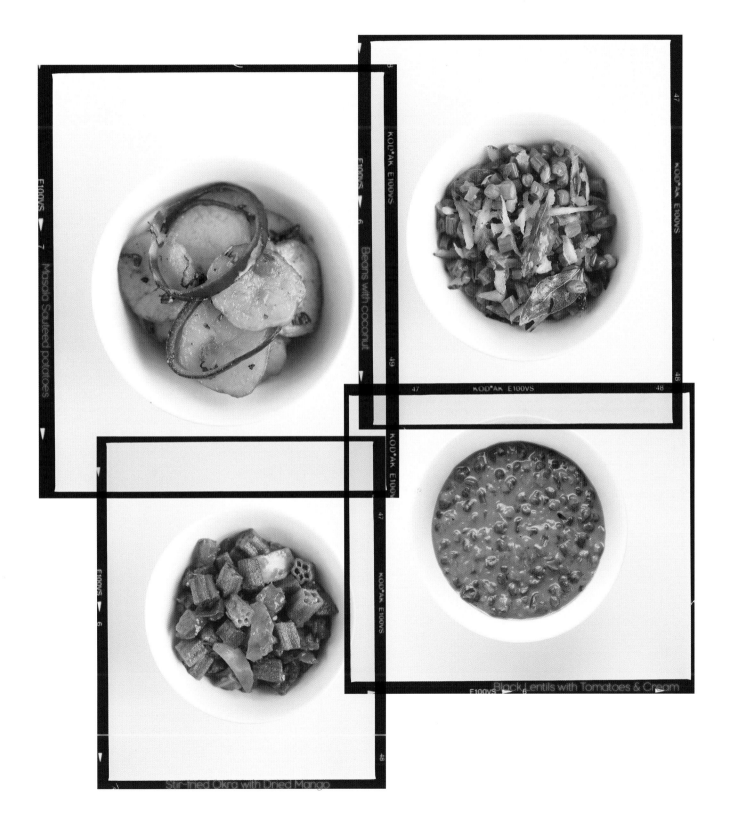

Masala Sautéed potatoes

Beans with coconut

Stir-fried Okra with Dried Mango

Black Lentils with Tomatoes & Cream

BLACK LENTILS WITH TOMATOES AND CREAM

SERVES 4

This is a traditional rich, earthy Punjabi dish unmodified by us in any way. At The Cinnamon Club we serve over a gallon of it each day. Once we have boiled up the ingredients together in a huge vat, we leave it simmering in the embers of the tandoor oven at the end of the night so that when we come in the next morning, it is cooked.

Drain the lentils and put them in a pan with the water. Bring to the boil and simmer for about 1 hour, until the lentils are thoroughly tender but not completely broken down. Add the ginger and garlic pastes, salt and chilli powder and simmer for 10 minutes longer. Add the tomato purée, then stir in the butter a little at a time. Simmer gently for 15 minutes, until the lentils are thick, but take care that the emulsion does not split (i.e. that the butter does not separate from the lentils).

Add the garam masala, dried fenugreek and sugar. Check the seasoning and then stir in the cream.

250g/9oz/1½ cups black urid lentils, soaked
in lukewarm water in a warm
place overnight
1 litre/1¾ pints/4 cups water
1 teaspoon Ginger Paste (see page 30)
1 teaspoon Garlic Paste (see page 30)
1 teaspoon salt
1 teaspoon red chilli powder
2 tablespoons tomato purée
150g/5oz/²⁄3 cup slightly salted butter, diced
1 teaspoon garam masala
½ teaspoon crushed dried fenugreek
leaves (just rub them between
your fingers to crush them)
½ teaspoon sugar
2 tablespoons single cream

RAJASTHANI FIVE-LENTIL MIX

SERVES 4

It's worth an excursion to an Asian grocery store to buy all the lentils for this dish but it's not absolutely essential. You can make it very successfully with fewer than five types of lentil, or even with just one.

2 tablespoons yellow moong lentils (split yellow mung beans)
2 tablespoons toor dal
2 tablespoons chana dal (split yellow chickpeas)
2 tablespoons white urid lentils
2 tablespoons split red lentils
¼ teaspoon ground turmeric
½ teaspoon salt
I tablespoon chopped fresh coriander
a squeeze of lemon juice

Mix the lentils together and rinse them in a sieve under cold running water. Place in a bowl, cover with cold water and leave to soak for 20 minutes, then drain.

Put the lentils in a saucepan with 500ml/18fl oz/2½ cups water and the turmeric and salt, bring to the boil and skim off any scum from the surface. Reduce the heat, cover and cook gently until all the lentils except the chana dal have broken down and are very tender.

For tempering, heat the ghee or oil in a frying pan, add the cumin seeds and dried chilli and let them crackle.

Then add the garlic and sauté until golden brown. Add the onion and when it, too, turns golden brown, add the spices and sauté for a minute. Stir in the tomato and cook until soft. Pour this mixture over the lentils, bring to the boil and simmer for 8–10 minutes. If the mixture begins to dry out, add some boiling water and keep stirring to prevent sticking. Stir in the coriander and lemon juice.

For tempering:

3 tablespoons ghee or oil
I teaspoon cumin seeds
I dried red chilli, broken in half
2 garlic cloves, chopped
I large onion, finely chopped
¼ teaspoon ground turmeric
½ teaspoon red chilli powder
I teaspoon garam masala
½ teaspoon salt
I tomato, chopped

WILD MUSHROOM AND SPINACH STIR-FRY

SERVES 4

If you have trouble in finding any wild mushrooms, you could substitute with well-flavoured cultivated ones, such as chestnut, portabello or oyster.

Heat the oil in a pan over a medium heat and add the cumin seeds. When they start to crackle and change colour, add the onions and sauté until golden brown. Add the mushrooms and toss until they begin to wilt. Add the chilli powder, ground cumin and salt and cook, stirring, for a couple of minutes. Add the chopped tomatoes and cook for 5–6 minutes, until the juices have evaporated. Add the spinach and cook, stirring constantly, until wilted. Sprinkle in the garam masala and fenugreek and check the seasoning.

4 tablespoons vegetable or corn oil
2 teaspoons cumin seeds
2 large onions, finely chopped
225g/8oz/2½ cups wild mushrooms, such as shiitake and oyster, sliced
100g/4oz/1¼ cups button mushrooms, sliced
1 teaspoon red chilli powder
½ teaspoon ground cumin
1½ teaspoons salt
3 large tomatoes, roughly chopped
400g/14oz fresh spinach, washed
¼ teaspoon garam masala
¼ teaspoon powdered dried fenugreek leaves

LENTIL BEAN SALAD

SERVES 4

This is a traditional lentil salad from the state of Maharashtra. Unusually the lentils are just soaked and not boiled at all which gives them a great freshness.

Put the kidney beans in a pan of water with half the salt, bring to the boil and boil hard for 10 minutes. Reduce the heat and simmer until the beans are tender but still hold their shape. Drain and leave to cool.

Wash the green and yellow mung beans, drain well, then mix them with the kidney beans, grated carrot, lemon juice and the remaining salt. To temper the salad, heat the oil in a small pan and add the mustard seeds. When they crackle, add the curry leaves and as they start to wilt, pour everything on to the salad and mix well.

50g/2oz red kidney beans, soaked in lukewarm water overnight in a warm place, then drained
1 teaspoon salt
50g/2oz green mung beans, soaked in lukewarm water overnight in a warm place, then drained and left for a couple of days until they germinate
50g/2oz split yellow mung beans, soaked in lukewarm water for 30 minutes, then drained
1 carrot, grated
juice of 1 lemon

For tempering:
1 tablespoon vegetable or corn oil
¼ teaspoon mustard seeds
1 sprig of fresh curry leaves

MIXED GREENS
WITH MUSTARD

SERVES 4

The Punjabis' favourite vegetable dish is sarson ka saag – a spicy purée of mustard leaves, often eaten with cornmeal bread. If you visit an Asian food shop you should find these leaves very easily. Otherwise you can use greens or cabbage and mix them with other leaves, as we have done here, adding wholegrain mustard to give the same effect.

Remove the stalks from the spinach, mustard and chard, then wash and drain the leaves. Chop them roughly, or simply tear them, then set aside.

In a wok or large frying pan, heat the oil to smoking point and stir in the cumin seeds and garlic. Almost immediately add the onion and sauté until golden. Add all the leaves and let them wilt quickly. When they are wilted but not discoloured, stir in the tomato. Add the wholegrain mustard, salt and sugar and mix well. Check the seasoning, stir in the ginger strips and serve.

200g/7oz/5½ cups baby spinach leaves
100g/4oz/3 cups fresh mustard leaves
100g/4oz/2½ cups red chard leaves
2 tablespoons mustard oil (or use
    sunflower oil mixed with ½
    teaspoon English mustard)
1 teaspoon cumin seeds
2 garlic cloves, finely chopped
½ onion, chopped
1 large tomato, deseeded and cut
    into 1cm/½ inch dice
2 tablespoons wholegrain mustard
½ teaspoon salt
a pinch of sugar
2.5cm/1 inch piece of fresh ginger,
    cut into thin strips

ROASTED AUBERGINE CRUSH

SERVES 4

In this traditional Punjabi dish, the aubergines are cooked twice – first roasted and then sautéed. Aubergines are used throughout much of India; sliced and fried in several regions, mashed with mustard oil, raw onions and chillies in Bengal, and simmered with coconut milk in the south.

Brush a little oil over the aubergines, then place them on a baking tray and roast in an oven preheated to 200°C/400°F/Gas Mark 6 for 10 minutes. Turn the aubergines over and cook for a further 10–20 minutes, until they are soft and the skin is wrinkled. Leave until cool enough to handle, then peel off the skin and mash the flesh to a pulp with a fork.

Heat the oil in a frying pan, add the cumin seeds and when they begin to crackle, add the garlic. When the garlic begins to colour, add the onion and sauté until golden brown. Add the chilli powder and ground cumin and cook for 30 seconds. Stir in the tomatoes and cook until soft.

Now add the ginger and green chillies, followed by the mashed aubergine, and cook, stirring, over a high heat for 2 minutes. Add the salt and fresh coriander and sprinkle in the garam masala. Cook for 30 seconds, then remove from the heat.

2 large aubergines
2 tablespoons vegetable oil, plus extra for brushing
1 teaspoon cumin seeds
3 garlic cloves, chopped
1 large onion, finely chopped
1 teaspoon red chilli powder
1 teaspoon ground cumin
2 tomatoes, chopped
2.5cm/1 inch piece of fresh ginger, finely chopped
2 green chillies, finely chopped
1 teaspoon salt
1 tablespoon chopped fresh coriander
¼ teaspoon garam masala

RAJASTHANI SANGRI BEANS

SERVES 4

Sangri beans are part of the staple diet in the arid land of Rajasthan. They have a straw-like appearance and, when cooked with local ker berries and kummat seeds, a unique nutty texture and taste. We have been importing these beans, berries and seeds to The Cinnamon Club ever since we first opened. Currently they cannot be found anywhere else in Britain and, while we can hardly claim to have converted all our diners into sangriholics, the dish has a passionate following. Although at the time of writing the chances are that you won't be able to obtain these mysterious beans, we have included the recipe in homage to their singular character. French beans could, at a stretch, be used as an alternative.

Heat the mustard oil in a large pan until it reaches smoking point, then add the ghee. Once it melts, add the cumin seeds and red chilli and let them crackle. As the seeds start to change colour, add the garlic and sauté quickly. Add the onion and cook until golden, then add the ground spices and sauté for a minute, stirring constantly to prevent them burning. Add the tomatoes and cook until the moisture from the tomatoes has evaporated and oil starts to separate from the mixture.

Add the sangri beans, ker berries and kummat seeds and sauté for a couple of minutes. Add the salt and yoghurt and stir until the mixture returns to a simmer. Pour in the hot water and cook, stirring, for 10–15 minutes, until the beans and berries have almost doubled in size and have soaked up most of the liquid from the sauce. Stir in the chopped coriander, sugar and lemon juice.

1 tablespoon mustard oil
1 tablespoon ghee
1 teaspoon cumin seeds
1 dried red chilli
1 tablespoon chopped garlic
1 large onion, finely chopped
½ teaspoon ground cumin
½ teaspoon ground coriander
1 teaspoon ground turmeric
1 teaspoon red chilli powder
2 tomatoes, finely chopped
75g/3oz/2½ cups dried sangri beans, rinsed, soaked in cold water for 3 hours and then drained
25g /1oz/½ cup ker berries, rinsed, soaked in cold water for 3 hours and then drained
25g /1oz/⅓ cup kummat seeds, rinsed
1 teaspoon salt
6 tablespoons plain yoghurt
100ml/3½fl oz/scant ½ cup hot water
1 tablespoon chopped fresh coriander
a pinch of sugar
juice of ½ lemon

BREADS

LAYERED PARATHAS

MAKES 8

This is a rich and delicious bread with a lovely crumbly texture though it does need quite a lot of ghee for a full flavour. If preferred, the ghee could be replaced with vegetable oil.

400g/14oz/3½ cups wholemeal flour
2 teaspoons salt
1 teaspoon carom seeds and/or
  ½ teaspoon black onion seeds
200ml/7fl oz/⁷/8 cup water
2 tablespoons vegetable or corn oil
5 tablespoons ghee or clarified butter

Set aside about 4 tablespoons of the flour and put the rest in a bowl. Add the salt, ajowan and/or black onion seeds, water and oil and knead until it comes together into a smooth, stiff dough. Cover with a damp cloth and leave to rest for 20 minutes. Divide the dough into 8 portions, shape them into balls and leave to rest for another 15 minutes.

Flatten each ball lightly with the palm of your hand. Sprinkle some of the reserved flour on it and roll out into a circle about 20cm/8 inches in diameter. Brush the top with ghee and sprinkle with a little more flour. Fold the dough in half to make a semi-circle, then brush with more ghee and sprinkle with flour. Fold again to give a small layered triangle.

Roll out each triangle to make a large triangle, taking care not to roll the dough too thin or you will lose the layers in the bread – roughly 3mm/⅛ inch thickness is fine.

Heat a heavy-based frying pan or a flat griddle over a high heat, place one of the triangles in it and cook for 2–3 minutes, until the dough begins to dry out and colours underneath. Turn and cook the other side, then reduce the heat to medium. Brush the top of the bread with ghee and turn it over again until it develops a deeper colour. Brush the top and turn again. You will notice that as the bread cooks it puffs up, opening out the layers. The application of ghee and flour between the layers facilitates this. Cook the remaining breads in the same way, wrapping them loosely in foil to keep warm while you wait for the rest to be done.

NAAN BREAD

MAKES 16

This popular bread is usually made by slapping a disc of dough on to the side of a tandoor oven. If you ever meet someone claiming to be a tandoori chef, check his right forearm; if there's any hair on it, he's lying to you. Generation after generation of tandoori chefs have forsaken this sign of manhood so that others may eat naan bread. Now Vivek and I can proudly reveal a new way of making naan without tears.

Mix the flour, baking powder and salt together in a bowl. Whisk together the milk, eggs and sugar, then add this mixture to the flour and knead lightly to make a soft dough (take care not to overwork the dough or it will become too stretchy). Cover with a damp cloth and leave to rest for 15 minutes.

Pour the oil over the dough and turn it a few times so it is evenly coated. Divide the dough into 16 pieces, roll out each one into a circle about 9cm/3½ inches in diameter, then gently stretch out one side to form the traditional teardrop shape. Alternatively just roll them into 10cm/4 inch circles.

Preheat the oven to 220°C/425°F/Gas Mark 7, placing a baking tray in it to heat up. Place the naan breads on the hot tray and bake for 4–5 minutes, until they are starting to brown in patches. You might need to turn the bread to colour both sides.

750g/1lb 10oz/6½ cups plain flour
1½ teaspoons baking powder
1 tablespoon salt
400ml/14fl oz/1¾ cups whole milk
2 eggs
3 tablespoons caster sugar
3 tablespoons vegetable oil

BAKARKHANI

MAKES 16

This is a traditional rich, slightly spiced bread, which crisps up to take on an almost biscuit-like consistency.

250ml/8fl oz/1 cup milk
50g/2oz/¼ cup caster sugar
a pinch of saffron strands
½ teaspoon fennel seeds
1 teaspoon sesame seeds
1 teaspoon melon seeds (available in
   Asian shops)
2 black cardamom pods
2 tablespoons ghee or clarified butter,
   plus extra for brushing
500g/1lb 2oz/4½ cups plain flour
1½ teaspoons salt

Put the milk in a pan, bring to the boil and add the sugar, saffron, fennel seeds, sesame seeds, melon seeds and black cardamom pods. Simmer for 5 minutes, then stir in the ghee or butter and leave to cool.

Put the flour in a bowl, add the salt and mix well. Now gradually add the milk mixture, taking out the cardamoms. Knead until it comes together into a smooth, stiff dough, then cover with a damp tea towel and leave to rest for 20 minutes.

Divide the dough into 16 balls and roll each one out on a lightly floured surface into a 7.5cm/3 inch circle. Heat a heavy-based frying pan or a flat griddle over a high heat, place some of the breads in it and cook for 2 minutes, until the dough begins to dry out and colours underneath. Turn and cook the other side, then reduce the heat to medium. Brush the top of the breads with ghee or butter and turn them over again until they develop a deeper colour. Brush the tops and turn again. Cook the remaining breads in the same way.

MISSI ROTI

MAKES 8

Missi Roti is a northern Indian bread. Though not as widely known as naans and parathas, it gives more of a spicy kick as an accompaniment to a meal.

Mix the chickpea flour and plain flour together. Remove 3–4 tablespoons of the flour mix and set aside for dusting. Add the salt, ginger, green chillies, coriander, ajowan seeds, red chilli powder, ground turmeric, red onion and spring onion and mix well. Add the oil and water and knead until everything is combined into a stiff dough. If the dough feels slightly soft, knead in some more flour. Cover with a damp cloth and leave to rest for 15–20 minutes.

Divide the dough into 8 pieces and shape into balls. Roll out each one into a circle15cm/6 inches in diameter.

Heat a large, heavy-based non-stick frying pan or a flat griddle over a high heat and place a round of dough in it. Cook for 3–4 minutes, until the dough starts to dry out and is lightly coloured underneath. Turn on to the other side and repeat. Reduce the heat to medium, brush the top of the bread with some of the ghee or butter, then turn it over and cook until the colour has deepened. Brush the top again, turn over and repeat. Cook the remaining breads in the same way.

300g/11oz/2¾ cups gram (chickpea) flour
200g/7oz/1¾ cups plain flour
25g/1oz/⅛ cup salt
1 teaspoon finely chopped fresh ginger
2 green chillies, finely chopped
a large pinch of finely chopped fresh coriander
1 teaspoon ajowan seeds
½ teaspoon red chilli powder
½ teaspoon ground turmeric
1 red onion, finely chopped
1 spring onion, finely chopped
2 tablespoons vegetable or corn oil
250ml/8fl oz/1 cup water
3 tablespoons ghee or clarified butter

CHUTNEYS AND DIPS

TOMATO AND ONION SEED CHUTNEY
TOMATO AND COCONUT CHUTNEY
TAMARIND CHUTNEY
GREEN COCONUT CHUTNEY
PAPAYA CHUTNEY
CURRIED YOGHURT DIP
MANGO AND MINT CHUTNEY
MUSTARD AND TOMATO SAUCE
CUCUMBER YOGHURT
SPICED ONION YOGHURT

GREEN COCONUT CHUTNEY

SERVES 4

The traditional south Indian coconut chutney; this version is from the southern state of Karnataka.

Put the coconut, coriander, mint, chillies, chana dal and salt in a blender or food processor and blend to a soft, spoonable consistency. To temper the chutney, heat the oil to smoking point and add the curry leaves and mustard seeds. As soon as they start to crackle, add the chutney and remove the pan from the heat.

I coconut, grated (see page 227)
50g/2oz fresh coriander leaves
20g/¾oz fresh mint leaves
4 green chillies, chopped
2 tablespoons roasted chana dal
I teaspoon salt

For tempering:
I tablespoon vegetable or corn oil
¼ teaspoon mustard seeds
IO fresh curry leaves

TOMATO AND COCONUT CHUTNEY

SERVES 4

Our take on the traditional coconut chutney with it's inspiration taken from Andhra where the use of chillies, tomato and yellow lentils makes a beautiful contrast to the classic coconut chutney.

Heat the oil in a pan and add the fennel seeds and curry leaves. When they crackle, add the onions and sauté until golden. Now add the tomatoes and chilli powder and cook until the tomatoes have softened. Stir in the grated coconut and cook until all the liquid has evaporated. Remove from the heat and leave to cool. Place in a blender with the roasted chana dal and a little water and purée until smooth. Mix in the salt.

To temper the chutney, heat the oil to smoking point and add the curry leaves and mustard seeds. As soon as they start to crackle, add the chutney and remove from the heat.

I tablespoon vegetable or corn oil
¼ teaspoon fennel seeds
2 sprigs of fresh curry leaves
2 onions, chopped
6 tomatoes, chopped
¼ teaspoon red chilli powder
I fresh coconut, grated (see page 227)
25g/Ioz roasted chana dal
I teaspoon salt

For tempering:
I tablespoon vegetable or corn oil
IO fresh curry leaves
¼ teaspoon mustard seeds

TAMARIND CHUTNEY

SERVES 4

One of the most versatile and widely used chutneys in north India used in almost any street snack one could encounter.

Place the tamarind paste, bay leaf and cardamom pod in a pan and bring to the boil. Add the jaggery or sugar and cook, stirring, over a medium heat for 15 minutes, until glossy. Stir in the chilli, ginger and salt, then strain through a sieve and leave to cool. Serve as a dip – it's particularly good with Tandoori-style Seared Tuna (see page 37) or Sweet Potato Cakes with Ginger, Fennel and Chilli (see page 68).

150g/5oz tamarind paste
1 bay leaf
1 black cardamom pod
50g/2oz jaggery or molasses sugar
1 teaspoon red chilli powder
1½ teaspoons ground ginger
¼ teaspoon salt

TOMATO AND ONION SEED CHUTNEY

SERVES 4

This is Vivek's mother's recipe. Its the way that people used to keep tomatoes to have when tomatoes were out of season. As a child he had many a meal just with a fried poori or paratha and this sweet spiced tomato spread.

Heat the oil in a pan and add the onion seeds, bay leaf and dried red chillies. When they crackle, add the chopped tomatoes and cook until soft. Stir in the chilli powder, sugar and raisins and simmer for 15 minutes, until the liquid has almost all evaporated and the chutney turns thick and glossy. Cool before serving.

2 tablespoons vegetable or corn oil
½ teaspoon black onion seeds
1 bay leaf
2 dried red chillies
500g/1lb 2oz tomatoes, deseeded and chopped
1¼ teaspoons mild red chilli powder
200g/7oz granulated sugar
1 tablespoon raisins

PAPAYA CHUTNEY

SERVES 4

Essentially a spiced conserve from west Bengal which, because of its transparent glaze, is also referred to as 'plastic chutney'.

Place all the ingredients except the sugar in a saucepan and bring to the boil. Simmer for 5 minutes, then add the sugar, reduce the heat and cook gently for 15 minutes, until the syrup has thickened and the papaya has turned glossy and translucent. Leave to cool before serving.

I green papaya, peeled, deseeded
  and thinly sliced
150ml/¼ pint white vinegar
¼ teaspoon black onion seeds
I dried red chilli
¼ teaspoon fennel seeds
I tablespoon raisins
I bay leaf
100g/4oz granulated sugar

CURRIED YOGHURT DIP

SERVES 4

Heat the oil in a pan and add the mustard seeds. When they crackle, add the curry leaves and let them wilt. Add the ginger and green chilli and sauté for 30 seconds, then stir in the turmeric.

Pour this tempering into the yoghurt, add the salt and sugar and mix well.

2 tablespoons vegetable oil
¼ teaspoon mustard seeds
10 fresh curry leaves
1cm/½ inch piece of fresh ginger,
  finely chopped
I green chilli, finely chopped
½ teaspoon turmeric
200g/7oz Greek yoghurt
I teaspoon salt
½ teaspoon sugar

MANGO AND MINT CHUTNEY

SERVES 4

A simple dip combining the freshness of mint with the sweetness of mangoes.

Put all the ingredients in a liquidiser and blend until the mint leaves are well puréed. Strain through a sieve.

2 ripe mangoes, peeled, stoned
  and puréed (or use 100ml/3½fl oz
  canned mango purée)
leaves from a 200g/7oz bunch of
  fresh mint
juice of I lemon

MUSTARD AND TOMATO SAUCE

SERVES 4

This sauce is particular to West Bengal, where it is served with street snacks such as Bengali Spiced Vegetable Cakes (see page 70).

Simply mix the ingredients together.

100ml/3½fl oz tomato ketchup
2 tablespoons Dijon mustard
4 tablespoons water

CUCUMBER YOGHURT

SERVES 4

This is our version of Cucumber Raita with lots more cucumber than normal which is gently bound by a thick, spiced yoghurt.

Peel the cucumber, cut it in half lengthways, then scoop out and discard the seeds. Cut the flesh into 5mm/¼ inch dice, place in a colander and sprinkle with the salt. Set aside for 30 minutes, then gently squeeze out the water.

Place the cucumber in a bowl, add the roasted cumin seeds and yoghurt and mix well.

I medium cucumber
I teaspoon salt
½ teaspoon cumin seeds, roasted (see page 33)
4 tablespoons Greek yoghurt

Variation: Cucumber Yoghurt Sauce
Whisk together all the ingredients, then stir in one quantity of Cucumber Yoghurt (see opposite).

100g/4oz Greek yoghurt
3 tablespoons water
I teaspoon cumin seeds, roasted and ground (see page 33)
10 fresh mint leaves, chopped
½ teaspoon sugar
I teaspoon salt

SPICED ONION YOGHURT

SERVES 4

Often, yoghurt accompanies a curry dish to quell the effects of hot spices. But yoghurt can do more than act as a fire extinguisher. Here we make it with ginger and onion.

Put all the ingredients except the yoghurt into a bowl and mix well. Set aside for 2 minutes, then gradually stir in the Greek yoghurt.

2 red onions, finely chopped
2.5cm/I inch piece of fresh ginger, finely chopped
2 green chillies, finely chopped
I teaspoon salt
I teaspoon sugar
I sprig of fresh mint leaves, shredded
75g/3oz Greek yoghurt

DESSERTS

COCONUT ROLL COCONUT ICE-CREAM AND COCONUT BRÛLÉE WITH FENNEL CARAMEL SAUCE CARROT TOFFEE PUDDING SEMOLINA FRITTERS WITH RUM AND RAISIN ICE-CREAM WARM CHOCOLATE MOUSSE STEAMED MANGO RICE CAKES WITH WILD BERRY SORBET CARROT HALWA SAMOSAS SOUTH INDIAN RICE PANCAKES WITH CINNAMON AND APPLE WARM APPLE LASSI WITH CHAMPAGNE GRANITA SPICED BANANA TARTE TATIN MANGO AND GINGER MOUSSE COCONUT CRÈME CARAMEL SAFFRON POACHED PEARS WITH CINNAMON ICE-CREAM PASSION FRUIT TART SPICED PUMPKIN BRÛLÉE MANGO BRÛLÉE FIG AND WALNUT CHEESECAKE CHILLED RASPBERRY SOUFFLÉ SORBETS

COCONUT ROLL, COCONUT ICE-CREAM AND COCONUT BRÛLÉE WITH FENNEL CARAMEL SAUCE

SERVES 8

We have incorporated three very different ways of using coconut in this dessert, each taking an element of western pastry practice.

First make the ice-cream. Put the milk, cream, sugar and liquid glucose in a pan and bring slowly to the boil, stirring occasionally to dissolve the sugar. Stir in the desiccated coconut and coconut milk, then remove from the heat. Whisk the egg yolks together in a bowl, then gradually whisk in the milk mixture. Freeze in an ice-cream machine according to the manufacturer's instructions. Alternatively, pour into a shallow container and place in the freezer until semi-frozen, then transfer to a chilled bowl and whisk well to break down ice crystals. Return to the container and place in the freezer again. Repeat this process 3 or 4 times, then leave until set firm.

For the coconut brûlée, put the cream and sugar in a pan and bring to the boil, then stir in the desiccated coconut and coconut milk and remove from the heat. Whisk the eggs and egg yolk together in a bowl and gradually whisk in the cream mixture. Pour into 8 ramekins and place in a roasting tin half full of hot water. Bake in an oven preheated to 120°C/250°F/Gas Mark ½ for 30 minutes or until just set.

Leave to cool, then chill before serving.

To make the coconut rolls, heat the ghee or butter in a pan, add the fresh coconut and desiccated coconut and fry over a medium heat until light brown. Add the raisins, evaporated milk and sugar and cook for 5 minutes. Remove from the heat and leave to cool. Lay out the pastry sheets and brush them with melted butter. Cut each sheet into quarters. Place an eighth of the filling diagonally across the centre of each piece of filo, fold in the 2 sides, then fold the top over and roll it up.

For the fennel sauce, put the sugar in a small, heavy-based pan and heat gently, stirring occasionally, until melted. Raise the heat and cook without stirring until it becomes a dark brown caramel. Boil the water separately, then gradually pour it into the caramel, standing well back in case it splutters. Simmer until the sauce has a light, syrupy consistency, then add the fennel seeds and remove from the heat.

Sprinkle the Demerara sugar over the coconut brûlées and caramelise with a blowtorch or under a very hot grill. Deep-fry the coconut rolls in hot oil for about 3 minutes, until brown and crisp, then drain on kitchen paper. Put a coconut roll, a brûlée and a scoop of ice-cream on each of 8 serving plates and pour a little of the warm fennel sauce around.

For the coconut ice-cream:
200ml/7fl oz/⅞ cup milk
200ml/7fl oz/⅞ cup single cream
50g/2oz/¼ cup granulated sugar
3 tablespoons liquid glucose
40g/1½ oz/½ cup desiccated coconut
2 tablespoons coconut milk
2 egg yolks

For the coconut brûlée:
300ml/½ pint/1¼ cups double cream
50g/2oz/¼ cup granulated sugar
1 tablespoon desiccated coconut
1 tablespoon coconut milk
2 eggs
1 egg yolk
40g/1½ oz/¼ cup Demerara sugar

For the coconut rolls:
2 tablespoons ghee or clarified butter
1 fresh coconut, grated (see page 227)
40g/1½ oz/½ cup desiccated coconut
1 tablespoon raisins
150ml/¼ pint/⅔ cup evaporated milk
2 tablespoons granulated sugar
2 sheets of filo pastry
a little melted butter for brushing
oil for deep-frying

For the fennel caramel sauce:
100g/4oz/½ cup granulated sugar
3 tablespoons water
½ teaspoon fennel seeds

CARROT TOFFEE PUDDING

SERVES 4-6

Sweet, rich and sensual, this combination of sugar and spice is for those with strong palates and sweet tooths.

50g/2oz/¼ cup granulated sugar
1½ tablespoons water
100g/4oz/1 cup plain flour
¼ teaspoon baking powder
½ teaspoon ground ginger
1 carrot, grated
150g/5oz/²/3 cup unsalted butter
100g/4oz/1 cup icing sugar
2 eggs
a little caster sugar

For the caramel sauce:
100g/4oz/½ cup granulated sugar
2 teaspoons water
25g/1oz/2 tablespoons unsalted butter, diced
100ml/3½fl oz double cream

Put the granulated sugar and water in a small, heavy-based pan and heat gently, stirring occasionally, until the sugar has melted. Raise the heat and cook without stirring until it forms a golden caramel. Remove from the heat and leave to cool.

Mix together the flour, baking powder, ground ginger and grated carrot and set aside. In a separate bowl, beat the butter and icing sugar together until fluffy, then beat in the eggs one at a time. Mix in the cooled caramel and then fold in the flour mixture.

Butter 4–6 deep muffin tins, dariole moulds or tea cups and sprinkle them with a little caster sugar to coat the sides evenly. Fill them about a third full with the pudding mixture, then bake in an oven preheated to 180°C/350°F/Gas Mark 4 for 20 minutes, until well risen and golden brown.

Make the caramel sauce. Put the sugar and water in a small, heavy-based pan and place over a low heat, stirring occasionally, until the sugar has melted. Raise the heat and cook

without stirring until it turns into a golden brown caramel. Gradually stir in the butter, standing well back in case the hot caramel splutters. Remove from the heat, stir in the double cream and set aside.

Leave the puddings to cool in their moulds for 5 minutes, then turn out on to serving plates. Serve topped with the caramel sauce and, if you wish, with cream or Rum and Raisin Ice-cream (see page 169).

SEMOLINA FRITTERS WITH RUM AND RAISIN ICE-CREAM

SERVES 8

The contrast between the hot and crispy fritters with the sweet ice cream makes for a stunning dessert combination.

First make the ice-cream. Soak the raisins in half the rum until plump. Put the milk, cream, liquid glucose and sugar in a pan and bring slowly to the boil, stirring occasionally to dissolve the sugar. Stir in the remaining rum, then remove from the heat. Lightly whisk the egg yolks together in a bowl, then gradually whisk in the milk mixture. Freeze in an ice-cream machine until the mixture is set but still soft. Mix in the soaked raisins and then freeze until firm. If you don't have an ice-cream machine, pour the mixture into a shallow container and place in the freezer until semi-frozen, then transfer to a chilled bowl and whisk well to break down ice crystals. Return to the container and place in the freezer again. Repeat this process 3 or 4 times, then stir in the raisins and leave until set firm.

For the fritters, heat the ghee or butter in a heavy-based pan, stir in the semolina and fry slowly until golden. Add the cashew nuts and fry for another 2–3 minutes. Then gradually pour in the evaporated milk and water, stirring constantly with a strong spatula to avoid lumps and prevent the mixture sticking to the bottom of the pan. Once the mixture becomes smooth, add the sugar and raisins. It will turn liquid after the sugar has been added, so cook gently for about 10 minutes, until it thickens up. Pour into a baking tray and leave to cool, then divide into 24 portions. Mould them into egg shapes or balls, dip them in the beaten egg, then roll in the breadcrumb and almond mixture until well coated. Chill until firm.

Just before serving, deep-fry the semolina fritters in hot oil for about 3 minutes, until golden. Drain on kitchen paper and serve straight away, with a scoop of the rum and raisin ice-cream.

75g/3oz/⅓ cup ghee or clarified butter
250g/9oz/1½ cups coarse semolina
1 tablespoon cashew nuts
100ml/3½fl oz/scant ½ cup evaporated milk
600ml/1 pint/2½ cups hot water
150g/5oz/²⁄3 cup granulated sugar
1 tablespoon raisins
oil for deep-frying

For the rum and raisin ice-cream:

40g/1½oz/¼ cup raisins
2 tablespoons dark rum
250ml/8fl oz/1 cup milk
250ml/8fl oz/1 cup single cream
4 tablespoons liquid glucose
50g/2oz/¼ cup granulated sugar
3 egg yolks

For coating:

1 egg, lightly beaten
100g/4oz/2 cups fresh breadcrumbs mixed with 50g/2oz/²⁄3 cup ground almonds

WARM CHOCOLATE MOUSSE

SERVES 4

Break the chocolate into small pieces and put it in a deep pan with the butter and the espresso, if using. Melt over a very low heat, stirring frequently. Remove from the heat, add the egg yolks and stir well.

This deeply sensual dessert is certain to have your guests groan with pleasure at the warm, smooth and creamy mousse, enlivened further with an aromatic ice cream.

Whisk the egg whites until they form stiff peaks, then gradually whisk in the sugar until you have a glossy, stiff meringue. Fold the meringue gently into the chocolate mixture. Pour into 4 ramekins or tea cups and chill thoroughly (this ensures that the centre stays soft and moist during cooking).

Bake in an oven preheated to 180°C/350°F/Gas Mark 4 for 10 minutes, until the mousse has risen to the brim of the moulds and is beginning to firm up on the sides; the centre should be moist but warm. Serve immediately, with a flavoured ice-cream such as cinnamon (see page 179).

125g/4½oz/4½ squares good-quality dark chocolate
35g/1¼oz/2 tablespoons unsalted butter, softened
1 tablespoon strong espresso coffee (optional)
3 eggs, separated
40g/1½oz caster sugar

STEAMED MANGO RICE CAKES

SERVES 4

Idli (south Indian rice cakes) are traditionally a breakfast dish or afternoon snack, where they are served with the vegetable broth of sambhar. Here we have simply added mango to the rice cake mixture. Accompany with the Wild Berry Sorbet on page 184.

Put the idli mix in a bowl and add the water, followed by the mango purée and vegetable oil. Mix together to give a smooth batter, then leave to rest for 10 minutes.

Add the diced mango to the batter and pour it into 8 lightly greased small shallow bowls. Place in a steamer, cover and steam over a high heat for 15–20 minutes, until the dumplings are firm to the touch and the texture is almost spongy. Remove from the steamer, turn out on to 4 serving plates and serve with the Wild Berry Sorbet.

100g/4oz/⅓ cup idli mix (available from Asian shops)
4 tablespoons water
125m/4fl oz/½ cup canned mango purée
1 teaspoon vegetable or corn oil
1 ripe mango, peeled, stoned and cut into 1cm/½ inch cubes
Wild Berry Sorbet, to serve (see page 184.)

SOUTH INDIAN RICE PANCAKES
WITH CINNAMON AND APPLE

SERVES 4

Using an instant dosa mix, which is available from Asian grocer's shops, this is a quick and easy dessert to make. It is an adaptation of the more traditional breakfast dosa.

200g/7oz packet of dosa mix
2 tablespoons vegetable or corn oil
a little ghee or clarified butter
4 teaspoons caster sugar

For the cinnamon and apple filling:
15g/½oz/1 tablespoon butter
2 green apples, such as Granny Smiths, peeled, cored and cut into 1cm/
   ½ inch dice
50g/2oz/¼ cup caster sugar
¼ teaspoon ground cinnamon

Prepare the dosa mix according to the instructions on the packet, then set aside.

For the filling, melt the butter in a pan, add the apples and toss for 3–4 minutes over a low heat. Now add the sugar and cook until the apples are soft and dry. Stir in the ground cinnamon, remove the pan from the heat and set aside.

To make the pancakes, spread a quarter of the oil over a large, heavy-based frying pan or a flat griddle and place over a medium heat. Pour a quarter of the batter into the centre of the pan and, using the back of a ladle, spread it out quickly with an outward circular motion to form a pancake about 20cm/8 inches in diameter.

Drizzle a touch of ghee or clarified butter and sprinkle a teaspoon of sugar around the edge of the pancake and cook over a low heat for a couple of minutes, until golden underneath. Spoon a quarter of the apple filling into the centre of the pancake and then roll or fold it. Using a spatula, transfer the pancake to a plate. Repeat with the remaining batter to make 4 pancakes altogether. Serve hot, with ice-cream.

CARROT HALWA SAMOSAS

SERVES 4

Carrot halwa is one of India's favourite sweets, where the aroma of cardamom really serves to lift the grated carrot. It is usually served on its own but in our recipe we wrap it in filo to make samosas.

100g/4oz ghee/½ cup or clarified butter
500g/1lb 2oz carrots, grated
100g/4oz/½ cup caster sugar
1 heaped tablespoon raisins
250ml/8fl oz/1 cup evaporated milk
seeds from 3 green cardamom pods, ground
2 sheets of filo pastry
a little melted butter for brushing
oil for deep-frying (optional)

Heat the ghee or butter in a pan, add the grated carrots and cook gently for 10 minutes, until the juice from the carrots has evaporated. Add the sugar and raisins and cook until the sugar has melted. Add the milk and cook over a medium heat, stirring constantly, for about 10 minutes, until the mixture looks like orange fudge. Stir in the cardamom, spread the mixture out on a baking tray and leave to cool.

Take a filo pastry sheet, cut out 2 strips 20cm/8 inches long and 7.5cm/3 inches wide and brush with melted butter. Place a spoonful of carrot fudge near the top of each one, then take one corner of the pastry and fold it over the carrot mixture in a triangular shape. Continue folding until you reach the end of the strip and have a neat triangle. Brush the edges with a little melted butter to seal, then brush

the triangle all over with more butter. Repeat with the remaining mixture and filo to make 4 samosas.

Deep-fry the samosas in hot oil for about 3 minutes, until golden brown and then drain on kitchen paper. Alternatively bake for about 10 minutes in an oven preheated to 190°C/375°F/Gas Mark 5. Serve hot, with ice-cream.

SPICED BANANA TARTE TATIN

SERVES 4-6

This is a wonderful dish and very easy to prepare. It should be quite sweet, with the caramel bringing out the flavours of the banana which in turn is enhanced by the delicate aromatic softness of the cinnamon.

4 bananas
I teaspoon ground cinnamon
I50g/5oz puff pastry
Cinnamon Ice-cream (see page I79),
   to serve

For the caramel:
I50g/5oz/²/3 cup granulated sugar
5 tablespoons water
I5g/¹/2oz/I tablespoon unsalted butter

To make the caramel, put the granulated sugar and water in a small, heavy-based pan and heat gently, stirring occasionally, until the sugar has melted. Raise the heat and cook, without stirring, until it forms a dark golden caramel. Add the butter, standing well back in case it splutters, then simmer for 8 minutes. Remove from the heat and pour into a 20cm/ 8 inch cake tin to coat the base. Leave until cool and set.

Peel and slice the bananas and arrange them in overlapping circles on top of the set caramel. Sprinkle the cinnamon on top. Now roll out the puff pastry to about 3mm/¹/8 inch thick and cut out a 23cm/9 inch round. Cover the bananas with the pastry, tucking the edges down inside the tin. Bake in an oven preheated to 190°C/ 375°F/Gas Mark 5 for about 15 minutes, until the pastry puffs up and turns light brown. Remove from the oven and invert the tart on to a plate so the bananas are on top. Serve hot, with the Cinnamon Ice-cream.

WARM APPLE LASSI WITH CHAMPAGNE GRANITA

SERVES 4

This elegant dish combines flavours of sweetened apples, slightly sharp aromatic yoghurt and the tingle of frozen Champagne. Serve in a tall glass and encourage guests to delve down with their spoons all the way to the bottom to get the three sensations together.

4 green apples, such as Granny Smiths, peeled, cored and cut into quarters
75g/3oz/⅓ cup caster sugar, plus 2 teaspoons
3 tablespoons water
200g/7oz/⅞ cup Greek yoghurt

seeds from 3 green cardamom pods, ground

For the Champagne granita:
300ml/½ pint/1¼ cups Champagne
1 tablespoon caster sugar
3 tablespoons water

For the granita, simply mix the Champagne, sugar and water together, stirring until the sugar has dissolved, then pour into a dish and freeze until solid. The mixture will form brittle crystals and clear ice. Scrape it up with a fork to form small granules, like ice shavings. Return to the freezer and then scrape it up again just before serving.

Place the apple quarters in a baking tray and sprinkle the 75g/3oz caster sugar and the water over them. Cover with aluminium foil and bake in an oven preheated to 180°C/350°F/ Gas Mark 4 for 15 minutes or until the apples are soft. Blend to a smooth purée in a food processor and set aside. Mix the Greek yoghurt with the ground cardamom and 2 teaspoons of sugar.

To serve, just take 4 old-fashioned tumblers or highballs, pour in enough warm apple purée to fill each one by a quarter, then cover with the yoghurt mixture. Top with the granita and serve immediately.

SAFFRON POACHED PEARS WITH CINNAMON ICE-CREAM

SERVES 4

This has been a very popular dessert at the restaurant. Boiling fruit with saffron is not a traditional Indian culinary custom but it's falttering to see that other restaurants have followed our trend in doing so. The Saffron adds a beautiful colour to the pear and gives off that special aroma that only saffron has. The yoghurt stuffing provides a fun element of surprise for guests.

Make the ice-cream. Put the milk, cream, liquid glucose, sugar and cinnamon stick in a pan and bring slowly to the boil, stirring occasionally to dissolve the sugar. Remove from the heat. Lightly whisk the egg yolks and ground cinnamon together, then gradually whisk in the milk mixture, removing the cinnamon stick. Pour into an ice-cream machine and freeze. Alternatively, pour into a shallow container and place in the freezer until semi-frozen, then transfer to a chilled bowl and whisk well to break down ice crystals. Return to the container and place in the freezer again. Repeat this process 3 or 4 times. Leave until set.

Peel the pears and put them in a bowl of water to prevent discolouration. Put the sugar, water and saffron in a saucepan in which the pears will just fit, then bring slowly to the boil, stirring to dissolve the sugar. Add the pears, reduce the heat and poach until the pears are tender but still slightly firm. Remove from the poaching liquid and leave to cool.

Mix together all the filling ingredients. Using a small scoop or an apple corer, carefully core the pears from underneath. Stuff with the filling, then place each pear on a serving plate and drizzle over a little of the poaching liquid. Serve accompanied by the cinnamon ice-cream.

4 William pears (not too ripe)
175g/6oz/¾ cup caster sugar
1 litre/1¾ pints/4 cups water
a generous pinch of saffron strands

For the cinnamon ice-cream:
200ml/7fl oz/⁷⁄8 cup milk
200ml/7fl oz/⁷⁄8 cup single cream
4 tablespoons liquid glucose
50g/2oz/¼ cup granulated sugar
1 cinnamon stick
3 egg yolks
1 teaspoon ground cinnamon

For the filling:
100g/4oz/½ cup Greek yoghurt
1 tablespoon icing sugar
1½ tablespoons raisins
10 fresh coriander leaves, shredded

MANGO BRÛLÉE

SERVES 6

This is a less challenging form of brûlée than the pumpkin (page 182) and would be a delicate end to a less spicy meal.

325ml/11fl oz/1⅓ cups double cream
50g/2oz/¼ cup granulated sugar
150ml/¼ pint/⅔ cup canned
  mango purée
1 egg
3 egg yolks
50g/2oz/¼ cup Demerara sugar

Put the cream, sugar and mango purée in a pan and bring to boiling point, stirring occasionally. Whisk the egg and egg yolks together in a bowl and slowly pour in the mango mixture, whisking constantly. Pour the mixture into 6 ramekins and place in a roasting tin half full of hot water. Bake in an oven preheated to 120°C/250°F/Gas Mark ½ for 30 minutes or until just set. Remove from the roasting tin, leave to cool and then chill.

Sprinkle the Demerara sugar on top and caramelise with a blowtorch or under a very hot grill. Leave until the top has become crisp, then serve.

PASSION FRUIT TART

SERVES 6

Fresh passion fruit is readily available in supermarkets these days, but a canned purée will suit your purposes fine for this fantastic dish.

6 ripe passion fruit (or 5 tablespoons bought passion fruit purée)
125g/4½oz/½ cup caster sugar
3 eggs
100ml/3½fl oz/scant ½ cup double cream

For the pastry:
100g/4oz/½ cup unsalted butter, softened
100g/4oz/1 cup icing sugar
225g/8oz/2 cups plain flour
1 egg, lightly beaten
1 egg yolk, for brushing

First make the pastry. Whisk the butter and sugar lightly together, using a hand blender or a whisk. Add the flour and egg and mix very lightly with your fingertips until you get a crumbly dough. Wrap in clingfilm and chill for 30 minutes.

Roll the dough out thinly and use to line a 25cm/10 inch loose-bottomed tart tin. Cover with aluminium foil, fill with baking beans and bake in an oven preheated to 180°C/350°F/Gas Mark 4 for 15 minutes. Remove the foil and beans and brush a thin coating of egg yolk over the pastry. Return to the oven for 5 minutes, then leave to cool.

For the passion fruit filling, cut the passion fruit in half, scoop out the insides and press through a sieve into a bowl (reserve some of the seeds for garnish). Whisk the sugar and eggs together until the sugar has dissolved, then whisk the cream and passion fruit purée into the mixture. Pour the filling carefully into the pastry case and bake in an oven preheated to 120°C/250°F/Gas Mark ½ for 20 minutes, until the filling is just set. Leave to cool, then serve chilled, garnished with a few passion fruit seeds if you have them.

SPICED PUMPKIN BRÛLÉE

SERVES 6

Though pumpkins are not typically used in desserts, we find that the boldness of the flesh stands up very well to the spices in the brûlée.

Put the diced pumpkin in a pan with the granulated sugar and 2 tablespoons of water and cook gently until soft. Leave to cool, then blend to a purée in a food processor.

Put the cream and caster sugar in a saucepan and bring to the boil, then whisk in the pumpkin purée, taking care that the purée is added only when the cream comes to boil, otherwise the cream may separate. Leave until luke-warm, then gradually whisk in the eggs, egg yolks and ground spices. Pour the mixture into 6 ramekins and place in a roasting tin half full of hot water. Bake in an oven preheated to 120°C/250°F/Gas Mark $^1/_2$ for 30 minutes or until just set. Remove from the roasting tin, leave to cool and then chill.

Sprinkle the Demerara sugar on top and caramelise with a blowtorch or under a very hot grill. Leave until the top has become crisp, then serve.

150g/5oz/$^7/_8$ cup peeled pumpkin flesh, diced
75g/3oz/$^1/_3$ cup granulated sugar
350ml/12fl oz/1½ cups double cream
75g/3oz/$^1/_3$ cup caster sugar
2 eggs
3 egg yolks
2 teaspoons mixed ground cinnamon, black pepper and cardamom (use equal quantities of each)
50g/2oz/¼ cup Demerara sugar

FIG AND WALNUT CHEESECAKE

SERVES 6

There is nothing obviously Indian in this dish, however we simply love the fig and walnut combination, which works so successfully for a cheesecake and makes for a great end to a spicy meal.

For the base, mix together the biscuit crumbs and melted butter to give a crumbly consistency. Spread the mixture with your fingers over the base of a 20cm/8 inch springform cake tin and chill.

Place a small, heavy-based pan over a low heat, add 1 tablespoon of the sugar and leave until melted. Raise the heat and cook without stirring until it has turned into a light brown caramel. Mix in the walnuts, remove from the heat and leave to cool. Now crush the walnuts coarsely.

Mix the cream cheese with the fennel seeds, fold in the whipped cream and set aside.

Put the egg yolks, lemon zest and remaining sugar in a large bowl and place over a saucepan of gently simmering water, making sure the water is not touching the base of the bowl. Whisk constantly, preferably with an electric beater, until the mixture has doubled in volume and is thick enough to coat the back of a spoon. Remove the

CHILLED RASPBERRY SOUFFLÉ

Though soufflés are never the easiest things to make they are invariably worth the effort and none more so than this stunning raspberry version.

bowl from the heat. Squeeze out excess water from the soaked gelatine and fold it into the egg yolk mixture.

Whisk the egg whites until they form stiff peaks. Fold them into the cream cheese mixture, then very lightly fold in the egg yolk mixture. Finally, sprinkle the chopped figs and crushed caramelised walnuts on top and lightly fold them in too.

Pour this mixture into the cake tin on top of the biscuit base. Smooth the top with a palette knife and place in the fridge until set. To serve, remove the side of the tin and cut the cheesecake into wedges.

75g/3oz/⅓ cup caster sugar
75g/3oz/¾ cup walnuts
500g/1lb 2oz/2¼ cups cream cheese
1 teaspoon fennel seeds,
    coarsely pounded
5 tablespoons double cream,
    lightly whipped
3 eggs, separated
grated zest of 1 lemon
5 gelatine leaves, soaked in cold
    water for about 5 minutes
75g/3oz/½ cup dried figs coarsely
    chopped

For the base:
75g/3oz/¾ cup digestive biscuits,
    crushed into crumbs
25g/1oz/2 tablespoons butter, melted

Put the raspberries in a heavy-based pan with 100g/4oz of the sugar and 3 tablespoons of water. Heat gently until the mixture comes to the boil and the raspberries soften. Continue cooking for 20–25 minutes, stirring occasionally, until the mixture is thick, then leave to cool. Blend to a purée in a food processor and press through a sieve to extract the seeds.

Whisk the egg yolks together in a mixing bowl, then gradually whisk in the raspberry purée, followed by the cream. Place the bowl over a pan of gently simmering water, making sure the water does not touch the base of the bowl. Cook, stirring, for 25–30 minutes, until the mixture is thick enough to coat the back of the spoon. Remove from the heat and cool slightly. Meanwhile, soak the gelatine in cold water for 5 minutes.

Squeeze out excess water from the soaked gelatine and whisk the gelatine into the raspberry mixture. Leave to cool to room temperature.

In a large bowl, whisk the egg whites until stiff, then gradually whisk in the remaining sugar until the mixture forms soft peaks. Gently fold this meringue into the raspberry purée, pour it into 4 individual bowls or one large one and chill until set.

200g/7oz/1 cup fresh raspberries
175g/6oz/¾ cup caster sugar
3 egg yolks
3 tablespoons double cream
2 sheets of gelatine
4 egg whites

SORBETS

SERVES 4

For the berry, mango or peach sorbet, put all the ingredients in a saucepan and bring to the boil. As the mixture comes to the boil, skim off any scum from the surface, then remove the pan from the heat and leave to cool. Chill thoroughly. Place in an ice-cream machine and freeze according to the manufacturer's instructions. Alternatively, pour into a shallow container and place in the freezer until semi-frozen, then remove and stir briskly with a fork to break down ice crystals. Return to the freezer and repeat this process 3 or 4 times, then leave until the sorbet is set firm.

For the lemon and mint sorbet, put the sugar and water in a heavy-based pan and heat gently, stirring occasionally, until the sugar has dissolved. Raise the heat and simmer gently for 20 minutes to give a light syrup. Add the lemon zest and juice, mint and liquid glucose and leave to cool. Chill thoroughly, then freeze as described above.

WILD BERRY SORBET

100ml/3½fl oz/scant ½ cup each of raspberry purée, blackberry purée, blueberry purée and blackcurrant purée (made by puréeing fresh fruits in a food processor, then straining through a sieve)
400ml/14fl oz/1¾ cups water
100g/4oz/½ cup caster sugar
3 tablespoons liquid glucose

MANGO SORBET

200ml/7fl oz/⅞ cup canned or fresh mango purée
200ml/7fl oz/⅞ cup water
20g/¾oz/1½ tablespoons caster sugar
2 tablespoons liquid glucose

PEACH SORBET

200ml/7fl oz/⅞ cup peach purée (made by puréeing fresh peaches in a food processor, then straining through a sieve)
200ml/7fl oz/⅞ cup water
20g/¾oz/½ tablespoons caster sugar
2 teaspoons liquid glucose

LEMON AND MINT SORBET

200g/7oz/⅞ cup caster sugar
200ml/7fl oz/⅞ cup water
grated zest of 1 lemon
200ml/7fl oz/⅞ cup lemon juice
2 tablespoons shredded fresh mint
1½ tablespoons liquid glucose

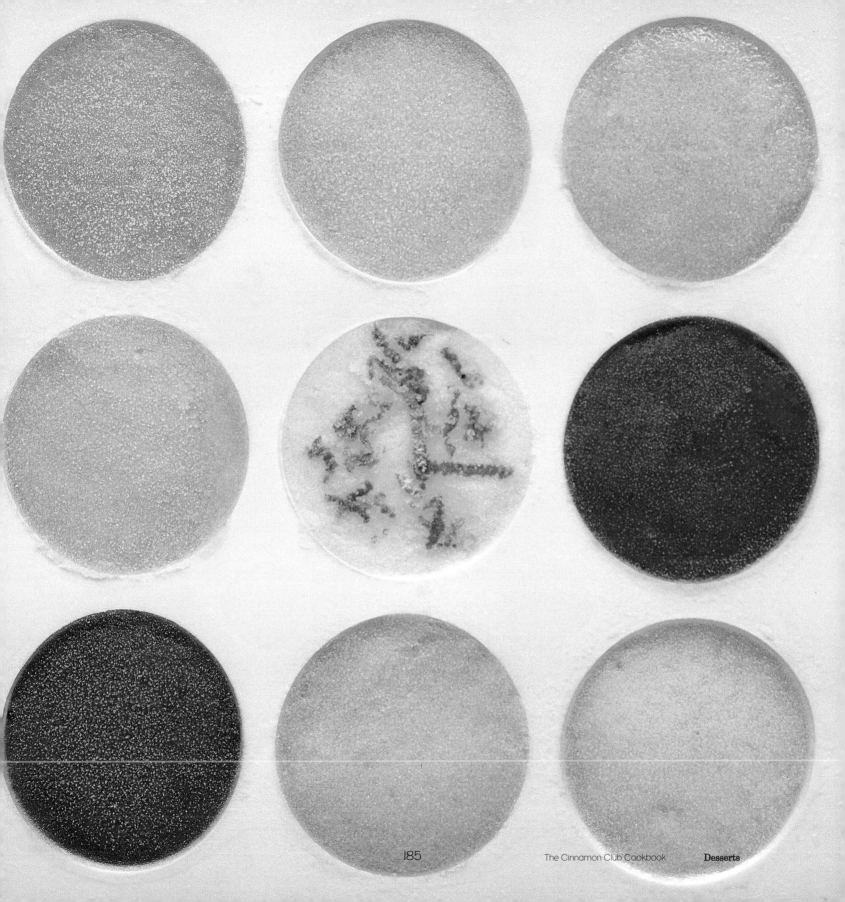

BREAKFASTS

Kedgeree with Poached Eggs and Smoked Haddock
Bombay Scrambled Eggs with Layered Bread
Haleem
Sambhar (South Indian Lentil Broth)
Dal poori
Potato-stuffed Parathas
Bombay Spiced Vegetables with Cumin Pao
Ham and Egg Dosas
Dosas with Spiced Vegetables
Dosas with Spiced Shrimps
Idli (South Indian Steamed Rice Dumplings with Smoked Salmon)
Uttapam (Rice Flour Pizzas)

KEDGEREE WITH SMOKED HADDOCK

This classic Raj dish is derived from the popular kichri *– rice and lentils cooked with ginger and onions. The British adapted the dish by adding eggs and smoked fish. It then made its way back to Britain as a breakfast dish, championed by, amongst others, Queen Victoria.*

Put half the smoked haddock in a pan, add enough milk to cover and bring slowly to the boil. Remove from the heat and set aside.

Heat the oil and butter in a pan, add the onion and sauté until golden brown. Add the ginger and turmeric and cook for 1 minute, then add the fish stock or water. Toss in the boiled rice, then fold in the salt and chopped egg whites. Flake the cooked haddock, removing any skin and bones, and add it to the pan with the coriander. Remove from the heat and keep warm.

Cut the remaining smoked haddock into 4 portions and heat it under a grill (or in a frying pan with a very little oil) for 2–3 minutes.

Meanwhile, for the poached eggs, pour the water into a shallow pan, add the vinegar and salt and bring to a gentle simmer. Carefully break in the eggs and poach until the whites coagulate and a thin film is formed over the yolk. You must take care that the water does not boil or the eggs will be ruined. Lift the eggs out with a slotted spoon and drain on kitchen paper.

To serve, put the rice in a bowl, the haddock on top and the poached eggs on top of that.

200g/7oz smoked haddock
a little milk
1 tablespoon vegetable or corn oil
25g/1oz butter
1 onion, chopped
4cm/1½ inch piece of fresh ginger, finely chopped
1 teaspoon ground turmeric
2 tablespoons hot fish stock or water
175g/6oz/1 scant cup basmati rice, cooked
1 teaspoon salt
whites from 2 hard-boiled eggs, chopped
1 tablespoon chopped fresh coriander

For the poached eggs:
1 litre/1¾ pints/4 cups water
2 tablespoons white vinegar
1 teaspoon salt
4 eggs

BOMBAY SCRAMBLED EGGS WITH LAYERED BREAD

SERVES 4

This Parsee dish is known in India as akuri and is the most popular breakfast dish we serve at The Cinnamon Club.

Heat the oil in a large pan, add the cumin seeds and let them crackle. Add the onion and sauté over a medium heat, stirring constantly, until golden brown. Now add the ginger and green chillies and stir for a minute. Add the salt, turmeric and red chilli powder and stir quickly to prevent the spices burning. In less than a minute, add the tomato and stir for a minute or two.

Add the beaten eggs and cook over a low heat, stirring constantly with a whisk or a wooden spatula, until the eggs are softly scrambled. Stir in the chopped coriander and serve on top of the parathas.

4 tablespoons vegetable or corn oil
½ teaspoon cumin seeds
I onion, finely chopped
I tablespoon finely chopped
    fresh ginger
2 green chillies, finely chopped
2 teaspoons salt
I teaspoon ground turmeric
½ teaspoon red chilli powder
I tomato, deseeded and finely diced
12 eggs, lightly beaten
2 tablespoons finely chopped
    fresh coriander
4 Layered Parathas (see page 154)

HALEEM

SERVES 4

This ancient Muslim dish is a rich broth of lentils and spiced lamb. It's a hearty meal, popular during the month of Ramadan to break a fast, but in Muslim parts of India such as Hyderabad and Old Delhi, and throughout Pakistan and Bangladesh, it's sold in restaurants all year round. It makes a wonderful weekend brunch dish. If you are buying your lamb from a butcher, ask for the leg bone to be chopped up and given to you so that you can add it to the pot; the juices from the marrow greatly enrich the dish. If you have difficulty finding the lentils and wheat, you could just buy a country soup mix from supermarkets that contains a good blend of pulses.

Heat the ghee or clarified butter in a wide, heavy-based pan, add the whole spices and onions and sauté until golden. Add the ginger and garlic pastes and sauté quickly for 2–3 minutes, adding a little water if necessary to prevent sticking. Add the lamb and cook over a high heat for 15 minutes, until browned all over.

Add the soaked lentils and the wheat and let them cook in the meat juices for 10 minutes, then add the chilli powder, turmeric, salt and the ground cumin and cook over a low heat for 5 minutes. Add the boiling water and simmer gently for 15–20 minutes, stirring occasionally. If the broth gets too thick, add more water. It should be neither as thick as porridge nor as thin as a soup. Check the seasoning, add the garam masala, then sprinkle the mint on top. Serve with bread.

75g/3oz/⅓ cup ghee or clarified butter
3 green cardamom pods
6 cloves
2 bay leaves
4 cinnamon sticks
3 red onions, sliced
3 large onions, sliced
1 teaspoon Ginger Paste (see page 30)
1 teaspoon Garlic Paste (see page 30)
500g/1lb 2oz boned leg of lamb,
  cut into 1cm/1/2 inch cubes
50g/2oz/⅓ cup white urid lentils,
  soaked in cold water for 30 minutes,
  then drained
50g/2oz/⅓ cup chana dal (yellow split
  peas), soaked in cold water for 30
  minutes, then drained
100g/4oz/²/3 cup dahlia or
  bulgar wheat
1 teaspoon red chilli powder
1 teaspoon ground turmeric
1½ teaspoons salt
1 teaspoon cumin seeds, roasted
  and ground (see page 33)
500ml/18fl oz/2¼ cups boiling water
½ teaspoon garam masala
2 tablespoons chopped fresh mint

SAMBHAR (SOUTH INDIAN LENTIL BROTH)

SERVES 4

This broth makes a hot, slightly sour accompaniment to the otherwise dry and slightly bland dosa and idli based breakfast dishes. It has the consistency of a medium-thick soup and can be just as easily and successfully served on its own with simple, plain boiled rice.

150g/5oz/⅞ cup toor dal
½ teaspoon ground turmeric
2 teaspoons salt
1 tablespoon vegetable or corn oil
1 sprig of fresh curry leaves
1 red onion, sliced
10 small shallots, roughly chopped
50g/2oz/¼ cup green beans, cut into
  2.5cm/1 inch lengths
2 carrots, cut into 2.5cm/1 inch chunks
2 baby aubergines, quartered
  (otherwise use ordinary aubergines)
2 tablespoons Sambar Masala
  (see page 32)
3 tablespoons tamarind paste
½ teaspoon red chilli powder
1 teaspoon sugar

For tempering:
1 tablespoon vegetable or corn oil
1½ teaspoons mustard seeds
1 dried red chilli
¼ teaspoon asafoetida
1 sprig of fresh curry leaves

Wash the lentils in cold running water, then leave to soak for 15 minutes. Drain well and put them in a heavy-based pan with 600ml/1 pint/2½ cups of water. Bring to the boil, skim off any scum from the surface, then add the turmeric and half the salt and simmer for 30 minutes.

Meanwhile, heat the oil in a separate pan, add the curry leaves and onion and sauté until the onion is soft. Add the shallots, green beans, carrots and aubergines and sauté for 5 minutes. Now add the Sambar Masala, tamarind and chilli powder and cook for another 5 minutes. Add this mixture to the simmering lentils and stir well, adding a little water if the mixture is too thick. Simmer until the vegetables are soft, then add the sugar and the remaining salt.

To temper the mixture, heat the oil in a small pan and add the mustard seeds. When they crackle, add the dried chilli, asafoetida and curry leaves, give them a stir and pour the mixture over the broth. Mix well and then serve.

DAL POORI (FRIED PUFFED BREAD WITH SPICY LENTIL FILLING)

MAKES 12

This is a great brunch dish and a pretty good hangover cure, too – the golden filling has a nice little kick to it. Dal poori is often sold as a street snack in India and can also be found made with a spiced potato filling, such as the one used for the stuffed parathas on page 194.

For the filling, put the drained lentils in a pan with 600ml/1 pint of water and simmer for 20 minutes or until they are just tender and the water has evaporated. Put the lentils in a food processor with the green chillies and ginger, blend to a paste and set aside. Heat the oil in a frying pan and add the cumin seeds. As they crackle, add the asafoetida, if using, stir-fry quickly for a minute or two, then add the chilli powder and turmeric and sauté for another minute. Add the lentil paste and cook, stirring constantly, until the moisture has evaporated and the mixture is very thick. Stir in the salt and sugar, then check the seasoning and adjust if necessary. Remove from the heat and leave to cool.

To make the dough, put all the ingredients in a bowl and mix to a smooth, stiff dough. Cover with a damp cloth and set aside for 20 minutes. Divide the dough into 12 portions, then divide the lentil mixture into 12 as well. Flatten each ball of dough slightly with the palm of your hand and push your thumb into the centre to make an indentation. Place the filling in the hole and then pull up the dough all round it so the filling is completely enclosed. Be sure to seal the edges, and make sure there aren't any cracks, or the stuffing will come out while rolling the poori.

On a lightly floured surface, roll out each poori into a circle about 10cm/ 4 inches in diameter, turning it over occasionally and making sure the filling doesn't become exposed.

Heat some oil in a deep-fat fryer or a deep saucepan and fry the poori one at a time for about 2 minutes, turning once, until golden. Drain on kitchen paper and serve immediately, with pickles or Green Coconut Chutney (see page 161).

100g/4oz/ $2/3$ cup white urad lentils, soaked in cold water for 20 minutes, then drained
2 green chillies, chopped
2.5cm/1 inch piece of fresh ginger, chopped
1 tablespoon vegetable or corn oil
½ teaspoon cumin seeds
a pinch of asafoetida (optional)
½ teaspoon red chilli powder
1 teaspoon ground turmeric
1½ teaspoons salt
1 teaspoon sugar
oil for deep-frying

For the dough:
300g/11oz/2¾ cups plain flour
½ teaspoon black onion seeds
1 teaspoon salt
1 teaspoon sugar
2 tablespoons ghee or clarified butter
125ml/4fl oz/1 cup water

POTATO-STUFFED PARATHAS

MAKES 8

One of the most popular Punjabi breakfast dishes. Dip the bread into spicy pickle and yoghurt if you are feeling adventurous.

Put the flour and salt in a bowl. Add the oil and water and knead until it comes together into a stiff dough. Cover with a damp cloth and leave to rest for 20 minutes. Meanwhile, for the filling, put the boiled potatoes into a bowl and roughly mash in all the remaining ingredients.

Divide the dough into 8 pieces and shape them into balls. Do the same with the stuffing. Take a ball of dough, make an indentation in the centre, and keep pressing and rotating the dough in your hand until the cavity is a little larger than the ball of stuffing. The edges of the cavity should be slightly thinner than the rest of it. Place the ball of stuffing in the cavity and bring together the edges of the dough so the stuffing is completely covered. Make sure there aren't any cracks or the stuffing will come out while rolling the paratha. Lightly dust with flour, gently flatten the dough

with your hands, then roll out into a 20cm/8 inch round, turning it over occasionally and making sure that the filling doesn't become exposed. Repeat with the remaining dough balls and filling.

Heat a heavy-based frying pan, preferably cast iron, over a low to medium heat and put a paratha in it. Cook for about 2–3 minutes, until it just starts to colour underneath, then turn it over and cook the other side. Brush the top with a little of the ghee or butter, turn it over and cook until the colour has deepened. Brush the top again, turn over and repeat. Place on a foil-lined plate and cook the remaining parathas in the same way. Keep the pile of parathas warm by wrapping them loosely in foil.

Serve with pickles and with Greek yoghurt that has been lightly salted and thinned with a little water.

500g/1lb 2oz/4½ cups chapati flour
1 teaspoon salt
2 teaspoons vegetable oil
250ml/8fl oz/1 cup water
3 tablespoons ghee or clarified butter

For the potato filling:
250g/9oz Desiree potatoes, boiled
 until tender, then peeled
3 green chillies, finely chopped
1cm/½ inch piece of fresh ginger,
 finely chopped
50g/2oz/1 cup fresh coriander,
 finely chopped
1 onion, finely chopped
1½ teaspoons dried pomegranate
 seeds, crushed (optional)
1 teaspoon red chilli powder
1 teaspoon salt

BOMBAY SPICED VEGETABLES WITH CUMIN PAO

SERVES 4

Pao bhaji *is common throughout much of India and is often enjoyed as a breakfast dish. A pao is like a fluffy bun and is used to scoop up a tangy purée of vegetables. In Bombay, where the dish originates, you can see it being made by street vendors on huge griddles.*

First make the cumin pao. Put the yeast and sugar in a small bowl, add the water and milk and mix until the yeast has dissolved. Set aside in a warm place for 15 minutes, until frothy. Add half the beaten egg to the mixture and whisk well.

Sift the flour and salt into a bowl and add the cumin seeds. Pour in the yeast mixture and mix to a smooth dough. Finally, mix in the melted butter. Cover the bowl with clingfilm or a damp cloth and leave the dough in a warm place for 30 minutes or until doubled in size.

Knock back the dough and divide it into 8 balls. Arrange them on a well-greased baking tray about 2cm/³⁄4 inch deep, placing them 1cm/¹⁄2 inch apart. Press the balls lightly so that they just touch each other, then cover with clingfilm or a damp cloth and leave in a warm place for 30 minutes, until they have doubled in volume. Brush with the remaining egg and sprinkle some cumin seeds on top. Bake in an oven preheated to 180°C/350°F/Gas Mark 4 for 25 minutes, until golden brown. Remove from the oven and brush with a little oil.

For the spiced vegetables, heat the ghee or butter in a large frying pan or on a flat griddle, add the cumin seeds and garlic and allow them to crackle. As the garlic starts to change colour, add the onion and sauté until golden. Add the carrot and sweat for a couple of minutes, then add the cauliflower and do the same, stirring constantly. Now add the green pepper and cook for 2 minutes. Add the green beans and cook for 1 minute, then stir in the cumin and chilli powder and sauté for a minute longer. Next add the puréed tomatoes and cook for about 10 minutes or until they have reduced to a coating consistency. Quickly stir in the masala and add the grated boiled potato – just enough to bind the vegetables together and give a smooth mixture.

Finally add the chopped ginger and green chilli, sprinkle in the fresh coriander and finish with the butter and lemon juice. Serve hot, with the cumin pao.

I tablespoon ghee or clarified butter
I teaspoon cumin seeds
I teaspoon finely chopped garlic
¹⁄2 onion, finely chopped
I small carrot, cut into 5mm/¹⁄4 inch dice
100g/4oz/1¹⁄2 cups cauliflower florets, finely chopped
¹⁄2 green pepper, cut into 5mm/¹⁄4 inch dice
50g/2oz/¹⁄4 cup fine green beans, cut into 5mm/¹⁄4 inch dice
¹⁄2 teaspoon ground cumin
I teaspoon red chilli powder
3 large, ripe tomatoes, puréed in a blender
I teaspoon Pao Bhaji Masala (see page 32)
about 50g/2oz/¹⁄4 cup boiled potato, grated
¹⁄2 teaspoon finely chopped fresh ginger
I green chilli, finely chopped
I tablespoon chopped fresh coriander
15g/¹⁄2oz/I tablespoon butter
juice of ¹⁄2 lemon

For the cumin pao:
10g/¹⁄4oz/I tablespoon fresh yeast
1¹⁄2 tablespoons caster sugar
100ml/3¹⁄2fl oz/scant ¹⁄2 cup water
2 tablespoons milk
I egg, lightly beaten
250g/9oz/2¹⁄4 cups plain flour
I teaspoon salt
I teaspoon cumin seeds, plus a few extra to garnish
15g/¹⁄2oz/I tablespoon butter, melted
oil for brushing

IDLIS (SOUTH INDIAN STEAMED RICE DUMPLINGS) WITH SMOKED SALMON

SERVES 4

Like the dosa, the idli has travelled from its native southern India across the rest of the country as a wholesome snack, often served for breakfast. The rice flour mix is usually placed in a special idli steamer but you can use an egg poacher to exactly the same effect. They are traditionally steamed plain and then have a sambhar lentil mix poured over them, but at The Cinnamon Club we like to serve them with smoked salmon and coconut chutney. The traditional preparation for the rice flour mix is cumbersome and very time consuming so unless you are feeling particularly adventurous you would be better off simply picking up a packet of idli mix, which is readily available in most Asian grocery shops.

100g/4oz/⅓ cup idli mix
150ml/¼ pint/⅔ cup warm water
1 teaspoon vegetable oil, plus a little
    for brushing
4 tablespoons Green Coconut Chutney
    (see page 161)
4 slices of smoked salmon

Put the idli mix in a bowl and gradually mix in the water and oil to make a smooth batter. Leave to rest for 10 minutes.

Bring some water to a simmer in an egg poacher and lightly brush the cups with a touch of oil. Pour the batter into the cups until they are two-thirds full and cover. Steam over a medium heat for 15 minutes, until the dumplings are firm to the touch and the texture is almost spongy.

Turn out the idli, spread the chutney over them and top with a slice of smoked salmon.

DOSAS WITH SPICED VEGETABLES

SERVES 4

A classic southern Indian dish eaten at any time of day. You can have pretty much whatever you like inside.

For the spiced vegetables, heat the oil in a pan and add the mustard seeds. When they crackle, add the dried chillies and chana dal. Let the dal turn golden, then add the curry leaves and cook until they begin to wilt. Add the onions and sauté until soft. Raise the heat, add the carrots, French beans and peas and stir-fry for 3 minutes. Add the turmeric, green chillies and ginger and sauté for another minute. Finally, add the salt and grated potatoes and mix well.

Make up the dosa mix according to the instructions on the packet. Spread a little oil over a large, heavy-based frying pan or a flat griddle and place over a medium heat. Pour a quarter of the batter into the centre of the pan and, using the back of a ladle, spread it out quickly with an outward circular motion to form a pancake about 20cm/8 inches in diameter. Cook until crisp and golden underneath, then slide it on to a plate and spoon some of the spiced vegetable mixture into the centre. Either roll it up or fold it into a triangular parcel. Make the remaining dosas in the same way, then serve with the Sambar and Green Coconut Chutney.

200g/7oz packet of dosa mix (available from Asian shops)
a little oil
Sambar (see page 32) and Green Coconut Chutney (see page 161), to serve

For the spiced vegetables:
2 tablespoons vegetable or corn oil
½ teaspoon mustard seeds
2 dried red chillies, broken in half
½ teaspoon chana dal (split yellow chickpeas)
2 sprigs of fresh curry leaves
2 red onions, chopped
50g/2oz/¼ cup carrots, finely diced
50g/2oz/¼ cup French beans, finely diced
50g/2oz/scant ½ cup peas
½ teaspoon ground turmeric
2 green chillies, chopped
1cm/½ inch piece of fresh ginger
1¼ teaspoons salt
250g/9oz floury potatoes such as Desiree, boiled until tender, then peeled and grated

Variation:

DOSAS WITH SPICED SHRIMPS

Make the dosas as above but substitute the following filling:

2 tablespoons vegetable or corn oil
¼ teaspoon mustard seeds
¼ teaspoon cumin seeds
1 sprig of fresh curry leaves
1 large onion, chopped
200g/7oz/1¼ cups shrimps, chopped
1 teaspoon red chilli powder
¼ teaspoon ground turmeric
2.5cm/1 inch piece of fresh ginger, finely chopped
3 green chillies, finely chopped
1 teaspoon salt
1 medium-sized Desiree potato, boiled until tender, then peeled and grated (optional)

Heat the oil in a pan, add the mustard seeds and let them crackle. Then add the cumin seeds, curry leaves and onion and sauté until golden. Add the shrimps and toss, adding the chilli powder, turmeric, ginger, green chillies and salt. Cook for 2–3 minutes – no longer, or the texture of the shrimps will be spoiled. If there is any moisture in the pan, mix in the grated boiled potato and toss until dry.

HAM AND EGG DOSAS

SERVES 4

In this recipe we have combined the basic Western ham and egg breakfast with the southern Indian dosa ingredientss.

200g/7oz packet of dosa mix
    (available from Asian shops)
a little vegetable or corn oil
8 slices of honey-roast ham
4 eggs
Green Coconut Chutney (see page 161)
    and Sambhar (see page 192), to serve

Make up the dosa mix according to the instructions on the packet. Spread a little oil over a large, heavy-based frying pan or a flat griddle and place over a medium heat. Pour a quarter of the batter into the centre of the pan and, using the back of a ladle, spread it out quickly with an outward circular motion to form a pancake about 20cm/8 inches in diameter. Dot the edges of the pancake with a little oil and then break an egg on top of it and leave until the egg sets. Meanwhile, warm 2 slices of ham under a grill for 2–3 minutes. Top the egg with the grilled ham and neatly fold the pancake over from 3 sides to cover the ham and egg and form a triangle.

Lift the pancake out of the pan with a spatula. Repeat with the remaining batter to make 4 dosas altogether. Serve with the Green Coconut Chutney and Sambhar.

UTTAPAM (RICE FLOUR PIZZAS)

SERVES 4

It was the southern Indians who first popularised this simple dish. As with pizza, half the fun is to be had with experimenting with your own toppings.

200g/7oz packet of dosa mix (available from Asian shops)
a little vegetable or corn oil
½ red onion, finely chopped
⅓ red pepper, finely diced
⅓ yellow pepper, finely diced
I tomato, skinned, deseeded and finely diced
2 tablespoons finely chopped fresh coriander
Green Coconut Chutney (see page I6I) and Sambhar (see page I92), to serve

Make up the dosa mix according to the instructions on the packet. Spread a little oil over a large, heavy-based frying pan or a flat griddle and place over a medium heat. Pour about 2–3 tablespoons of the batter into the centre of the pan and, using the back of a ladle, spread it out quickly with an outward circular motion to form a pancake about 10cm/4 inches in diameter.

Dot the edges of the pancake with a little oil and sprinkle with some of the chopped vegetables and coriander to form a colourful topping. Cook over a low heat for about 4 minutes, until golden underneath. Turn over and cook the other side for another 3–4 minutes. Repeat with the remaining batter to make 8 pancakes altogether. Serve with the Green Coconut Chutney and Sambhar.

COCKTAILS

CINNAMON BELLINI,
ROSE PETAL BELLINI,
LYCHEE BELLINI,
MANGO VANILLA LASSI,
KIWI RASPBERRY LASSI,
PEACH APPLE LASSI,
LASSI CAIPIRHINA,
STRAWBERRY,
RASPBERRY &
ORANGE LASSI,
INDOBRIT, SUTRA,
MELON GUSSA.
MANGO MARTINI,
BOLLYWOOD MARTINI,
CINNAMON CLUB
MARTINI

CINNAMON BELLINI

15ml cinnamon tea (made with cinnamon
    tea bags, then allowed to cool)
5ml cinnamon syrup (available from
    good off-licences)
10ml Goldschlager (available from
    most good superstores)
10ml apple juice
Prosecco or Champagne

Put some ice in a cocktail shaker and
add the cinnamon tea, cinnamon
syrup, Goldschlager and apple juice.
Shake vigorously, then strain into a
Champagne flute. Top up with
Prosecco or Champagne.

ROSE PETAL BELLINI

15ml rose syrup (available from
    Indian shops)
5ml Goldschlager
15ml lychee purée (if you can't find this,
    use lychee juice)
Prosecco or Champagne
rose petals
rose water

Put some ice in a cocktail shaker and add
the rose syrup, Goldschlager and lychee
purée. Shake vigorously, then strain into
a Champagne flute. Top up with Prosecco
or Champagne. Garnish with rose petal
and a few drops of rose water.

LYCHEE BELLINI

20ml lychee purée or juice
10ml lychee liquor
5ml apricot brandy
10ml pineapple juice
Prosecco or Champagne
a peeled fresh lychee

Put some ice in a cocktail shaker and
add the lychee purée, lychee liquor,
apricot brandy and pineapple juice.
Shake vigorously, then strain into a
Champagne flute. Top up with Prosecco
or Champagne. To finish, carefully drop
the peeled lychee into the flute.

LASSI COCKTAILS

SERVES 1

Lassi is a traditional yoghurt-based drink common to much of India. It's a refreshing drink that many enjoy as a meal accompaniment. At the Cinnamon Club we devised some cocktails that are based on lassi but frothed to make the consistency lighter and through which we layer vodka and fruit. It makes for a stunning-looking drink with a superb combination of flavours.

MANGO VANILLA LASSI	KIWI RASPBERRY LASSI	PEACH APPLE LASSI

MANGO VANILLA LASSI

Layer one (mango)
35ml Absolut mandarin vodka
20ml mango purée, plus a slice of
  mango to garnish
10ml mango syrup
30ml apple juice

Layer two (vanilla lassi)
35ml Stolichnaya vanilla vodka
50ml very low fat stirred yoghurt
15ml vanilla syrup
10ml gomme syrup
4 ice cubes

Put some ice in a cocktail shaker and add all the ingredients for the mango layer. Shake vigorously, then strain into a tall glass, half filled with ice.

Put all the ingredients for layer two in a blender and blend thoroughly, until the lassi takes on a creamy consistency. Slowly pour the lassi on to the mango base, creating 2 layers. Garnish with a slice of mango.

KIWI RASPBERRY LASSI

Layer one (raspberry)
35ml Stolichnaya raspberry vodka
25ml raspberry purée (if you can't find
  any, just blitz a punnet of fresh raspberries in a blender)
50ml cranberry juice

Layer two (kiwi lassi)
35ml Absolut citron vodka
50ml very low fat yoghurt
½ kiwi fruit, peeled and diced, plus a
  slice of kiwi to garnish
15ml gomme syrup
4 ice cubes

Put some ice in a cocktail shaker and add all the ingredients for the raspberry layer. Shake vigorously, then strain into a tall glass, half filled with ice.

Put all the ingredients for layer two in a blender and blend thoroughly, until the lassi takes on a creamy consistency. Slowly pour the lassi on to the raspberry base, creating 2 layers. Garnish with a slice of kiwi fruit.

PEACH APPLE LASSI

Layer one (peach)
35ml Archer's Peach Schnapps
25ml peach purée (if you can't find this,
  simply blitz a peeled, stoned ripe
  peach in a blender)
50ml cranberry juice

Layer 2 (apple lassi)
35ml Pomme Vert liquor
50ml very low fat stirred yoghurt
15ml Gomme syrup
20ml apple juice

Put some ice in a cocktail shaker and add all the ingredients for the peach layer. Shake vigorously, then strain into a tall glass, half filled with ice.

Put all the ingredients for layer two in a blender and blend thoroughly, until the lassi takes on a creamy consistency. Slowly pour the lassi on to the peach base, creating 2 layers. Garnish with a slice of peach or apple.

With this cocktail the base always remains the same. We have used a classic Brazilian drink called a Caipirhina for this drink and added an Indian twist with a fruit lassi layer.

LASSI CAIPIRHINA

4 brown sugar cubes
1 lime, cut into 6 wedges
40ml Cachaca
   (Brazilian cane sugar rum)
10ml dark rum
crushed ice

Place the sugar cubes in an old-fashioned glass. Squeeze the juice of the lime segments over the sugar cubes and add 3 of the segments to the glass. Using a long pestle, grind the sugar cubes and lime segments until the sugar has dissolved. Add the Cachaca and dark rum. Fill the glass full with crushed ice and stir carefully (do not over stir, or the ice will melt).

The next stage of the drink is the lassi layer. Below are recipes for three different flavours.

STRAWBERRY LASSI

Place all the ingredients in a blender and whiz until the ice and fruit are liquidised. Slowly pour the lassi on to the Caipirhina base to form 2 layers. Garnish with a strawberry and 2 straws.

50ml low-fat stirred yoghurt
4 strawberries, plus 1 to garnish
10ml crème de fraise
15ml gomme syrup
5 ice cubes

ORANGE LASSI

Prepare in the same way as the strawberry lassi.

50ml low-fat stirred yoghurt
10ml Absolut mandarin vodka
10ml fresh orange juice
15ml gomme syrup
6 ice cubes
a slice of orange, to garnish

RASPBERRY LASSI

Prepare in the same way as the strawberry lassi.

50ml low-fat stirred yoghurt
9 raspberries, plus 1 to garnish
10ml Stolichnaya raspberry vodka
15ml gomme syrup
5 ice cubes

INDOBRIT

Put some crushed ice in a cocktail shaker, add the raspberries, rose syrup, elderflower cordial, Bacardi limon, pear cognac and cranberry juice. Shake vigorously, then pour into a long glass. Top up with soda water and garnish with rose petals.

SERVES 1

10 fresh raspberries (crush the
    raspberries to a purée)
10ml rose syrup
40ml Bacardi limon
20ml Xante pear cognac
25ml cranberry juice
soda water
a few rose petals, to garnish

SUTRA

Put 6 white seedless grapes and 6 black seedless grapes into a mixing glass. Using a pestle crush the grapes to extract their juice. Now add the vodka, Chambord, syrup and lime juice. Shake the ingredients with ice, then strain into a tall glass filled with ice. Top the drink up with soda water and garnish with 3 grapes.

SERVES 1

6 white seedless grapes
6 black seedless grapes
50ml Absolut vodka
15ml Chambord
10ml gomme syrup
5ml lime juice
soda water
3 grapes, to garnish

MELON CUSSA

Put the gin, citron, Midori, melon purée, lime juice and syrup into a cocktail shaker and add some ice. Shake vigorously, then strain into a tall glass with ice. Top up with apple juice and garnish with a small slice of melon.

SERVES 1

25ml Plymouth gin
25ml Absolut citron
15ml Midori
30ml fresh melon purée (made by
    puréeing some ripe honeydew
    melon in a blender)
10ml lime juice
10ml gomme syrup
apple juice
a small slice of melon, to garnish

CINNAMON CLUB MARTINI

SERVES 1

Put the vodka, Thandi and mint leaves into a cocktail shaker. Using a long pestle, slowly crush the mint leaves to release their flavour, then add the cream. Add some ice to the shaker and shake vigorously. Strain into a chilled martini glass. To finish the drink, slowly pour khalua into the martini glass using the incline as your guide. This should give the drink 2 layers. Sprinkle some cocoa powder on top and serve with a short straw. Stir before drinking, so the flavours mingle.

30ml Absolut vodka
5ml Thandi (available from most good Indian food stores)
4 fresh mint leaves
20ml single cream
kahlua
cocoa powder

BOLLYWOOD MARTINI

SERVES 1

Put all the ingredients in a cocktail shaker filled with ice. Shake well, then strain into a chilled martini glass. You can leave this drink ungarnished but it does look attractive with a slice of starfruit.

35ml Stolichnaya vanilla vodka
10ml cherry brandy
5ml coconut syrup
15ml fresh raspberry purée
20ml cranberry juice

MANGO MARTINI

SERVES 1

If you can't find mango purée it is very easy to make your own. Peel a ripe mango and slice away the flesh, being careful not to cut too close to the stone to avoid getting fibres in the purée. Place the flesh in a blender and blitz to a purée.

Put all the ingredients in a cocktail shaker filled with ice. Shake well, then strain into a chilled martini glass and garnish with a slice of mango.

40ml Absolut mandarin vodka
25ml fresh mango purée, plus a slice of mango to garnish
15ml mango purée
20ml apple juice

MATCHING WINE WITH SPICE

At The Cinnamon Club we have produced an extensive wine list designed to balance and enhance the flavours of our dishes. We have done this by breaking down the wines into different categories that are both recognisable in themselves, and yet also fit with certain spice blends. There is, of course, no definitive answer, no universally accepted solution as to which wine best suits which dish as so much rests on a particular individual's palate and preference. In the restaurant we are happy to offer our own recommendations based on our research whilst still acknowledging that half the fun is to be had through personal experimentation.

The main element of wine is, of course, the grape. To list all of them would be a lengthy and dull process, but in general certain grape varieties are known to produce certain styles in specific parts of the world where particular and appropriate climatic and soil conditions are present. What follows is a guide to matching specific styles of wines with the range of spices found in Indian cooking so that both the wine and the food can be allowed to perform to their best.

Laurent Chaniac
Cinnamon Club wine buyer

FRESH AND DRY WHITES

This particular style lays emphasis on the acidity of the wine. The overall impression should be one of great freshness with a clean fruit finish.

This is a style that is ideal for the early part of a lunch or dinner but remember that too much acidity during the evening might keep you awake through the night. One of the qualities of this style of wine is that it acts as a very good palate cleaner.

Soils play a major factor in producing the fresh and dry style of wine, in particular volcanic, chalk, clay, limestone and sand stone. The altitude of the vineyards is also a key factor; the higher they are, the longer the ripening period. And as at every 100 meters above sea level the temperature tends to fall by about 1 degree celsius so the extra time needed to ripen the grapes results in a higher acidity.

Look out for wines made from the Semillon grape from Bergerac sec AOC in the south west of France and from the lower part of the Hunter Valley in Australia. In the north east of Italy in the Veneto region, the Soave produced by Anselmi, Pieropan and Stefano Inama are excellent. But beware of the mass-produced wines of the Veneto – they can be so clean and pure, almost sterile, that they seem to lack any fruit at all. The wines from the Trentino – Alto Aldige produce some very fresh wines whilst in the Alsace region the choice should be Riesling from vineyards situated on the limestone hills.

In Germany, wines from the microclimate of Pfalz are spicy and powerful. German wines in the 18th and 19th centuries were famous and expensive all around Europe; they then went out of fashion, though now they are beginning to be rediscovered.

Match a fresh and dry wine with a spice mix that contains acidic or sweet characteristics. The first match can be described as a marriage in harmony and the second a marriage in contrast.

When citrus is predominant in a dish and is paired with a fresh and dry white wine, the two acids balance each other on the palate and there is a neutralising effect that encourages the wine and the dish to harmonise. If the dish has a sweet flavour, the freshness of the wine cuts through it and if there are traces of heat from chilli, the spices will lift the fruity elements of the wine and those flavours will then persist on the palate.

FRAGRANT WHITES

One of the most expressive styles of wine; the fruits tend to be very upfront on the nose and palate and the acidity in contrast moderate and never sharp. The intensity of the fruits in these wines can be related best to perfume, while the soft acidity and little residual sugar in them, up to 6 to 8 grammes per litre, make for a very elegant style of wine.

Grapes to look out for include Riesling, Tokay Pinot Gris, Chenin Blanc Sec and Sauvignon Blancs from certain regions. Conditions that allow for the slow ripening of the grape with moderate temperatures in the vineyards is important. Temperatures that are too high would hinder the winemaker achieving the correct amount of acidity to balance the wine. Regions where these grapes do best are Germany, Alsace, Australia Clare Valley, and Tasmania for the Riesling; Alsace, Austria, Luxembourg for the Tokay Pinot Gris; South Africa and Loire Valley in France for the Chenin Blanc.

The heat in Indian cuisine is generated by peppercorn, chilli, clove and cardamom. If these spices are dominant in a spice mix they work very well with wines such as these that are fragrant with just a little residual sugar. The heat from the spice mix tends to be neutralised by the acidity in the wine and as a consequence the fruit of the wine has all the space it needs to show on the palate.

SOFT, SUBTLE AND AROMATIC WHITES

The dominant element in these wines is one of a gentle ripe fruit balanced with very soft acidity, achieved by a particular fermentation process called "malolactic" which transforms one acid into another by softening the acidity.

The most suitable vineyards are those located in plains where soils are rich and water reasonably abundant. In order for the grapes to mature with the right sugar content to produce a generous wine it is important that the vines should not have to suffer to get nutrients and water.

These vineyards tend to be located in countries and regions where the climate is warm during the ripening season of the grape. In Europe they can be found in the central and north plains of Italy, in Spain, in the south of France in the Languedoc Roussillon and the south of the Rhone Valley and in the USA and Australia.

The grapes that best produce the elegant style without too much ripeness are the Pinot Gris from north and central Italy and the Roussane and Marsanne blends from the Southern Rhone.

FRUITY WHITES

Richness, ripeness and power are the main words to illustrate this style of wine. Low in acidity, they produce intense fruit on the palate. The maturing of the grapes takes place in locations with higher than average temperatures and it is the wine maker's task to produce a balanced wine from these imbalanced conditions.

Look out for wines from California and from the states of South Australia, Queensland and Western Australia as well as the Languedoc Roussillon region in southern France.

The grapes usually used are the Chardonnay, Roussane, Marsanne, Viognier and Pinot Blanc. Sometimes the wines can be partially fermented in oak barrels but the process has to be controlled very carefully as there is a tendency to produce overly powerful wines with little complexity or subtlety.

Intense and fruity wine should be matched with dishes that are hot. The fruit of the wine should be intense enough to be able to cope with the heat. Avoid barrel fermented white wines as they tend not to work with hot spices – the combination can result in a bitter after taste with the oak all too often overpowering the fruit elements.

JUICY REDS

These are red wines which put an emphasis on fruit combined with freshness – any traces of acidity in the wines should be regarded as a fault. The fruit can be intense but not ripe and more importantly supported by minerals taken from the soil.

The type of soil plays a key role here; with the best being well drained, where the root of the vine struggles to find water. As the roots have to grow deeper than usual to find the nutrients in these conditions they struggle down deep to bring up the mineral element into the fruit. Soils that are stony, sandy or made of decomposed granite or limestone with iron have properties that do not allow the water to remain stagnant on the topsoil. If some of these soil conditions are combined with long summers and cool winters, the freshness of the wine will be present and the intensity of the fruit determined by the yield production and the grape type. Shiraz, Shiraz blended with Cabernet Sauvignon, and Pinot Noir produce distinguished wines in these conditions which are best found in the Alsace and Rhone Valley region in France, in Coonawarra and Tasmania in Australia and in New Zealand.

The finesse of these wines demand gentle spicing. Chillies can be present in the spice mix only as long as they are used as a seasoning and not as a dominant spice. The presence of onion, carom seeds and turmeric will play a very interesting trick on the character of the wine: carom and turmeric are traditionally used in medicine to fight acidity problems in the stomach and so when matched with this style of red wine, a softening of the freshness on the palate takes places whilst the fruit becomes much more opulent.

ELEGANT AND FIRM REDS

This is a style of wine characterised by an intensity of fruit supported by firm tannins and gentle freshness. The fruit should be reasonably ripe in order to have sufficient freshness. Here the skill of the wine maker is absolutely crucial; the elements involved in achieving this style are difficult to balance and are best realised with a climate that has four clearly defined seasons.

Vineyards are generally located on soils poor in nutrients where the vines have to suffer to feed, thus bringing extra complexity to the wine. Wine fermentation plays a key role here; if the fermentation is encouraged quickly in high temperatures it will allow the wine to have more intense fruit but less complexity. Conversely, if the fermentation takes place in cooler conditions over a longer length of time the wine will tend to have more complexity.

This style of wine is very well represented in Western Europe but also in the New World where the vineyards are located in high altitudes or near cold seas thus tempering an otherwise too warm climate. Good examples can be found in Bordeaux where the Cabernet Sauvignon, Cabernet Franc and Merlot grapes are mainly used. Also in Burgundy with the Pinot Noir and in the northern Rhone valley where the wines are a blend of Syrah, Mourvedre, Carrignan and Grenache. In Northern Italy, the Tuscany region produces some excellent wines with the Rosso di Montalcino, the Sangiovese, the Cabernet Sauvignon and Merlot grapes leading the way. In the north east of Italy Rondinella and Corvina Veronese do very well. In Spain the Ribera Del Duero produces some excellent wines mainly based on Tempranillo. In Portugal the region of the Douro Valley

and the Alentejo stand out, where the grapes used are Touriga Nacional, Roriz and Cabernet Sauvignon.

In Australia the Coonawarra and MacLaren Vale regions produce wines from Shiraz, Cabernet Sauvignon and Merlot. In the USA the wines from the west coast by the Russian River and Carneros on the upper part produce very good Pinot Noir.

The best dishes to match with this style of wine can certainly have intense flavours though chilli must not be a dominant flavour and must only be used as seasoning. It is important that the tannins do not react to the heat from the spices as the flavours will simply become overbearing and would then destroy the fruit element of the wine. An ingredient like tamarind complements the flavours from the *terroir* while spices like onion seeds and ajowan are a good match as they also tend to soften the tannins making the wine more approachable.

WARM AND SPICY REDS

These are wines of great intensity. Their freshness depends on the skill of the winemaker and an early picking. The tannins tend to be integrated in the fruit element of the wine. The warm summer conditions help to produce wines that are rich, allowing the grapes to develop a spicy element. To develop this style of wine, the vines needs to grow on a fertile topsoil and the under layers tend to be calcareous or volcanic, sometimes with sand deposits to ensure good drainage.

The main grape varieties used are Cabernet Sauvignon, Merlot, Grenache, Shiraz, Mourverdre, Carignan, Tempranillo, Malbec, and Mataro and are found in South Australia, Northern California and Southern Rhone in France as well as in Argentina and Chile. Probably the best examples are to be found in Argentina where the Malbec give some fantastic results though the Shiraz, Mourvedre and Carignan in the southern Rhone can be equally stunning.

The extra ripeness found in these wines is often the direct result of water irrigation systems. Controlling the irrigation in wine making ensures that the sugar content in the grape can be controlled allowing the fermentation to produce a sufficient amount of alcohol: other than the grape variety, this is the main reason why wines from the new world can be so powerful in alcohol and rich in fruits and yet so low in acidity.

The richness of these wines means they can handle dishes that have very intense flavours. A delicate heat from chillies will match warm and spicy wines only if their tannins do not have a dry finish. Spices like ginger, turmeric, ajowan and fresh berries have natural acidity in their sequence of flavours and they play an important role in the spice mix balancing the heat from the chilli and spice from the cloves, reflecting on the wine positively.

BIG, RIPE AND BOLD REDS

This final style of wine expresses what strength, power and intensity are to wine. Their colour is normally very dark and their texture silky. On first impression, whether on the nose or palate, they come across as fruit driven. However their complexity is revealed with sequences of spices such as mint dark chocolate or cinnamon and vanilla. Their tannins tend to be very soft and lend support to the fruit. The alcohol can be very high, sometimes up to 14.5% due to very hot summer conditions which allow the grapes to produce a natural sugar content later to be transformed into alcohol.

The best example of these wines can be found in the new world and the southern part of Italy but generally speaking the new world sets the standard. Districts like the Barossa Valley and Coonawarra in Australia and the Napa, Dry Creek, Alexander and Sonoma Valleys in California are the ambassadors of this style. In the Barossa valley the king grape is the Shiraz followed by the Cabernet Sauvignon and Merlot. In the Coonawarra the Cabernet Sauvignon and Merlot are dominant. In California the best grapes to achieve this rich style are the Zinfandel, the Cabernet Sauvignon, Merlot and Cabernet Franc. In Europe in the district of Puglia located in the south east of Italy the vineyards literally cook under the baking sun and until recently were not condusive to producing fine wines - this has now changed with the recent introduction of less productive grape varieties and better irrigation systems so that grapes such the Primitivo, Negroamaro and Sangiovese can now produce wines of real quality.

Due to the fact that these wines are heavily concentrated with very soft and discreet tannins, they are ideal to match with hot dishes. Spices like fennel, cumin, cloves and chilli have some of the most persistent flavours in Indian cooking and they require some powerful red wines to match.

If you take a classic pickling spice mix composed of cumin, onion, fennel, carom, and mustard seeds, and then mix it with star anise and then combine it with a grape such as a Cabernet Franc from a very hot climate a wonderful alchemy will take place; the grape will tend to release aromas of eucalyptus and liquorice which then marry perfectly with the flavours from the pickling spice mix.

GLOSSARY

AJOWAN

Ajowan (also know as carom) is a close relative of dill, caraway and cumin. When chewed on its own, it has a bitingly hot and bitter taste, though when cooked with other ingredients, its taste mellows. Particularly good with fish and seafood dishes, root vegetables and green beans. Usually sold in most Asian stores in whole form. It's used quite sparingly in cooking so no need to buy too much.

ASAFOETIDA

Asafoetida is dried latex from several species of giant fennel. It has an unpleasant smell like pickled eggs due to the presence of sulphur compounds. On its own it tastes horrible. Used in several Indian savouries. Sold as powder or granules and can keep well for up to a year.

BANANA LEAVES

Often used to wrap fish/meat etc. before steaming. The stalk is removed and often sold in boxes in Asian or Thai shops.

BOTTLE GOURDS

Small hard skinned vegetables from the courgette family. The outer skin has a shiny surface, dark bottle green colour and a waxy surface, which is scraped before use. Its availability is quite restricted to northern India, though can be found in certain Indian stores.

CARDAMOM PODS
(GREEN AND BLACK)

The dried fruit of an herbaceous plant of the ginger family. The fruits are picked just before they ripen and dried in drying houses or in the sun. They are shaped like oval capsules containing hard dark brown seeds that are sticky and cling together. The best varieties are bright lime green colour, unblemished and unopened.

It is best to buy fresh whole pods with the freshness sealed in. It keeps well for up to 6 months if stored whole in a dry, clean, jar and kept in a dark place. Cardamom is versatile and is used both in sweets and savoury dishes.

CHANA DAL
(YELLOW SPLIT PEAS)

Gram, sometimes better known as Bengal gram, is the most commonly grown lentil in India. They are obtained from pods containing 2 or 3 lentils. They are dried, then husked and left whole, split or ground into flour. They are matt and yellow, similar to yellow lentils but are bigger, coarser, and stronger in taste with a nutty sweet aroma and flavour. Can be stored in airtight jars for up to 4 months.

Roasted chana dal are whole yellow lentils which have been dry roasted and which then puff up like popcorn, splitting open the dark brown husk. The husk is removed and the lentils are then spilt and sold separately as Roasted chana dal.

CHAPATTI FLOUR

Wholewheat flour used in bread making.

CHAT MASALA

A spice mix made with cumin, dried ginger, mint powder, pepper, asafoetida and salt, sprinkled on kebabs and used in various chaats to add zing to the dish.

CHILLI

Chillies are the fruits of the capsicum species and have distant relatives like tomatoes and eggplant. They are cultivated mostly in tropical and sub-tropical countries. There are various different varieties available and the fieriness and pungency is dependent on the variety in question.

For dried chillies the fruits are picked when ripe and then dried in great mounds in the sun or in huge driers.

When buying fresh chillies, look for crisp, unwrinkled ones that are waxy and green or red. Make sure they are bright and unbroken. As with most dried spices, powdered chilli loses its power and sparkle after a few months.

Whole dried chillies can be stored for up to a year in a dark place. Exposure to light spoils the colour.

At The Cinnamon Club we use a lot of Kashmiri chilli powder which is the brightest and most aromatic of all chilli powders, without pungency or heat. It can be used liberally to achieve a bright red colour in marinations and curries without making the dish unbearably hot. Yellow chilli powder is similar to turmeric in colour and the has pungency of a common chilli powder. We use it in recipes when we don't want to alter the colour of the dish.

COCONUT

Coconuts are large, brown hairy fruits with a hard woody shell and a creamy white kernel. To remove flesh from the shell, lightly tap the coconut from all sides with a heavy knife – alternatively heat the entire shell on a gentle flame on all sides so that when the coconut is broken the flesh falls away easily.

The water inside makes a refreshing drink. Fresh coconut flesh has a sweet nutty flavour and oily aroma. The texture is crisp and crunchy and used both in sweet and savoury dishes. The creamy kernel finds varied uses in cooking as a base for sauces, dressings, pastes, desserts etc.

Coconut is available fresh, flaked as milk or creamed. When buying fresh coconut shake it to establish that it has water. If there is no water, then probably the flesh is tough and dry. Fresh coconut can keep for up to a week, flesh can be grated and frozen for 3 months. Flaked or powdered coconut should not smell oily.

CORIANDER

The coriander plant bears whitish pink flowers, which mature into seeds. The leaves are fragile, the stem pale green and tender. The seeds, which constitute the spice, are round and have fine longitudinal ridges. The herb and spice are completely different from one another with regards to aroma and flavour. The leaves taste and smell fresh; the seeds on the other hand, have a sweet, heady aroma with a subtle whiff of pine and pepper. Suitable to almost every savoury Indian dish, coriander the spice and the herb is used daily in curries, chutneys, soups and drinks. Roasted ground coriander is an indispensable item in the spice box.

CUMIN SEEDS

Cultivated in western Asia where the main producing countries are India, Iran, Indonesia, China and the south Mediterranean.

The strong aroma is modified by frying and roasting. Cumin is used whole or ground in most vegetable preparation and for tempering and is a major constituent in the basic spice mixture.

Black or royal cumin seeds are dark brown, long and very thin, found in Central Asia and Northern India.

CURRY LEAVES

Curry leaves are native to India and Sri Lanka and thrive in tropical climate. The leaves are almond shaped with a strong curry like odour, tasting slightly bitter but pleasant and aromatic. Available fresh or dried in most Asian stores.

Curry leaves are an important ingredient in south Indian cooking, where they are used to flavour meats, fish, vegetables and breads. Also ground with coconut and spices to make chutneys. Curry leaves have limited use in north Indian cooking where they are used mainly to flavour or temper lentils.

DRIED MANGO POWDER

Known as Amchoor, am means mango and choor means powder, mango powder is made from raw sour green mangoes. The unripe fruits are peeled and cut into thin slices, and dried in the sun, which are then either powdered or used dried. The dried mango looks like fine slices of shrivelled wood, light brown in colour; the powder is camel coloured. Amchoor has a tangy and sour taste and is used as a souring agent in north Indian cooking for chutneys, soups, vegetables, marinades and pickles. Available only in Asian stores, the slices need to be used within 6 months – the powder will keep up to a year in an air tight container

FENNEL SEEDS

Fennel is the dried ripe fruit of a biennial or perennial herb known as saunf. They are dried for storage and turn to a dull greenish yellow. Fennel is native to the Mediterranean but also grows in other parts of the world.

A common and much loved spice in India, fennel adds richness to meat gravies, sweetness to desserts and special zest to vegetables. It is used powdered or whole. When dry-roasted it grinds more easily. It is also used in pickles and chutneys in north India. Available in any supermarkets either dried, fresh or on stalks.

FENUGREEK

Known as *methi*, fenugreek is grown around the Mediterranean, Argentina, France and India.

The spice consists of small, hard, yellow seeds. The whole plant has a pronounced, aromatic odour and the seeds have a bitter smell of curry and are generally roasted to reduce bitterness.

The seeds are available whole, crushed or powdered while the fresh stalks with leaves are sold in every Indian food shop. The dried fenugreek leaves known as *kasoori methi* are sold in packs. Dried fenugreek leaves are used to flavour all sorts of Indian savouries and curries. Dried seeds are widely used in southern Indian cookery in breads, chutneys, batters and lentils.

GARAM MASALA

Garam masala literally means hot spice and is a mixture of several spices roasted and ground to a fine powder. Each region of India has its own version of garam masala.

Used whole or ground, depending on the recipe, the basic blend includes cloves, cinnamon, cardamom, peppercorns, bay leaf, mace, cumin seeds and coriander seeds. Garam masala has a rich, warm fragrance and tastes hot and aromatic. Commercially produced garam masala is a poor substitute.

CHEE

Ghee is the purest form of butter fat. In the days when there was no refrigeration, milk was converted to ghee to lengthen storage life. Basically clarified butter, it is made from the milk of cows and buffaloes; in India buffalo milk is preferred because of its high fat content. Because of its unique flavour there is no substitute for ghee which is used as a fat for cooking, flavouring dishes and on its own with rice and bread. See recipe on page 33.

GRAM FLOUR

Also known as chickpea flour and 'besan', this is the most commonly used flour after rice and wheat flour in Indian cooking, obtained from husking and then grinding the gram lentils into a powder. The degree of fineness varies depending upon use. Chickpea flour is used in sweet as well as savoury dishes. It's advisable to buy a 1 lb/450g pack and store in an airtight jar for up to 6 months.

GREEN MOONG LENTILS

Whole moong beans or green gram, are small, oval and olive green in colour. When split they are small, flattish and yellow. Whole moong beans have a stronger flavour than the split ones and are rather chewy and musky. Yellow moong are easy to cook and don't really require soaking. The moong bean plant grows all over India as a rain fed crop.

JAGGERY

Known as gur, jaggery is dehydrated sugarcane juice similar to molasses and is mostly produced by small cultivators. Jaggery is not purified and hence has all the quality of the juice itself. Jaggery ranges from mustard yellow to amber in colour, depending on the quality of sugarcane juice. It is sticky but can be crumbled easily, and has a heavy, caramel like aroma, which is slightly alcoholic, like sweet sherry or port. It can be procured from any Indian or Thai store and is used mainly as a sweetener. Jaggery is as important as sugar in Indian cookery with a unique flavour. Demerara sugar is the closest equivalent.

KASUNDI MUSTARD

A ready-made mustard commonly used and available in Bengali cooking. Mustard seeds are soaked in vinegar and made into a paste with mustard oil and the addition of dried raw mango. This prepared mustard adds its characteristic flavours to numerous dishes from the region. It can be replaced with Dijon or any other prepared grain mustard.

KEWRA WATER AND ROSE WATER

Essences have been a part of Indian cookery since antiquity. The attars of the mughal emperors of India were famous and rare flowers would be grown in the royal green houses to be converted into perfume, some of these ended up in the kitchen. Floral essences are the most popular. The rose reigns supreme, closely followed by screw pine or kewra. The best blooms are selected and the essence is distilled. This is then mixed with water to make rose water and kewra water. Both these essences are readily available in Indian stores and can be stored for up to a year. They are used to flavour biryanis, pulaos, kebabs, desserts and sweets.

KOKUM BERRIES

These sour berries, also called Black Mangosteen, are sold dried and used in Keralan curries as a souring agent.

MOONG LENTILS
(MUNG BEANS)

Also known as green gram, these are the most versatile of all lentils. They are used either in the skin or husked. There is also a variety which is split but left in the skin.

Whole moong lentils are small, oval and olive green in colour. Whole lentils are stronger in flavour and musky. Yellow, split lentils are extremely easy to cook, and easy to digest.

MUSTARD LEAVES

The fresh green leaves from the mustard plant used either on its own or mixed with spinach to make a vegetable. It's sometimes also blanched and made into a paste to be used for various marinades in tandoori cooking.

MUSTARD OIL

Mustard oil is extracted from mustard seeds. Greatly favoured in Bengal and eastern India, certain Punjabi dishes get their flavour from this strong smelling, viscous oil.

MUSTARD SEEDS

There are three main varieties of mustard; white, brown and black. All three varieties grow in India. The seeds of the plant are the spice. White mustard seeds are pale tan in colour and have a smooth matt finish. Black mustard seeds are larger than the other two. The seeds are sharp, nutty, slightly bitter and aromatic in taste. Their heat is often misjudged, so be careful when adding them to recipes. Mustard paste has a unique flavour that hits you in the nose and then sings in your veins. In southern India and along the coast mustard seeds are used for tempering. In Bengal mustard seeds are crushed to pastes and used in fiery marinades and curries. Also widely used for pickling.

PANEER CHEESE

Indian version of set cottage cheese made by separating the whey from the milk by the addition of lemon juice to curdle it. When the whey is separated the solids are collected in a muslin cloth and tied and pressed under a heavy weight for a few hours until the solids set.

On its own, paneer tastes quite bland but is widely used in India as an alternative to meats for vegetarians. If unavailable, substitute with cottage cheese if using as a filling, having first drained through muslin to remove some of the moisture.

POMEGRANATE SEEDS (DRIED)

The pomegranate is an ancient fruit and has been a symbol of plenty and prosperity from the earliest times. The ripe fruit is plucked and the seeds separated and dried in the sun to make *anardana*. When dried the seeds turn reddish brown and are sticky and are then powdered or sold whole. They have a sour smell and a dry taste with a note of astringency. Used in north Indian cookery to add tang to chutneys, curries and stuffing.

RATTAN JYOTH

The bark of a tree used to give Rogan Josh its characteristic colour, it imparts a deep red colour to the oil to which it is added. Rogan Josh literally translated for the Hindustani means red juice.

Rattan jyot is rarely available outside India, and even then in only the most specialised stores.

SAFFRON

The costliest of all spices, saffron is the dried stigma of a perennial bulb. India and Spain are the largest producers of saffron. The best saffron is rich in colour and highly fragrant. Pure saffron is believed to colour and flavour 70,000 times its weight in liquid. The taste is slightly bitter but richly perfumed.

Saffron enhances savoury food as well sweet. A few strands soaked in a little warm water or milk and added along with the liquid to the dishes adds a fragrant richness.

SANDALWOOD

The wood of the sandal wood tree, finds extensive usage in perfumery and manufacture of soaps etc. The powder of the wood or its paste is used in cooking mostly with mild aromatic spices and delivers a delicate perfumed aroma to a dish.

STAR ANISE

Star anise is the fruit of a tree of the magnolia family and grows mainly in China and Vietnam. Dried star anise is hard and has eight hollow boat-shaped petals, which form a perfect star holding shiny seeds. Though it is not related to aniseed the spice is similar in flavour though the sweet aromatic taste is more prominent. Generally used in rice dishes, in teas and in succulent meat curries.

TAMARIND

Nowadays tamarind paste is readily available in many Indian and oriental stores. Tamarind is one of the main souring agents in Indian cookery and is used abundantly in south Indian cookery in lentils, chutneys and curries.

TOOR DAL

Also known as yellow lentils (lens culinaris), it is a deep rooted and shrubby perennial grown from seed. The lentil comes from seeds that are removed from pods by drying. In some cases the seeds are slightly oiled to increase the shelf life. Outside of India, you will mostly come across oiled varieties of these lentils. This is the most commonly used lentil in India and the Hindi term 'dal-roti' has come to mean a staple, everyday food.

TURMERIC

One of the most versatile and traditional spices used in Indian cooking, turmeric is at the very heart and soul of any Indian curry. Turmeric is a member of the ginger family and grows best in tropical climates. Fresh turmeric root resembles ginger and can be easily peeled. The roots are sold fresh, dried and powdered. It is ground turmeric that is generally used in cooking. Turmeric is used in virtually every Indian meat, lentil and vegetable dish. It is also an excellent preservative hence its extensive use in pickles. It can be added to foods for its colour, taste or as a thickening agent.

URAD LENTILS

Urad Dal, also known as black gram, is used whole in North Indian cooking and split in South Indian.

Whole black lentils are small and oblong, sometimes flecked with dark green or grey. When they are split, they are creamy white. Black lentils have a strong musky smell and rich heavy taste. When split, they have a much more subtle aroma.

Whole lentils are too heavy to use everyday, so buy small quantities and store in airtight jars for up to 4 months.

WHITE POPPY SEEDS

Poppy is obtained from the seed of an annual plant which bears large leaves and flowers with a purple centre. When cooked they impart a nutty aroma. Their graininess often gives distinct texture to Indian dishes.

Poppy seeds are always sold whole and are simple to grind at home, though dry roasting them makes this task easier. Indian cookery mostly uses cream coloured seeds as the grey ones alter the colour of the finished dish. Store in a dry, clean jar.

WHITE URAD LENTILS
Refer to urad lentils

YELLOW MOONG LENTILS
Refer to green moong lentils

YOGHURT

There are numerous varieties of yoghurt available on the market and one of them, Greek yoghurt is a good substitute for the hung or drained yoghurt that is used in India, where it is used for marinations - the thickness of the yoghurt coating and enriching the meat. Natural yoghurt on the other hand is used in sauces and other dips where the thickness is not relevant – indeed the thinner the yoghurt the longer it can be cooked without the fat separating.

SOME SUPPLIERS OF INDIAN PRODUCE

United Kingdom
London
Indian Spice Shop
115-119 Drummond Street
020 7916 1831
Mon-Sat 9.30am-9.30pm, Sun 10am-9pm

Taj Stores
112-14a Brick Lane, E1
020 7377 0061
Daily 9am-9pm.

Green Village
10a Carlton Terrace, Green Street, E7
020 8503 4809
Daily 8am-7pm

Kishan The Mill Shop
20 Carlton Terrace, Green Street, E7
020 8471 0008
Mon-Sat 9am-7pm, Sun 10am-6pm

Sunfresh
11-12 Carlton Terrace, Green Street, E7
020 8470 3031
Daily 8am-7pm

Fudco
184 Ealing Road, HAO
020 8902 4820
Mon-Sat 9.30am-6.30pm, Sun 10.30am-6.30pm

V.B & Sons Cash and Carry
218 Ealing Road, HAO
020 8902 8579
Mon-Fri 9.30am-6.45pm, Sun 11am-5pm

Dokal & Sons
133-135 The Broadway, UB1
020 8574 1647
Daily 9am-8pm

Sira Cash and Carry
128 The Broadway, UB1
020 8574 2280
Daily 8am-8pm

United Kingdom
Spicyfoods Cash and Carry
460 London Road, Croydon CRO 2SS
020 8684 9844

OK Cash & Carry
253 Canterbury Road, Gillingham, ME7 5XE
01634 572123

Bhullar Brothers Ltd.
44 Springwood Street, Huddersfield HD1 4BE
01484 531607

Indian & Continental Foods
69 Princes Avenue, Hull HU5 3QN
01482 346915

Asian Food Centre
175 Staines Road, Middlesex TW3 3LF
0208 5707346

Medina stores
27 Debeauvoir Road, Reading RC1 5NR
01189 268627

Atif's Cash & Carry
Walton Road, Woking
01483 762774

Some US Suppliers
Dowel Quality Products (mail order available)
91 First Ave. (between 5 & 6 St.), New York
212-979-6045
Daily 11am-1am

Foods of India (mail order available)
121 Lexington Ave. (between 28 & 29 St.), New York
212-683-4419
Mon-Sat 10am-8pm, Sun 11am-6pm

Kalustyan's (mail order available)
123 Lexington Ave. (between 28 & 29 St.)
212-685-3451
Mon-Sat 10am-8pm, Sun 11am-7pm

Useful US Website:
www.indianfoodsco.com
"Making the cuisine of India yours"

INDEX